BOLD LOVE

DR. DAN B. ALLENDER
DR. TREMPER LONGMAN III

NAVPRESS

A MINISTRY OF THE NAVIGATORS
P.O.BOX 35001, COLORADO SPRINGS, COLORADO 80935

The Navigators is an international Christian
organization. Jesus Christ gave His followers
the Great Commission to go and make
disciples (Matthew 28:19). The aim of The
Navigators is to help fulfill that commission by multiplying laborers for Christ in
every nation.

NavPress is the publishing ministry of The
Navigators. NavPress publications are tools
to help Christians grow. Although publications alone cannot make disciples or change
lives, they can help believers learn biblical
discipleship, and apply what they learn to
their lives and ministries.

Some of the anecdotal illustrations in this
book are true to life and are included with
the permission of the persons involved. All
other illustrations are composites of real
situations, and any resemblance to people
living or dead is coincidental.

Unless otherwise noted, all Scripture in
this publication is from the *Holy Bible: New
International Version* (NIV). Copyright © 1973,
1978, 1984, International Bible Society. Used
by permission of Zondervan Bible Publishers.
Another version used is the *New American
Standard Bible* (NASB), © The Lockman Foundation 1960, 1962, 1963, 1968, 1971, 1972,
1973, 1975, 1977.

Printed in the United States of America

FOR A FREE CATALOG OF
NAVPRESS BOOKS & BIBLE STUDIES,
CALL TOLL FREE 1-800-366-7788 (USA)
or 1-416-499-4615 (CANADA)

CONTENTS

ACKNOWLEDGMENTS

If imitation is the highest form of compliment, then I owe thanks to many that I have borrowed from in terms of ideas and spirit. James Dobson's *Love Must Be Tough* opened my eyes to the strength of love. Os Guinness in a lecture on "Fool Making" from 1 Corinthians 1 helped me understand the importance of surprise in undermining arrogance. M. Scott Peck compellingly described evil in *People of the Lie* and advised us to reflect on evil as a daily reality rather than as an occasional aberration. Frederick Buechner's *The Gospel as Tragedy, Comedy and Fairy Tale* deepened my tears, laughter, and wonder in the gospel. I am indebted to writers and pilgrims I've never met.

I am also grateful for a community of colleagues and staff that continue to support me in my growth and productivity: Precious Atchison, Cheryl Jones, Natalie Merilatt, Sue Rike, Al Andrews, Liam Atchison, Don Hudson, Tom Varney, and Joe Wall. Larry Crabb, my most passionate advocate and critic, has relentlessly offered me a living picture of bold love in our years of friendship. The turbulence and heartache of this dark world and odd profession is soothed by the honor of walking with him.

The staff of NavPress are supportive co-laborers in the wearisome task of making books. Traci Mullins, my editor and friend, guided me through the labyrinth of conceptual, syntactical, and grammatical mire with mirth and kindness.

The idea for this book occurred during our yearly vacation with David and Meg Dupee, Tremper and Alice Longman, and all our brood. I am deeply grateful for relationships that possess a history that precedes conversion and will stretch into an eternity of shared stories. Tremper, my co-author, was the one who introduced me to eternity and to the joy of learning. Our shared roots are deep.

I owe my wife, Rebecca, and my children, Anna, Amanda, and Andrew, my deepest, most abiding gratitude. This book is largely the fruit of my wife's unswerving commitment to offer us an exquisite taste of earthy, lively, transcendent love.

In Memoriam

O. Lee Allender
1929–1991

*Love anything and your heart will be wrung and possibly broken.
If you want to make sure of keeping it intact you must give it to
no one, not even an animal. Wrap it carefully round with hobbies
and little luxuries; avoid all entanglements. Lock it up safe in
the casket or coffin of your selfishness. But in that casket — safe,
dark, motionless, airless — it will change. It will not be broken; it
will become unbreakable, impenetrable, irredeemable.*
—From *The Four Loves* by C.S. Lewis

❖

*We are lovers in a dangerous time. Nothing worth having comes
without some kind of fight. We have to kick at the darkness until it
bleeds daylight.*
—Bruce Cockburn
"Love in a Dangerous Time"

❖

*The love for equals is a human thing — of friend for friend, brother
for brother. It is to love what is loving and lovely.*

The world smiles.

*The love for the less fortunate is a beautiful thing — the love
for those who suffer, for those who are poor, the sick, the failures,
the unlovely. This is compassion, and it touches the heart of
the world.*

*The love for the more fortunate is a rare thing — to love those
who succeed where we fail, to rejoice without envy with those who
rejoice, the love of the poor for the rich, of the black man for the
white man. The world is always bewildered by its saints.*

*And then there is the love for the enemy — love for the one
who does not love you but mocks, threatens, and inflicts pain.
The tortured's love for the torturer. This is God's love. It conquers
the world.*
—From *The Magnificent Defeat* by Frederick Buechner

FOREWORD

We'll never get it quite right until we're home. Only then will we be safe from damaging assault, uncorrupted by false values, and entirely free to live by design. But until then, God has made provision for our joy in the middle of adversity. He quietly stirs up a hunger for purity that is stronger than lust; and He empowers us to pursue other people, even ones who mistreat us, in the strength of forgiveness and restorative grace.

But supernatural joy, deep purity, and passionate love (the kind that survives abusive treatment) are in short supply in our Christian communities. We're better at singing about joy than sensing its reality when adversity hits. We're more inclined to resign ourselves to conceal impurities than to honestly confront our defeat. And we like to measure our spirituality in terms that never require us to face the deadness in our souls, which takes the passion out of our relationships.

There are signs, however, that God is on the move. Two trends in particular encourage me to think that an awakening

9

may be on the way. They give me hope as I continue on in a shallow, wicked world where nothing works the way it should. Perhaps that's why I'm glad that Drs. Allender and Longman have written *Bold Love*. They talk honestly about evil in a fashion that requires us to depend on God's supernatural power if we hope to survive this life with joy.

One hopeful trend is the renewed courage in many quarters to believe that God exists, imminently, that He might do something discernible and deep, that prayer provides a literal connection with Him—just as telephone wires reach another mere mortal—and that a unity among similarly connected people could weaken sectarianism without compromising distinctive convictions.

Call this trend *a recovery of the supernatural,* or of the reality of a relationship with God. And then realize that it has the potential to make us passionate about the right things. Can you imagine debating our differences candidly with legitimate zeal, without losing a burning passion for Christ that keeps us holding hands? Recovery of contact with the supernatural could promote the unity for which the Lord Jesus prayed just before He died.

The second trend involves a willingness to be done with pretense. For too long, we have maintained a confidence in the power of God's Word by pretending that things aren't as bad as they are and that God's call to love means something less than He intended. If we find the power to keep our relationships pleasant and our personal lives disciplined, then we congratulate ourselves for our maturity.

I've often wondered if the popularity of big churches, where the Sunday morning event is more important than everyday community, reflects a disillusionment with relationships more than a love for worship. And I've wondered, too, if exciting conferences, where speakers perform after reciting the stock disclaimer, "I've come here to minister, not perform," give us any more than a temporary rush without equipping us to move toward God through our private agony and failure.

But good things are happening. Big churches and exciting conferences are more often addressing the real problems of life and are encouraging ongoing community as the proper context for working through our heartbreak, rage, and doubt. We're coming to realize that a relationship with Christ is not intended to cover up the dark side of life, but rather to illuminate a path through it. And a few are seeing that true Christianity does not offer God as a higher power who solves our problems, but rather it exalts God as reason enough to persevere with purpose, hope, and joy.

This second trend — call it the *courage to struggle* — complements the first. It calls us into a battle where we will either be killed or put in touch with God. It calls us to engage God's enemy. And it reminds us that if we battle a different foe, we go it alone. When we take on merely those forces that work against our immediate comfort, and fail to engage the diabolical enemy who longs to rob God of glory, then God never becomes a reality — because He is waging war on a different front, where the battle is far more intense.

God's consuming preoccupation is to destroy evil through the power of sheer goodness made known through His perfectly righteous love. And, as every Christian knows, that takes some doing. God is relentlessly determined to erase every suspicion that He is not good and to bow every knee in confession that there is no glory greater than His.

Until He returns in full revelation of the power of His uncompromising love, He commands His followers to enter the reality of life (and to be bloodied by contact with evil). We are to be armed for battle with *a higher purpose than present enjoyment, a determined confidence that God is good no matter what happens, and the passion of a love bold enough to take on the real enemy.*

The courage to struggle against evil with the weapon of bold love needs to be encouraged. Its development will expose the lie of a moralism that tells us to insulate ourselves from the human heart by focusing on conformity to external standards. It will shatter the pretense of a legalism that reduces life to an orderly system where doing right things preserves us from having to walk through deep valleys of confusion, doubt, and pain. Coupled with the first trend — the recovery of the supernatural—this second one could unite us for battle against a common enemy and get us moving onward with the courage of supernaturally equipped soldiers.

Life is not easy. It can be good, but it is not easy. Bigger churches where we can hide and more exciting conferences that pump us full of adrenaline are not the answer. We must discover God's power to care about others when our heart is breaking; we must find God's love to reach out to lost people even though our pain continues. We must learn to live well in a community of people who are sometimes wonderful, too often unspeakably evil, and usually somewhere in between.

This book takes on the challenge of helping us find the power we need to live in our world without pretense. It destroys weak notions of forgiveness. It confronts shallow attempts to love. It exposes our inclination to make life work by not admitting when it doesn't. It moves us toward a despair that will either ruin us or drive us to the reality of God.

I know Dan Allender well. Like all of us, he is flawed and imperfect. But like only a few, he has an unflinching resolve to work through reality in his pursuit of God. Tremper Longman is one of a rare breed: an academic scholar who studies the text with the precision of a disciplined mind and, at the same time, an honest seeker after God who is not satisfied with passionless (and therefore irrelevant) accuracy.

A counselor who fights on the front lines and a scholar who supplies ammunition have worked together to produce a book, one of the few, that strengthens my hope: God is accessible to help us fight a good battle as we enter the reality of life.

—LAWRENCE J. CRABB, JR., PH.D.

FORGIVENESS:
An Intricate Mystery

Love. We use the word so easily and might even think we know a bit about it. Surely it's something we all want and, in our better moments, want to give. Yet there is no more demanding occupation than love.

Love, as a reflection of the glory of God, is the ground of being, the reason for existing, and the core of the gospel. It is the most basic staple of life; yet it is nearly impossible to wrap words around love's vastness, to describe how to be transformed by it, or to use it for the sake of another—especially in a world that hurts us regularly and often deeply. Writing a book about love seems almost presumptuous.

Then why would I take on such a task? Because the challenges and mysteries of love have captured me. Every day of my professional and personal life, I am compelled to answer the question, "What does it mean to love those who harm me?" As a psychologist—and even more, as a man who lives as a fallen person with other fallen people—I am faced with the daily, hourly, and moment-by-moment transgressions of others.

I am faced, as you are, with transgressions of love that cry for forgiveness and the unrelenting demand of God to forgive.

But there is a struggle for most of us in forgiving those who harm us. The greater the damage, it seems, the more difficult it is to forgive. If you are a Christian, you have a redeemed, but still sinful, heart that struggles to forgive. God's inexorable demand to forgive, to turn the other cheek, to offer one's coat to an enemy is at times infuriating, at other times illogical, and always costly beyond right or reason.

The requirement to forgive, therefore, may be honored as noble but impractical, dismissed as antiquarian, forgotten except in safe surroundings, or just as tragically, applied without wisdom or understanding. Forgiving others, the *sine qua non* of love, is not an easy subject to understand, let alone live. But there is no more important subject. It is, therefore, my purpose in this book to explore (I wish I could say answer) the question, What does it mean to love my enemy? — the one who sexually abused me; my spouse who is angry and insensitive; my friend who gossiped behind my back and damaged my reputation; my child who snarls at my offer to go for a walk; the surgeon or service station mechanic who fails to act in my best interest. The list is endless.

For every person, in every instance, either brief or interminable, cruel or civil, warm or hostile, there will be enough sin in all our relationships that forgiveness is required if they are to continue toward an end that is good. This book will discuss forgiving love — the kind that can deal with tragic and incomprehensible harm like sexual abuse, as well as the ordinary and explainable struggles, like insensitivity or impatience.

This is an awesome task for reasons that go beyond the enormity of the concepts. It is a sober enterprise due to personal reasons. There are three reasons why I have resisted writing this book. First, I don't consistently love well. If you were to ask my friends, students, clients, neighbors, and others how well I love, you would hear a mixed report. At times I love quite well — much as for a short period of time an alligator can outpace a horse — but more often than not, my legs are short, my skin scaly, and my expression intimidating. Like an alligator, I am not much of a long-distance runner.

Recently, a friend whom I respect told me I am a hypocrite—a far better speaker on friendship than a face-to-face friend. The rebuke came after I failed to expend the energy to call a mutual friend who was weeks away from dying. By my withdrawal, I deeply grieved the heart of a man who had meant a great deal to me.

There was, of course, a context to my neglect (there always is), ranging from busyness, travel, and ministry preoccupation to a quiet, deep hatred of death that likely lingers from experiences of loss at a young age. Yet, even with the context considered, the failure to love is without excuse. How can I write a book on love when I, at best feebly and at worst hypocritically, deny the very premise that I hope to present? The only answer I know to justify the continued writing of this book is my passionate desire to understand what is true and to grow in my practice of it, irrespective of how poorly I might sometimes model what I teach.

Equally, I know that like any redeemed man or woman, I long to know, at the depths of my being, the love of God and to offer refreshing water to any whose thirst has driven them beyond dull complacency and justified self-centeredness. And one of the first routes to comprehending what it means to love is to gain greater clarity about how poorly I do love. If that is true, I am well on the way. I can only hope for a richer taste of His kindness and mercy.

A second factor that has caused this book to be a struggle is the risk of misunderstanding. Many cherished notions about love and forgiveness will be challenged. I do not relish the idea of assailing beliefs that have been used by God to bring significant change, but the fact that certain beliefs have brought about good results does not make them true. I know Christians who have found comfort in Bible passages when the meaning had been twisted beyond comprehension or who have been forced to bear a perspective that was simply not to be found in the verse, yet they were encouraged or convicted as a result of their understanding. This does not justify sloppy interpretation, but it does warn (and reassure) us that God can and will use anything to accomplish His purposes.

Every author writes in the crucible of the culture. We are never free from the influence of our culture — reacting as defenders of the old convictions and naysayers of current trends, or just the opposite. I am no different. I do not believe forgiveness involves forgetting the past and ignoring the damage of past or present harm. To do so, even if it were possible, would be tantamount to erasing one's personal history and the work of God in the midst of our journey. The only way for the "forgive-and-forget mentality" to be practiced is through radical denial, deception, or pretense.

Many raised on the familiar chant, "forgive and forget," may already question this book's viability. I can only hope the reader will read further before labeling the book as heretical. The "forgive and forget" approach has included some important truths about forgiveness that should not, like the clean baby, be thrown out with dirty bath water. From this approach, we must learn the importance of radically putting aside the right to use the past harm to justify present sin. But we must not pretend that past harm never happened. I believe the past can be remembered for the well-being of the abuser. Facing the damage of the past can bring good into the present day relationship with the one who perpetrated significant harm. This complex issue will be addressed.

On the other hand, those who most likely would agree with my initial premise that it is neither desirable nor possible to forget the harm of the past are apt to argue that forgiving others cannot occur until we first learn to forgive ourselves and accept our humanness. A related belief is that you cannot learn to love others until you first learn to love yourself. This approach argues for a priority in learning to first take care of yourself, then you will be able to take care of others. Although there is a legitimate self-acceptance flowing from the gospel, nothing could be further from the premise of this book than the "me-first" attitude that fuels this thinking. Such self-interest contradicts the radical "other-centeredness" of the gospel and ignores the Lord Jesus' words that one will never find his life until he first loses it (Matthew 10:39).

The "take-care-of-yourself" movement has led many to justify self-centeredness. And yet, this approach has recognized many significant problems with the traditional understanding of love and forgiveness. The take-care-of-yourself movement properly refuses to think of dependent, fear-based compliance and rescuing behavior as love. I could not agree more. Love is far more than merely doing the right thing; in fact, many relationships are so bound by guilt, fear, and neediness that true love is impossible.

For example, many people ignore the harm done to them and call it "forgiving" the other. In fact, one reason it may be ignored is the fear of causing conflict. When fear of the other is the undergirding motive for turning the other cheek, it cannot be called love, or forgiving the other. A lot of activity that is seen as spiritual is infused with fear, pretense, and ritual. The take-care-of-yourself movement accurately sees the potential for what appears to be loving behavior to be based on a heart that is not concerned with love, but with protecting the self or others from difficult truths.

The two options discussed are not without merit, but both leave me empty. The first minimizes pain, and the second undervalues sacrifice. Something is wrong with our understanding of love and forgiveness if popular teaching encourages either (1) a self-righteous pardoning of the sinner based on denial and pretense or (2) a self-absorbed reclamation of the soul through the unbiblical act of forgiving yourself, rather than receiving God's forgiveness. The phrase "forgive yourself"—a reaction to the common experience of not "feeling" forgiven—disregards the fact that we are already forgiven if we have embraced the work of Christ's death and resurrection as our passover from God's righteous wrath.

If justification by faith has not moved us out of our self-contempt and poor self-esteem, then something other than a supposed failure to forgive ourselves is going on in the human personality that needs exposure and repentance. Self-affirmation designed to develop self-forgiveness and self-expression will only aggravate the problem. I am aware that I am running against the tide of popular opinion in these remarks. At this early point, I hope the offended reader will not dismiss this book as another example of codependent self-sacrifice that is encouraging a doormat view of Christian service.

A third concern that I feel as I write this book, far beyond the issue of misunderstanding, is the fear of promoting a response to sin that may release people to bash others in the name of loving confrontation. I would be heartbroken if I opened a door to honesty, sharing, and vulnerability that had nothing to do with long-sufferance, forbearance, and covering a multitude of sin. Let me illustrate my fear.

A friend recently saw his ministry and reputation sullied due to the unbiblical use of an "honesty intervention." The meeting was called to discuss ministry concerns; it turned into an inquisition of accusation and attack. He was recovering from a serious illness and was only recently released from a hospital stay where he almost lost his life due to the unusually high toxicity of a potent drug.

The "intervention" proceeded with feedback from a number of people. His level of defensiveness increased as the feedback intensified. Global accusations of being distant, hard, angry, closed, hurtful, and unbroken were lobbed into his lap, and he fulfilled his accusers' assessments by getting more confused and defensive. Finally, he could bear no more and walked out of the meeting. He said, "I finally lost it and I could not handle the hatred I felt from people who days earlier were at my bedside, bringing me magazines and marveling at my courage."

He was inaccurate. He did not lose it. He finally responded to an accurate sense that something was dreadfully wrong with their confrontation. He rightly chose to flee from an unbiblical intervention. Not all confrontations, even those represented as loving interventions, should be endured.

I personally know a number of his accusers. They are good people; they are not without wisdom and understanding. Yet they chose a context that was deplorable and procedures that violated the guidelines for dealing with major transgressions as detailed in Matthew 18. My friend was not without fault in the way he had handled people or decisions. He was possessive at times and then distant and aloof. He repeatedly gossiped about a staff member to others on the team. He could be pleasant and self-sacrificing at one moment, and soon after, complain about how used he felt. He was, and is, a normal sinner. He is also a man with an enormously good heart, willing to grow in wisdom, and deeply committed to the welfare of others.

In a room full of angry and hurt friends, reeling from exhaustion and prescription drugs, he was not at his best. No one could be. He was told by one man that he was being given "bold love" for his good. Again, I don't doubt the sincerity and good intentions of his accusers, but there was something grotesque about the event that I do not want to promote. For him to be assailed in the meeting for being defensive and hard sounds as absurd to me as accusing a drowning man of being untrusting when he is splashing wildly as he goes down for the second time.

What in the world is going on in our penchant for honesty and openness? Our day is so full of hypocrisy, pretense, and deception that we crave a sincere relationship with another person. One sad byproduct of this legitimate craving is an undisciplined tendency to let people know when we are hurt or offended. Obviously, there is a place for rebuke and honesty, but not as the primary staple of building or maintaining loving relationships. My friend was assaulted, at least in part, due to misapplication of material that I had taught on "bold love." It alternately breaks my heart and terrifies me that I might unleash a style of interaction that will harm others.

Bold love is not reckless or cruel. It is not beating up another in the name of sharing or intervention. *Bold love is courageously setting aside our personal agenda to move humbly into the world of others with their well-being in view, willing to risk further pain in our souls, in order to be an aroma of life to some and an aroma of death to others.* Boldly loving another with the energy of Christ (Colossians 1: 8-9) would never have produced the destructive confrontation that was thrust upon my friend.

The potential for abusing real love is enough to make a sensitive heart fear to love at all, beyond being nice and helpful. While love does not require less than kindness, it definitely requires more. The commitment to love often seems to be derailed by our insensitivity or lack of wisdom, but that can never serve as a reason to not venture to love more. It should, however, make us cautious and compel us to consider and reconsider our motives, timing, and concern for the other person before we decide how to handle his or her failures. No amount of fencing, clarifying, and restating will keep some from seeking to force the Kingdom's entrance through verbal violence. I can only prayerfully hope to limit the potential misuse.

The reader may wonder, with my admitted sense of inadequacy, concern, and dread, why I want this book to see the light of day. In part, I am a man under constraint to address the question of what it means to forgive. I am also privileged to be working on this project with a friend of twenty-five years. Dr. Tremper Longman III and I met in a music class in eighth grade. We soon became best friends. Our friendship continued and developed through high school, college, and seminary. During that time, his quiet, unrelenting pursuit of God opened the door to my conversion. We have remained inseparable friends.

Tremper's years of study at Westminster Theological Seminary and later at Yale University have equipped him as one of the foremost evangelical Old Testament scholars in the world today. His collaboration on this project—particularly his contribution of chapter 5—provides a unique opportunity for the reader to see how high-level biblical scholarship is not only helpful to front-line counseling and discipleship, but is required if Kingdom thinking is to intrude into the culture of our day. It is an unparalleled honor to have Tremper's involvement in this project.

Bold love is a powerful agent in the change process that can transform both the lover and the recipient. The passion of bold love is a gift that brings a hardened, defensive, enraged heart face to face with the unrelenting, piercing eyes of redemptive kindness. Tremper and I are privileged to encourage you to look into God's eyes.

PART ONE

The Battlefield of the Heart

❖

CHAPTER ONE

MIXED FEELINGS ABOUT LOVE:
What Drives a Human Heart?

S herry's father hated women. Every time she was with him, she was subjected to his tirades about her "frigid" mother and his "lesbian" customers. She was his one and only "pretty lady," and she carried the burden of his cruelty upon her weary, guilty shoulders. When she finally suggested to him after twenty years of being his surrogate spouse that his attitudes toward women, including her, might be damaging her soul, his well-chosen words cut like a cold dagger: "I thought you cared about me. I guess you're just a dyke like all the rest."

What would it mean for Sherry to forgive her father for years of abuse? Jesus said to "turn the other cheek." She'd already done that hundreds of times, yet she was getting pummeled beyond recognition by her father's verbal blows. She wanted to forget she even had a father. But the Bible said she was supposed to love him.

Patrick's wife was still the love of his life. After fifteen years of marriage, she could make him laugh like no one else, and as a hostess for his clients, she stole the show. Everyone loved a party when Penny was there. She had that magic touch, and Patrick was so proud of her. But whenever he tried to talk to her about what he

23

really felt, how much he wanted her for more than a laugh, how she hurt him and the kids with the endless public performances that stole her heart from them, she blew up. "Oh, don't be ridiculous! What do you want from me, anyway? You can be such a baby." Sometimes, she'd apologize later, but nothing ever really changed. The cycle of pain kept cutting deeper into Patrick's heart.

Patrick knew all about "forgive and forget." It was the only solution. He loved his wife. But could he really go on like this for the rest of his life? What about the kids? It was becoming harder to overlook Penny's caustic replies and soul-numbing contempt. Forgiving and forgetting wasn't getting their family anywhere. So what did God expect of him? What was love for a wife who just didn't care?

Jane's phone was ringing again. It was probably Carol. It seemed like it was always Carol. She was really having a rough time of it — had been for as long as Jane could remember. She needed someone to talk to, and Jane did love her. Carol could be so sweet, and she always listened to what Jane had to say and tried to follow her advice. But the resentment was building inside Jane. "How can she be so self-centered? All we talk about is her problems. What about me? What about a give-and-take relationship? I'm really getting sick of this."

But "love covers a multitude of sins." Sure, Carol could be selfish, but she was really struggling. Shouldn't Jane be a little more forbearing? She didn't want to resent Carol, but it was getting harder to forgive the daily ringing of the phone. She wasn't feeling much love anymore. What did God really want from her, anyway? She just wanted out.

MIXED FEELINGS ABOUT LOVE

All of us want out sometimes. Love is too hard; forgiveness seems impossible. Why try when our efforts to love seem to make matters worse? Even in our best relationships, the wounds of the battle hardly seem worth it sometimes. But it's hard for a human heart to live long or well without love.

Love offers life. It softens the dark moments and keeps the heartbeat of hope alive. Love is both a mysterious friend and, at times, a terrible disappointment. Love one day satisfies and the next seems to strip the heart bare before the cold winds of betrayal. If we are honest, we often have mixed feelings about love.

A woman I counseled told me in tears, "I hate love. I cannot live without it, but neither can I bear the bitterness of betrayal." Her life was not particularly hard or full of terrible loss. She was married, with two grown sons and a husband who was not cruel, nor deeply involved in her life. She had good health and sufficient funds to live as she desired — and a growing awareness of an ache in her heart.

Her emptiness, though remotely present through much of her life, became acute after a fairly routine event at church. She was involved for years in helping out in everything from the nursery to missions conferences. For two years, she was the vice-president of the women's ministry and thoroughly expected to take over the leadership once the current president retired.

When the president stepped down, my client's best friend, who had never been too involved nor consistent in ministry, but who was a vivacious and natural leader (and favored by the pastor's wife), was elected president. During the church service when her friend was announced as the new president of the women's ministry team, my client felt cold and numb. It felt like a hit-and-run accident. One minute she was laughing with friends as she interacted in fellowship, and the next she sat stunned and bloody — alone, abandoned, and friendless. As hard as she tried to tell herself it was not a big deal and that she was being petty and irrational, she still felt betrayed.

Her friend had betrayed her. She did not defer the position to the one who had done most of the work over the years. In the days to come, my client fluctuated between guilt and anger. Every time she thought about the night her friend accepted the position with modesty and quiet thrill, she felt nauseous. It seemed impossible to be kind, let alone love her friend and forgive her. What was she to do with her inner tumult? She knew the Word of God, "Love your enemies," but she never thought she would be called to love an enemy who, a day before, was a close friend.

THE HOPE FOR LOVE

Love, or even the hope of love, draws each person into the battle of life. Yet it is love, or the loss of it, that causes us to question our desire to live. We are caught on the horns of a dilemma. We want love and want to love, but we are often suspicious and cynical toward love as a seducer and a betrayer. Nevertheless, most of us continue to plod forward, hoping the next experience of love will be different.

What draws most people into the mainstream of work, homemaking, endless trips to little league, and cookouts with neighbors is the hoped-for possibility that maybe one day life will come together so that the confusion, loneliness, betrayal, and fears will all melt away, like wrinkles before the fountain of youth. We all know the fountain of youth is a dream and Eden a lost memory, but the hunger for a world where love reigns supreme — or at least, where my world is saturated with love — draws me into another day's activity. That hope works even when I'm aware only of the necessity of getting up to keep my job. Let me illustrate this struggling hope for love by telling you about one woman's life.

A single mother gets up at 5:30 a.m. to get herself ready for work, dresses her children, drops them off at a daycare center, fights morning traffic, hunts for a parking place, grabs a cup of coffee as she shoulders her way through the bustling hordes, glides behind her desk for a day of fighting petty office gossip, sexual innuendoes, and fragile male egos in order to make enough money for her struggling family. Why? Why does she do it day after day?

This single mother's first answer might be, "I am alone. I have to work to feed my family." She may feel this obligation of responsibility, but there is more. She would not persist in her daily grind unless she were somewhat motivated by love. She has kids to feed and clothe. She has a flute teacher to hire for her oldest daughter and new tennis shoes to buy for her youngest son's first T-ball game. Some of her reasons for laboring so hard may be based on anger — an "I-will-do-it-on-my-own" rage — but at some level, love draws her on.

Without love, she would wither and blow away.

Though her life revolves around love, perhaps it is a chronic refusal to love that actually drives her. Suppose she is involved in occasional bouts of immorality. Further, suppose her heart is full of hatred for her ex-husband, who left her for a younger woman. Her painful divorce has hardened her heart and closed her eyes to the gospel. She has turned her heart away from tenderness. In her growing toughness, she is less disposed to listen to her daughter's awkward teenage struggles and her young son's repetitive stories about baseball. Her heart hates the one who devastated her and is closing toward those who desperately need her compassion. She is a mystery of hardness and tenderness, distance and compassion. She is lonely, alone, and longing. Does love mean anything to her?

Would this woman say that love is her reason for existing? Does love serve as a category for evaluating her life? In one sense, love is what entices her on and, in turn, has hardened her through disappointment. Love is her reason for living, but she rarely considers the meaning of love or what love requires of her.

What might we tell her about love? About God's love? About what it means to be transformed by love and to love others from the perspective of God's love? The task is more monumental than most of us would have thought. What should I tell my client who is a single mother struggling with loneliness and immorality, exhaustion and hardness? Years ago, I would have spoken more glibly and surely than I do now. I would still tell her to put off immorality. I would neither then nor now soft-pedal the biblical command to forgive her ex-husband. I would encourage her to put aside her defensive hardness and self-protection.

My counsel is solid, but I wonder if my words would fall on nearly deaf ears. I'm afraid my advice (though true) might, in large measure, appear irrelevant to her daily concerns. How does loving others, especially those who have hurt her, relate to the daily grind of getting out of bed, making mortgage payments, and adjusting to the mayhem of the world around her?

THE POSSIBILITY OF LOVE

Love may be necessary for survival, but daily existence seems to make love impossible. Love is essential, but it seems maddeningly unreasonable. It is both what we desire and despise, wait for and ignore, work toward and sabotage.

Could it really be true that love, without divine intervention, is impossible? The old adage "to err is human, to forgive divine" implies that one should not expect much more than a sin-riddled mess — unless something occurs outside the normal channels of human relationship to bind up the wounds created by love's failure. Love is not possible, at least for long, without the healing work of forgiveness.

If my client finds the discussion of love impractical, what will she likely think about my counsel to forgive those who have wounded her and damaged her heart through love's betrayal? I want her to be so taken by the love of God that the murky fog of hatred is consumed by the irresistible brightness of the gospel. I fear, however, that any discussion of forgiveness and love will add a burden that increases the already long list of reasons to turn her back on the gospel and, instead, embrace its cheap but quickly enjoyed counterfeit in the arms of a lover.

Surely one of the reasons she'll feel the directive to forgive as a terrible burden is that she has been misinformed as to what forgiveness actually is in the context of the relationships that hurt her most. Before we take a lengthy journey into what it means to forgive, let me reflect on some of the misunderstandings that are, at times, associated with the topic of forgiveness.

I spoke to a woman whose daughter quit school midterm to join a Christian rock band, without talking to her or addressing the loss of tuition. The same week, her husband lost most of their retirement funds in a get-rich scheme promoted by a flamboyant Christian businessman. After all that had transpired, particularly with fellow believers, she vocalized her enormous pain and anger to her pastor.

In what felt like another crushing blow, he rebuked her, saying, "Bitterness is an even bigger problem than all youhave experienced. You must learn to forgive and forget; put these bad experiences behind you and get on serving God and others." His advice was tragic in that it had enough of a ring of truth to pass unobstructed and unchallenged into her heart. The forgive-and-forget approach to forgiveness left her hopeless.

She tried to repent, but she still felt hurt. She felt anger and wanted people to take responsibility for their sin. She felt that the Christian ministry that accepted her daughter in the music group should be exposed for sweeping young people into service without consulting their parents. She wanted the businessman disciplined for the patterns of deceit that had bilked many others in the church. She wanted her pastor to take seriously the deep struggles in her marriage and family. Instead, her pastor told her that forgiveness always involves putting the event in the past and pressing on, forgetting what lies behind.

Most of us, if we have been around the church for long, have probably had similar experiences. After years of being bludgeoned by others' misguided advice and by our own misinformed conscience, we are too weary, hesitant, or angry to enter the true battle toward forgiveness that brings life. The forgiveness of God means little to us, and forgiving others seems like leaping into an abyss of further harm.

How do we really view the idea of forgiveness? What have we done to derail the kind of forgiving love that enters the fray of betrayal and brokenness with a bold, courageous desire for the kind of reconciliation that redeems all the Evil One's efforts to destroy?

Forgiving love does not merely get one through tough times or give purpose to the daily grind of life. *Forgiving love is the inconceivable, unexplainable pursuit of the offender by the offended for the sake of restored relationship with God, self, and others.* It is the kind of love that has fallen on hard times in our self-oriented, take-care-of-yourself age. Few, if any, question the importance of love, but the idea that we need to love others rather than ourselves is more readily thought to be a symptom of a sickness called codependency.

Women are often told they love too much or love the wrong kind of man. Love is now a diagnostic criteria for measuring mental health. If you love the unlovable, let another person's desires take precedence over your own, or even worse, love someone who has hurt you, then you are likely love addicted, codependent, and emotionally unhealthy.

Without question, a common perversion of love is dependent, demanding, and soulless in its giving, so that, in fact, it ceases to be love. What an odd thought—love that is not loving. It is obvious that what we call love might be little more than a slightly veiled, self-interested demand for appreciation and respect. And what we call forgiveness might be a self-aggrandizing—or its tragic opposite, a self-destroying—avoidance of the offense in order to achieve an end other than biblical reconciliation. The difference between love and forgiveness and their counterfeits is obviously complex and bewildering.

The premise of this book is simple: *I will not live with purpose and joy unless I love; I will not be able to love unless I forgive; and I will not forgive unless my hatred is continually melted by the searing truth and grace of the gospel.* True biblical forgiveness is a glorious gift for both the offender and the offended. Few of us have ever understood what the Bible really means when it speaks of forgiveness, and clarity won't come immediately in the early chapters of this book. But keep reading. Forgiveness is even harder than we think it is—but infinitely more life-giving. If love offers life, forgiveness enables love.

THE CHARACTERISTICS OF LOVE

Love: The Preeminent Virtue

Love is unquestionably the highest calling a person can pursue. Love is the fulfillment of the law. Jesus shocked His biblically and theologically well-versed brethren by summarizing the law in two commandments: "Love the Lord your God with all your heart and with all your soul and with all your mind and with all your strength"; and "Love your neighbor as yourself" (Mark 12:30-31). He then stated, "There is no commandment greater than these" (verse 31). In one breath, He placed love above tradition and the sacrificial system, and brought all the commandments of God into alignment under the majesty of love. No wonder His adversaries no longer asked Him any more questions; He boggled their minds. I am stunned as well.

I am stunned that every word and story of the Old Testament, every law, every commandment, and every jot and tittle of truth can find its final completion in one word—love. Paul also viewed love as the summary of the Old Testament law. He stated, "The entire law is summed up in a single command: 'Love your neighbor as yourself'" (Galatians 5:14). Paul further elaborated that all laws, including the Ten Commandments, could find their fulfillment in one command: Love your neighbor as yourself.

> Let no debt remain outstanding, except the continuing debt to love one another, for he who loves his fellowman has fulfilled the law. The commandments, "Do not commit adultery," "Do not murder," "Do not steal," "Do not covet," and whatever other commandment there may be, are summed up in this one rule: "Love your neighbor as yourself." (Romans 13:8-10)

Love does no harm to its neighbor; therefore, love is the fulfillment of the law. It is wonderfully simple and grand—all of life's requirements summarized by the admonition to love God and your neighbor. Love is indeed not only the summary of the law, but by implication, the central measuring rod by which my life will be judged.

What is love? What is the nature of this thing called love that we are required to mirror in our relationships with others and even in our relationship with God? Jesus obliquely answered the question of what love is by pointing to Himself. He said, "A new command I give you: Love one another. As I have loved you, so you must love one another. By this all men will know that you are my disciples, if you love one another" (John 13:34-35). Love is described (1 Corinthians 13), illustrated (the good Samaritan, Luke 10:25-37), and commanded

(Luke 6:27-36), but it is never defined. The meaning of love is found in the person Jesus Christ and incarnated with definition and meaning by His death and resurrection.

Love is a sacrifice for the undeserving that opens the door to restoration of relationship with the Father, with others, and with ourselves. It is in the light of Christ's sacrificial, intentional, and transforming love that we are to define love. It is equally on this basis that we will be evaluated and, one day, judged.

Love: The Measuring Rod of Character

Love is the measure by which my life will be assessed. Such a measuring rod strips me of any self-importance. If I am judged on how I love and not on how many books I sell, seminars I give, and people I counsel, then at one level it does not really matter if I write, teach, or counsel. It matters only if I love. That seems so stark and unbending. Why can't I be judged on what I do well and do every day as a natural course of life? Why can't I be judged on how I run my business or how often I am involved in ministry activity? Most people do not mind being assessed on a wide variety of tests — including how they love — but it does not seem fair to be assessed on nothing more than the quality of how we have loved others. We want a broader foundation on which to stand.

For example, I recently had a tense argument with my wife about who would pick up our daughter at school. I was home, but working. She was busy and distracted. She felt that I could take a few minutes away from my computer terminal to do an errand, and I felt that she should understand that I was as much at work in my home office as when talking to a client in the office.

The argument became a sideshow of faultfinding and blameshifting. She stormed out of the house, while I went back to work on the topic of love. I wrote well that day (another evidence of mercy), but I am sadly aware that I lost, for a moment, intimacy with my wife and closeness with the Lord. The section I wrote after our war will be judged not on its literary merit or practical helpfulness, but on whether my heart was lovingly other-centered or hatefully self-centered.

The warning from Paul's opening words in 1 Corinthians 13 is haunting: "If I speak in the tongues of men and of angels, but have not love, I am only a resounding gong or a clanging cymbal. If I have the gift of prophecy and can fathom all mysteries and all knowledge, and if I have a faith that can move mountains, but have not love, I am nothing. If I give all I possess to the poor and surrender my body to the flames, but have not love, I gain nothing" (verses 1-3). Talent without love is deafening; spiritual discernment and power without love is debasing; and sacrifice of possession or body without love is defrauding.

It is pointless and worthless to live and not love. There will be no sweet sounds of joy or reward for living without love. So how do we know if we're really pressing on for the prize? Is love common and ordinary, or supremely rare and supernatural? Is it possible that many are involved in using talents, exercising power, and sacrificing enormous portions of money and flesh without being driven by a heart of love? I wonder if a great portion of our daily choices are made without a passing thought to whether our activity is consistent with a heart of love.

It is also quite possible to be consumed with concerns about our failure to love. Most of us know someone who is more haunted by their failure to love than by the effects of their failure in the lives of others. Sadly, many are consumed by a self-oriented absorption over failure that appears to be a legitimate conviction about sin, but may be another form of subtle self-protection that keeps one's heart out of the battle of true sacrifice.

Many seem either to ignore love as the foundation of daily decisions or become so overwhelmed by past failures that love is viewed as beyond the most remote possibility. Why would this be the case?

Love: False Presumptions
Love is the most essential, life-giving gift we offer to another human being. It is also the least-likely, -natural, or -consistent response that is offered in the mundane moments, let alone

during the difficult, soul-demanding struggles when we are threatened, reviled, and harmed. Rich moments of other-centered care and sacrifice are rare. Most people presume the desire to love is a natural human sentiment, but love is actually the exception, the extraordinary, and the life-altering surprise.

In most cases, love for one's infant child seems to contradict my premise that love is not natural, because in a mother's love and sacrifice there exists the most natural and wholesome other-centeredness known to human experience. In many cases, it is a mother's love for her nursing child that compels her to lose sleep and sacrifice her own comfort for her hungry infant. But is a mother's love necessarily universal or consistent on every occasion? Though it may be a paradigm of compassion, a mother's love is not to be viewed as infallible or motivated thoroughly by other-centered commitment.

Isaiah compares God's love to the most excellent form of love—the compassion of a mother for her infant: "Can a mother forget the baby at her breast and have no compassion on the child she has borne? Though she may forget, I will not forget you!" (Isaiah 49:15). It is inconceivable that a mother whose breasts are engorged with milk and whose maternal instincts are presumably oriented to her child could ever forget or neglect her child, but the evidence is irrefutable; it does happen. Even the purest form of love is not without failure or forgetfulness. If a mother's love may be flawed, how much more are the garden variety forms of love—husband and wife, parent and child, friend and friend—equally flawed and incomplete. Is love natural? Is it to be presumed that love will be recognized from our daily sacrifices for one another?

I was recently traveling by plane to teach a seminar on the topic of bold love. My seatmate observed my absorbed gaze, frustrated scribbling, and hurried additions to what already appeared to be a mound of paper mayhem. He asked, "Are you a lawyer?" I longed for any reason to put aside my final moments of preparation, so I answered his question. Soon we were talking about my trade and purpose for flying to Miami. When I told him I was addressing several hundred people on the topic of love and forgiveness, he peered over his bifocals, squinted, and replied condescendingly, "How nice. Love, huh? Well, I guess we all need to be reminded of the importance of love."

Our discussion soon revolved around what he viewed as the central, driving purpose in his life. He told me that what pleased him most about his grown children was their tenacity and doggedness in pursuing education, careers, and success. They had learned well from their father, and he was indeed proud. He later told me his three children had experienced five divorces, and he had grandchildren he had not seen for five years due to the acrimonious marital endings. His own two divorces seemed to trouble him little.

I eventually asked him how important it was to teach his children to love and remain doggedly committed to people. His response was highly illuminating. He said, "I never taught my children about love. I suppose I thought they would naturally pick up what needed to be learned about those things." Love, he told me, was noble and natural, therefore as basic to life as breathing. With more sad bravado than conviction, he added, "I taught my children to love by example, not by word. I hope that was enough."

It was difficult to tell him that it was not enough. Without question, he had taught his children something about love. It is almost impossible as a human being, unless one is thoroughly evil, not to live out love to some degree. But the emphasis of his life and instruction seemed to be bent toward success in finances and career, not sacrifice of soul for the sake of giving others a taste of God.

I wonder how often love is truly taught and lived as the central priority of life. I asked one of my children what she thought was the most important lesson I wanted her to learn about life. She replied, "Work hard, do your best, and don't lie." Those are worthy objectives to teach a child, but if internalized without a larger picture, they are the basis for crushing legalism and pharisaical arrogance. I wonder why my children apparently do not see the pursuit of love as the central purpose of life? Perhaps love is so rare, even in good homes, that other lessons about life are preeminent in the classroom of family living. We would do well to ask the hard question: Is love the most prized possession in our home, the most cherished character trait we pursue, and the most central lesson we teach in all that we do? The most optimistic answer, I fear, is "sometimes," the most realistic, "seldom." Love was never meant to be so incidental.

The false presumption that love is a common human sentiment springing naturally from pure hearts leads to another, that we already love quite well. Of course, we all fail to be sensitive at every moment. We sometimes lapse in our commitment, lie, gossip, and use those who have entrusted to us their secrets and souls. But overall, if the circumstances were known and our struggles were weighed, certainly any reasonable court in the land would find the facts overwhelmingly clear: We are innocent of a grave failure to love. No one could find us guilty of a felony, let alone a capital offense deserving death.

I have heard perpetrators of spousal abuse, child abuse, and immorality talk about their grievous harm to the victim in one breath and their love for the victim in the next. Without doubt, in less extreme situations, we often love and hurt the same person. But some are not able to admit or acknowledge with sorrow the tragic interplay of love and hate in the fallen human heart. Consequently, at times, when I have questioned whether or not there may be a discrepancy between their sin and their protestation of love, I am attacked or defensively retreated from as an enemy, not a friend.

When the question of failure to love is raised, it should be heard as the whisper of a friend, not the accusation of an enemy, because our failures can be the delicious entry into a new comprehension of God's grace. Unfortunately, we are often so committed to seeing our involvement with others as innocent and our presumption of goodness untarnished that we retreat from facing our own lovelessness. It seems inconceivable to most of us that relief can be found in facing our failure. In seeing what is in our heart, we might be further compelled to flee from our presumption of self-sufficiency and embrace the hope of relationships built on God's initiative and not on our performance. However, this kind of dependence requires a broken heart that has given up the demands of pride. Many are simply not ready for such loss of face.

There is an enormous drive within the fallen human personality that impedes the process of learning to love and an equally powerful force outside of every person that labors to destroy any effort to love. Every day I hear stories about Christian parents, spouses, pastors, bosses, ad infinitum that boggle my almost unflappable mind. I hear accounts of tragic sexual abuse, overwhelming neglect, emotional cruelty, and less tragic violations of love, which cumulatively add up to a thousand pinpricks that slowly bleed a person to death by drops. Complacency and presumption work hand-in-hand to blind even Christians to the importance of love and the inherent battle involved in learning to love. If we are to learn to love, we must begin with an acknowledgment that love is not natural and that love's failure is not easy to admit.

How then does God intervene in the human personality to remove the block to love and destroy the power of evil that hates love? The answer is found in an understanding of God's relentless, intrusive, incarnate involvement and His patient, forbearing forgiveness. The essence of Christianity is God's tenacious loyalty to redeem His people from the just penalty for sin.

Forgiving Love: The Essence of Christianity
Consider God's involvement with and long-suffering forgiveness of us. Nehemiah describes in a few verses the history of the repetitive pattern of having God's good gifts spurned and, in turn, how He wins His people back by His kindness and forgiving love:

> "In their hunger you gave them bread from heaven and
> in their thirst you brought them water from the rock;
> you told them to go in and take possession of the land
> you had sworn with uplifted hand to give them.
>   "But they, our forefathers, became arrogant and stiff-

necked, and did not obey your commands. They refused to listen and failed to remember the miracles you performed among them. They became stiff-necked and in their rebellion appointed a leader in order to return to their slavery. But you are a forgiving God, gracious and compassionate, slow to anger and abounding in love. Therefore you did not desert them, even when they cast for themselves an image of a calf and said, 'This is your god, who brought you up out of Egypt,' or when they committed awful blasphemies.

"Because of your great compassion you did not abandon them in the desert. By day the pillar of cloud did not cease to guide them on their path, nor the pillar of fire by night to shine on the way they were to take. You gave your good Spirit to instruct them. You did not withhold your manna from their mouths, and you gave them water for their thirst. For forty years you sustained them in the desert; they lacked nothing, their clothes did not wear out nor did their feet become swollen." (Nehemiah 9:15-22)

Let me review some of the key elements of this passage.

1. *God's response to hunger and thirst:* Provision of bread, water, and possession of the land.
2. *People's response to His kindness:* Arrogant, stiff-necked, and rebellious making of other gods and a return to slavery.
3. *God's response to hateful rebellion:* Forgiving, gracious, compassionate, slow to anger, and abounding in love. He did not desert nor abandon His people.

The pattern has been continually replayed since the fall of Adam and Eve into sin. God blesses; man uses and perverts; and then God disciplines, forgives, restores, and calls us into useful service. The pattern is tragic in its repetition, but overwhelmingly wonderful in its end. God wins, as do those who bear the mark of His forgiving love.

His long-suffering patience and forgiveness, however, are not offered without great cost to Himself. The cost is ultimately the sacrifice of His own beloved Son for the payment of sin. His forgiveness also involves a high price for the recipient. The cost is sacrifice as well, but of a wholly different order from His Son's shameful death on behalf of His brothers and sisters.

The cost for the recipient of God's grace is NOTHING — and no price could be higher for arrogant people to pay. Something within me (that feels noble) longs for a religion that requires payment. I may like an occasional free gift, but I cannot bear the loss of pride and swagger that occurs when I give my life and nothing is required. Grace is free, and that is disturbing. It is so distressing, in fact, that most who receive it work hard to find some way to preserve their arrogance by laborious piety. The often sincere, but arrogant, penance in many cases serves to retain their false pride and in turn to obligate God to act on their behalf.

Love seems to be constantly derailed by sin. Every effort to do good, to some degree, seems to flounder on the shoals of self-centeredness. A typical event illustrates the normal tragedy of well-meaning, yet self-centered, efforts to love.

My wife, Rebecca, and oldest daughter, Anna, were embroiled in a nasty discussion over Anna's homework. I decided to step in, like a tag-team exchange, to relieve Rebecca from the imbroglio. I saw her waning and exhausted by the interchange, so I mounted my white steed and, like a shining knight, rode into battle. Within minutes, I transformed a benign but unpleasant discussion into a high-stakes, emotional free-for-all that deepened Anna's anger and despair.

When Anna failed to take seriously my concerns — nothing is more irritating for a parent than to feel dismissed — my anger escalated. The angrier I got, the more sullen she became. My tone became louder, and my wife's frenzy reached new levels. Soon my daughter was furious, and my wife was disgusted with us both. I became incensed at Rebecca's frustration and livid over Anna's disregard. I soon stormed out of the room after one last childish show of temper. Act one had finished. Act two was about to begin.

I soon realized how foolishly I was behaving. I decided to apologize. I went up to Anna's room, and my wife said to me, "Are you planning more of the same?" She was wrong for her snide remark, but she certainly had a basis for it in my track record. Instead of accepting her unkind rebuke, I snarled at her, seconds before going into my daughter's room. Anna heard the unkind interchange between Rebecca and me. When I entered her room, she asked, "Are you and Mom fighting over me? Are you going to get a divorce?" I was exposed, saddened, and ashamed by my sin. So much for trying to help my wife and daughter. The curtain was ready to go up on act three.

The real battle that ensued was an internal struggle over whether to ever involve myself with my family again. If I do such harm when I mean to do good, why bother trying to love at all? I felt like a failure, a well-meaning bumbler. The problem, however, was worse than my bumbling. I was quietly demanding that my family be thrilled with my wise, strong involvement. I was demanding that my daughter be deeply moved to go after her homework with more vigor than I expect of myself when I clean the garage. I was sincere, but dead wrong. The guilt and confusion I felt over the debacle were strangely mixed with rage.

My conviction was not pure; I was still irked that I failed, not that I hurt my family or turned my back on God. I couldn't seem to manage more than a frail conviction entangled with self-centered guilt, nagging shame, and inner outbursts of rage, confusion, and deepening despair. I could either ignore my spiraling inner mess or cry out to God for forgiveness. The choice was between the hardness of denial or the suppleness of love. Was I willing to remain humbly and strongly involved with my family until restoration was won? In order for love to prevail, someone or something had to intervene to cut the cords of guilt, shame, rage, confusion, and despair from my frail heart.

In my sin, I felt contaminated and dangerous. I was isolated from my family, myself, and certainly from God. If love was ever to prevail, complete forgiveness was required. The flawed lover must be restored to the path of love after love has perished on the shoals of self-centeredness. At the deepest level, the taste of forgiveness must come from the One most offended in order for life and love to be restored. In every case of sin, it is God who is most hurt and offended by our refusal to love. It is His forgiveness that is central to any movement to love after love has been trampled under the muck of hatred.

This is true if the failure of love is in the giving (as in my case) or in the receiving. There are many who offer great gifts of love but are rebuffed and, in turn, refuse to deal with their own hurt, anger, and refusal to love again with an open heart. Many clients I work with in counseling have made an oath—sometimes conscious and usually unwitting—to never give again after a sincere, good gift was harshly rejected or thoughtlessly ignored.

A woman told me that when she was a child, she bought her mother an inexpensive gift of glass earrings. She spent hours making a card and wrapping the present. Before dinner, she gave the wonderful gift to her mother. Her usually distracted, self-absorbed mother patronized her daughter and told her she would open it later. After dinner, my client asked her mother if she had opened the gift. Her mother said, "Honey, I'm afraid I threw that little package away with the dinner trash. I hope you're not upset." Her mother typically ignored her daughter's joys and sorrows, and in turn, created a context where my client refused at a young age to offer her heart to any who might disappoint her or disregard her soul. Not only was the mother-daughter relationship profoundly empty, but my client's other relationships lacked the vigor of passion, openness, and involvement.

Love often succumbs to a cold death on the sharp rocks of disappointment. *Love cannot last long or live out its eternal purpose in human relationships without a foundation of forgiveness*—the forgiveness from God for our failure to love with a pure, other-centered heart, and forgiveness when the recipient of our love spurns our gift or uses our soul in an unloving fashion. Unless the fabric of our involvement with others is woven with the threads of forgiveness, love will suffer the corruption of denial, hardness, cynicism, and eventually hatred.

Given the reality of sin, love and forgiveness are inextricably bound together. God is continually, literally, second-by-second covering our sin under His Son's blood and forgiving us our sins. God cannot love us unless He forgives us and cannot forgive us without a commitment to love us. Love and forgiveness are equally bound together in all human relationships. I cannot hope to ever love someone unless I am committed to forgive him. I cannot hope to ever forgive him—that is, truly forgive him—unless I know the rich, incomprehensible joy of being forgiven.

Jesus discussed the intimate relationship between love and forgiveness with a Pharisee named Simon one night as they dined and drank together. At one point, Simon's party was disrupted by the appearance of a distasteful ex-prostitute who prostrated herself at the feet of Jesus, gently weeping and anointing His feet with her perfume.

Let me attempt to set the context. How would you like to have Billy Graham over to your home for dinner? Wouldn't your Christian, and even your unbelieving, friends be impressed? Imagine that as you serve him delightful hors d'oeuvres before the meal, a neighborhood teenager known for her wild immorality, reckless behavior, and offensive clothes saunters over to your porch, falls down at his feet, and begins to thank him for his ministry and his life. You might be confused, embarrassed, and perhaps outright offended that a thoroughly unacceptable gate crasher was wrecking your party. And then imagine that Dr. Graham gave his attention to the girl.

It was in that setting that Simon felt contemptuous toward the Lord. Didn't He know what kind of woman was touching His feet? What was His problem? He certainly was not as wise as He presented Himself.

To those thoughts, Jesus addressed His parable-question: Who will be more grateful, one who has been released from a small debt or one who has had a large debt canceled? Simon was trapped by both his private thoughts and the obvious conclusion of the question. Luke recorded Simon's reply: "I suppose the one who had the bigger debt canceled" (7:43).

He was correct. Jesus finished the conversation with Simon by summarizing the point of the story: "Her many sins have been forgiven—for she loved much. But he who has been forgiven little loves little" (verse 47).

Love is dependent on forgiveness. A formula can almost be structured from this concept. *The extent to which someone truly loves will be positively correlated to the degree the person is stunned and silenced by the wonder that his huge debt has been canceled.* Perhaps another way to say it is that gratitude for forgiveness is the foundation for other-centered love.

A hint may now be offered as to why grace is so demanding in its free offer—all that's required in response is stunned silence and overwhelmed gratitude. A stunned and grateful heart is free to love because it has been captured with the hilarious paradox that we are unlovely but loved, and unable to love but free to try without condemnation. And all efforts to love are made lovely and useful by a great Lover who superintends all our bumbling efforts and turns the dross of mixed motives to the gold of eternal intentions.

If this is true, why do so many seem to love so poorly? Part of the answer is that few are that silent or that grateful to God for the work of the Cross. Instead, most of us are somewhat irritated with God that He has not done more to resolve our struggles with an outstanding mortgage debt—or with the debt that is owed to us by a parent who abused us. To be honest, few Christians are that overwhelmed by the power of the gospel to save our souls from hell, because the unpleasant consequences of living in a fallen world feel too much like a hell in which God refuses to intervene.

If love is deeply bound to the work of forgiveness, both in the divine-human relationship and in human-human relationships, then it is imperative for us to understand in greater detail why forgiveness seems to mean so little to us. If we want to learn to love, we must first face the extent of our hatred for God and others.

CHAPTER TWO

TAKING OUR HATRED OUT OF THE CLOSET:
Why Don't We Love Better?

❖

T he pleasant, light-hearted interchange I was enjoying with a good friend suddenly ended with an intense glare and an angry turn of the shoulder. I was teasing her about her occasional lapses of logic and lack of awareness of time. I made a joke about her being a space cadet, and she erupted. It seemed as if I had set off a deep, internal earthquake of rage.

I was silenced and stunned by the intensity of her response. I attempted to talk about what occurred, but her response was a stony, cold silence, injected with an occasional sarcastic comment. I clearly had touched a nerve, and she reflexively responded with anger, hurt, and withdrawal. I was face to face with hatred.

At the moment of the attack, my friend, who cares for me, wished me harm. Her sarcastic comments were arrows meant to pierce my heart, and her stony silence was a club that attempted to bludgeon me into indifference. I knew she was hurt, but she was also murderous. I was aware that she felt intense shame, which she anesthetized with mega-doses of rage.

Is it accurate to say that at that moment, for whatever reason — legitimate or illegitimate — she hated me? We are friends; we care for one another. But when she stuck one of her barbs into my back, her love was eclipsed by her hatred.

Is it possible to love and hate the same person at the same moment? Even more important, is it possible to hate someone so deeply that love is obscured — to a point of being a functional nonentity, even though a molecule of love may still exist for the person? If that is possible in our relationships with one another, could a regenerate heart have even love for God crowded out by self-interest, fear of others, anger, rebellion, and hatred? I believe that it is not only possible, but the very reason why most of us love so poorly.

We must ask a difficult question: Why don't we love better? Perhaps, better said, why does forgiveness, at times, mean so little to us? Why are we so apt to forsake forgiveness or to forgive in such a tedious and mechanical manner that it neither touches the one forgiven nor deeply changes us?

Let me summarize the point of this chapter: Our unacknowledged and undealt-with commitment to find life apart from dependence on God, which is a form of subtle hatred of God, blocks our desire and commitment to love others. We will never love perfectly until we are without sin, glorified, and made perfect like Christ Jesus. The reason we do not love better, then, is our ongoing struggle with sin.

Love is derailed when our heart is turned against God. The direction of the heart is either one of love, gratitude, and worship or its opposite, hatred and self-justification for sin and adoration of the self. The dilemma is that hatred of God is rarely obvious or articulate. More often than not, our anger toward God is suppressed, denied, and redefined.

It is imperative to take our attitude toward God out of the closet and look at it in the light of His long-suffering kindness.

BUT I DON'T HATE GOD!

There are many sensitive Christians who will immediately balk at the idea that a believer might have a form of hatred toward

God. The thought that a redeemed heart could or would ever be angry at God, who sacrificed His Son on our behalf to provide us with forgiveness from our sins and a relationship with the Trinity, is repugnant to many. For a few moments, let me dialogue with the questions a sensitive believer might raise as objections.

How could any person hate God? First, let us consider the heart of the unbeliever. The unbeliever hates God (Romans 8:7). Whether the unbeliever is arrogant or humble in heart, deceitful or sincere in his relationship with others, the Scriptures say that we were all enemies of God before we were reconciled to Him through the death of His Son (Romans 5:10). We were enemies of the Cross because we believed that we could find life apart from relationship with God through our own wisdom and strength. Paul described the unbeliever as "foolish, disobedient, deceived and enslaved by all kinds of passions and pleasures. We lived in malice and envy, being hated and hating one another" (Titus 3:3). Living in hatred—hatred of God and others—is an inescapable reality for the blind, hardened, enslaved heart.

But I Can't Hate God Because I Am a Believer!
There are many who would suggest that it is not possible or even conceivable for a Christian to hate God because the old has passed away and the new has come. The old man is dead, and we are freed to love in the new way of the Spirit. I could not agree more. At the deepest part of my new identity in Christ, I love God and His law. The battle to subdue sin in my members, however, still rages—and the battle is intense.

What is the nature of the battle? Paul says it is the battle between his "inner being" and the "members of his body" (Romans 7:22-23). Paul makes a clear distinction between his inner being, which delights in the law of God, and his members, which wage against truth and entrap him in the slavery of sin.

I don't believe he was offering a technical and precise distinction that can be understood as referring to some actual element of our material or immaterial being. He is not saying that our mind is sinless but our hands are evil, nor is he arguing that our spirit is now pure but our soul is still under the sway of sin. I rather understand the distinction to be metaphorical, in that he is implying, irrespective of how it actually works or where it comes from, that we are a mysterious mixture of life and death, good and evil, and love and hatred. I am mixed up, but I can count on a wonderful fact—the deepest, strongest, most central part of me that will last through eternity is of God, goodness, and love. The other part may look stronger and have greater controlling influence at any one moment, but in reality, it will be swallowed up in a twinkling of an eye and I will be transformed into perfect, uncompromisable, undiluted humanness.

Paul understood the battle of the inner life to be one of a fight between two strong inclinations—a desire to do good and a desire to do evil. The fight is not one of two separate natures doing battle in a helpless body, but a deep desire to do good in the "inner being" and a sinful inclination within the "members of my body" that continually fight to regain control of the mind. The war is in the same heart.

I think of that as similar to the battle for an island during World War II. Once the troops landed and secured the beach, the island was essentially won. The enemy had no power to replenish its troops or send in reinforcements. The cost for sweeping the island of all opposing forces, however, was extremely high. The war was won, but countless tragic, bloody battles were yet to be fought. This is true for a Christian's heart. Victory is certain, but the heart must be restored to its full image in Christ, inch by precious inch and battle after tragic battle.

But isn't the believer a new creation? "Therefore, if anyone is in Christ, he is a new creation; the old has gone, the new has come!" (2 Corinthians 5:17). This passage is often used to imply that a Christian at regeneration is given an entirely new internal disposition, which is sinless, pure, and perfect. The assumption seems to be that I (that is, the real me) am without sin, and when I sin, it is really not me, but sin that is external to the perfectly pure new creature within me. The assumption is that I, as a new creation, am perfect.

However, the "new creation" passage is better understood as a description of our new relationship to the Kingdom of God. We were once aliens and strangers (in fact,
enemies) of the Kingdom of Light, but as a result of being
in Christ, we are part of a new creation, a new Kingdom.
As a result of being made citizens of a new country/crea-
tion/Kingdom, we are given the unbelievable opportunity
of being ambassadors of reconciliation. The passage is not a
statement about our new internal constitution, but a picture of
our newly created opportunity to stand in a radically different
relationship to God and those who are still in the kingdom of
darkness.

This can be compared to being grafted into a new vine.
The believer has been grafted into the vine, and over time, she
will have the capacity to bear fruit. At first, however, she is
an appendage, not a full-grown, mature, fruit-bearing branch.
If she abides in the vine (and the vine in her) then over time,
through careful pruning, she will eventually bear fruit. This
implies a process — a development from the day of attachment
to the vine to the day that her roots are imbedded in the vine,
then to the day that her branch buds, and finally to the day she
offers fruit to the tender Gardener who grafted her to the vine.
Upon grafting, her character, inclinations, and fruit-bearing
capacities are not immediately operative.

The same is true for a believer who is a new creation. The
new passport and new citizenship granted as a result of being
grafted to a new Kingdom do not immediately provide the
new immigrant with a facility in the country's new language,
customs, or ethos. Citizenship does grant a new status and,
in most cases, a deepened gratitude and new opportunities.
The same is true for conversion. The metaphor breaks down
in that citizenship does not involve an internal change. At the
point of regeneration, the Holy Spirit takes up its abode in
the internal world of the new believer, which creates a new
inclination to pursue God and to give to others. Indeed, a new
inclination is in operation — a working of the Holy Spirit with
the newly alive human spirit — but it is inconceivable that
all the perceptions and struggles of the past have vanished

at conversion. Consequently, it must be assumed that some, and in fact a great many, of the past perceptions and convictions will need to be torn down and rebuilt in the light of new creation ethics.

Am I a new creation? Of course, I am an adopted child of the reigning King. Am I a radically different person—inside and out—as a result of my new standing in the Kingdom of Light? Of course—I am grafted by the Spirit to the Vine. And, of course not—there is a significant developmental process of time and pruning before I am a radically changed, wonderfully fruit-bearing branch.

Why, Then, Don't I Feel Hatred Toward God?

Most Christians experience a variety of emotions toward God— on one hand, gratitude, awe, fear, delight, and comfort; on the other, confusion, irritation, loneliness, and coldness. In large measure, our feelings are related to our desire to either serve Him or to serve ourselves.

When I am thrilled with the reality of who God is and what He has done, I am filled with feelings that are consonant with any intimate relationship. I feel close, connected, engaged, passionate, and alive. On the other hand, when my heart is oriented toward securing life (or a cab, or a waitress to bring my bill, or a break from struggling with the thorns and thistles in my garden) through my own power and wisdom, I am serving another master, not God. The result will be feelings that are associated with a break in relationship—distance, loneliness, hurt, blame, and anger.

The Scriptures go further to describe our relationship with God as one that involves either love or hatred—and nothing in between. Jesus tells us, "No one can serve two masters. Either he will hate the one and love the other, or he will be devoted to the one and despise the other" (Matthew 6:24).

At the same time, emotions can be easily distorted or redefined as feelings that are more acceptable. Hatred can be reshaped as confusion, hurt, indifference, irritation, anger, or contempt. For example, I spoke to a man who felt confusion when others experienced him as hostile. When I pointed out that his anger might be hidden under confusion, he retorted with disdain, "Might it also be possible that I am confused?" His words were tight fists held in front of my face. The tension built to a near crescendo as I quietly looked into his angry eyes.

Finally, he shook his head and said, "I don't know. I don't know what I am feeling. I feel so confused with what I hear other people saying to me." His anger melted into uncertainty. He now felt an emotion that was not as alienating as anger and did not require the kind of strength that is needed to deal with conflict. Confusion allowed him to get off the hook of conflict and hide the intensity of anger.

Paul says that people have the capacity to "suppress the truth by their wickedness" (Romans 1:18). The writer of the book of Hebrews warns us to not be "hardened by sin's deceitfulness" (Hebrews 3:13). The believing heart has the capacity to be blind and hard, thus distorting or denying our inner world or the realities of the outer world, if for some reason it is too noxious to our senses.

Why don't we feel hatred toward God? First, a Christian does not always hate God because our heart's inclination has been transformed from being an enemy of God to being His adopted son or daughter. It is imperative to consider this thought: A Christian's hatred of God will always be temporary (though it may last far longer at levels of severity than we desire) and will eventually increase a sense of conviction and repentance. Second, when I am serving a false god, I may deceitfully justify my choice; therefore, the mold has transformed the raw reality of my rebellion into emotions that don't feel like hatred, but indeed are hatred. Or when I am serving another master, I may also ignore, deny, or suppress my hatred so that I am not aware of the raw rebellion pulsating through my veins. Opposition to God, in other words, is seldom immediately experienced as hatred.

Won't God Punish Me for My Hatred?
Finally, if I admit that I do not like God at times, won't He punish me and make me pay? Nothing could be further from the

truth. Let us begin with the assumption that the omniscient, all-seeing God already knows what I may not even be aware of feeling or thinking. Has God turned His back on me because of my foolish schemes to find life apart from Him? I believe the Cross displays an answer to that question. He has chosen to bear the high cost of turning me from my false gods to open the return to His gracious care.

The cold or hot heart that wrestles with God is far more pleasing to Him than the one that slowly cools toward Him in tepid pretense (Revelation 3:15-16). I have known Christians who struggle with strong fury toward God, who I believe are more pleasing to Him than others who dutifully obey and offer burnt offerings on the altar without thought or passion. Some of God's favored servants spoke to Him with words that might make many Christians shudder. Listen to one of them:

> O LORD, you deceived me, and I was deceived;
> > you overpowered me and prevailed.
> I am ridiculed all day long;
> > everyone mocks me.
> Whenever I speak, I cry out
> > proclaiming violence and destruction.
> So the word of the LORD has brought me
> > insult and reproach all day long. (Jeremiah 20:7-8)

Jeremiah felt deceived by God. The word *deceived* has a sexual connotation that implies seduction. Jeremiah felt seduced by God. God had promised him protection when he was called to be God's prophet, and the derision, mockery, and hatred of others did not seem consistent with God's commitment to keep him safe. Jeremiah was, at that moment, not fond of God.

God, however, did not crush Jeremiah for his hatred. God's intention was to flame the small fire that Jeremiah could not put out. God will not break a broken reed or put out a smoldering wick (Isaiah 42:3). His intention is to turn the hatred into passion and the passion into radical worship of Him and service to others.

WHAT DOES IT MEAN TO HATE GOD?

In its simplest definition, sin is hatred of God. Every time I set my heart in opposition to God, demand that life work according to my vision, and act in the power of my arrogance, I turn Him into my enemy. When do I feel most compelled to take life into my own hands and pursue the false gods of an Enemy kingdom? Some moments of opposition are conscious and overt. There are times I know that I want to say an unkind word to my wife because she has hurt me. I am fully aware the remark will be cruel; she deserves it. At that moment, I know God will be grieved by my sin, but I don't care. Revenge seems like it will be sweet enough to warrant the anguish I will cause all parties concerned. This is reprehensible hatred of my wife and God; I make them my enemies. And yet, if I am under God's grace through trust in Christ's shed blood, even during moments of intentional hatred, I remain His friend, albeit one that deeply grieves Him.

At other times, our opposition to God is not a conscious act of rebellion, but an unwitting resolve to take care of our pain in our own strength. I have a friend who is apt to be rash. When she is disappointed, she stomps around and vents her articulate steam. After a few moments, she is fine and forgets her concerns, but many around her tread lightly for hours for fear that another mini-quake might occur.

Does my friend know that she is angry at God? To a degree, but more often than not she is oblivious to her effects on others or to her feelings about a God who seems to allow the injustice that invokes her momentary bursts of pique. Her pattern is to occasionally roar and then quietly wait for others to respond. She is a wonderful friend, but she unwittingly, unconsciously rages at God in her demands for personal and relational perfection.

Sin, or hatred of God, is a defiant movement, sometimes unwitting and other times quite conscious, which refuses to depend on God for His direction and strength. In that sense, we become enemies of God whenever we seek to find satisfaction for our deepest longings apart from relationship with Him. James vividly describes the fury we have at others and at God when our desires go unsatisfied:

> What causes fights and quarrels among you? Don't they come from your desires that battle within you? You want something but don't get it. You kill and covet, but you cannot have what you want. You quarrel and fight. You do not have, because you do not ask God. When you ask, you do not receive, because you ask with wrong motives, that you may spend what you get on your pleasures.
>
> You adulterous people, don't you know that friendship with the world is hatred toward God? Anyone who chooses to be a friend of the world becomes an enemy of God. (James 4:1-4)

Turning God into an enemy can come at points of big decisions and huge consequences, or in the minute and minor. Let me give an example of the commitment to live life with quiet, subtle arrogance. By its relative triviality, the example will likely offend. Many readers may dismiss the thought that a form of hatred of God can be so small and incidental.

The other day, I bought a new pair of comfortable wool socks. The store's paper label surrounded the socks; I easily tore it off. The socks were still secured by a small plastic insert that kept them together. I tugged on the plastic and it did not give way to my gentle insistence. I pulled harder and it tenaciously resisted my intention of putting on my new socks. I got angry. I yanked the socks apart, and to my delight, the plastic snapped. My joy was short lived, however. To my chagrin, I noticed a small hole in my new socks. I was furious. I had been lazy. In fact, not only lazy, but presumptive ("I won't rip my socks"), foolish ("I can manage this task without getting up to get a pair of scissors"), and of course, arrogant ("I am too busy to be bothered by such mundane tasks"). I wanted my socks on and I wanted them on now. In one of the smaller moments of my day, I was invited to face my depravity.

Is it silly to say at the moment I ripped the hole in my

socks, "I hate God"? Most people probably think so. The only reason to call this event silly is the relative insignificance of the results. The consequence was minor; unfortunately, that is not always the case. The dynamics of sin were in place as I yanked the socks apart—a refusal to bow to wisdom and a commitment to find satisfaction from life on my own. Is that essentially different from the person who decides to have an affair or the one who chooses to gossip? The consequences are at times more tragic and long lasting, but in fact all foolishness, demandingness, and arrogance is, at core, hatred of God.

WHEN ARE WE MOST APT TO HATE GOD?

Let me again state the obvious point: A Christian is not God's enemy, nor will the Spirit of God permit, without deepening conviction, a rampant, unrestrained, bottomless hatred of God. The patterns of hatred—of others and God—will over time painfully recede and slowly be replaced by a growing desire to worship God in truth and wisdom and serve others in the new freedom of the Spirit. The good news is that hatred of God and others decreases as Christ takes the heart inch by inch. On the other hand, the battle rages even more intensely as progress is made. For many, the deepest growth in humble, joyful reliance on God will be in the context of the most bloody battles, which appear to be tragic losses and not glorious victories.

Hatred, as a final reality, is dead when persons accept Christ's sacrifice as their atonement for sin. The war is won. But the battle to replace hatred with love will be over only when we see Jesus in the flesh and become as He is (1 John 3:2). There are times during the battle when hatred plays a more powerful influence than gratitude and love. It is imperative to understand when we are most likely to overtly or subtly make God our enemy and labor to make life work in the manner that fits our demands. The two major contexts where hatred is easily incited are at crossroads of choice and in the face of injustice.

LIFE ISN'T EASY!

I spoke to a friend who was engaged in the awesome task of choice. It was four weeks and one day before Christmas, and he was twenty-four hours from the deadline to purchase a less expensive plane ticket. He could not decide whether he should go home to see his parents or stay and work to pay off more of his school debts. His parents wanted him to come, but could not help pay for the tickets. On the other hand, they had been quite critical of his decision earlier that fall to fly to see his girlfriend.

His parents were struggling financially and told him not to purchase any gifts. Once before, the same assertion was made and he chose to accede to their desire. For several years, both parents scolded him for failing to buy the other parent a small token of his appreciation.

Tom was in a bind. He could not responsibly afford to fly home, yet he could not emotionally afford not to fly home. He did not want to pay for his absence at the family Christmas celebration, yet he did not want to pay for an expensive flight home and the expected gifts.

Tom's family is not unusual. Their own reluctance to speak honestly and accept the consequences of a decision without punishing the one who makes an unpopular choice is common. As we talked over lunch, he wavered between confusion ("What is God's will? What is loving? What is the right thing to do?") and anger ("How can they put me in this bind? Don't they realize I am struggling financially? Why can't they accept my decision to break away from the family?"). The energy behind his angry confusion was the demand to be free from both the choice and the consequences of his choice.

Avoiding Choices
We are odd people. We will fight for freedom and die to protect our right to choose. On the other hand, every day we labor to avoid choice and hunger for someone or something to relieve the awesome burden of choice. Put simply, I will want to kill you if you take away my opportunity to choose and will hate

you if you require me to choose.

Some of us approach life with overt commitments to avoid choice (passivity) or perfect choice (perfectionism) so that the consequences of choice will not fall on our shoulders. Others make irresponsible choices (impulsion) or delay them (procrastination) so that excuses can be readily offered. Some make aggressive choices (intimidation) to keep others from being able to exert their freedom to choose. All of these approaches hate the burden of choice and attempt to sidestep the responsibility to deal with the consequences of choice.

I find that much of my reading, thinking, praying, and seeking counsel from wise friends is motivated by a desire to share the responsibility of choice with God and others. If I am in a community that will not tolerate current trends of fashion, then I need not concern myself with a whole range of difficult, ethical choices. If I know that I like moo goo gai pan, then I don't need to look over the complex, bewildering choices at a Chinese restaurant. I order what I know, which is often determined centrally by the desire to stick with the easiest choice. No wonder people flock to authoritarian and persuasive leaders — they relieve the anguish of choice — or to approaches of sanctification that lay out the rules for recovery and the stages for sanctification. We all want a well-lighted, paved, yellow brick road to life. And we feel rage when someone tells us that yellow brick roads lead only to Oz, not to freedom.

The anguish of choice ("Do I go home for Christmas?" "Do I tell my wife that she hurt me?" "Do I work overtime or do I spend more time with my kids?" "Do I go to a more progressive church or stay in my dull but orthodox congregation?") often exposes our fury at God. He has commanded me to love and holds me accountable to love perfectly (Matthew 5:43-48). But then I am faced with the confusion about what it means to love. Why can't He be clearer about what He wants from me? And why can't He be simple about how I am to appropriate His power to do what He wants me to do? Why can't He give me the wisdom, strength, and boldness to conquer doubt, inability, and fear? Why does He hold me accountable to be perfect and then not give me what I need to obey His will?

Most people would gladly crawl over broken glass if they knew it would restore a broken marriage or heal a drug-addicted teenager. Most people would kill to know what to do and how to get the strength to do it. And yet God often seems so silent. He commands us to love, but does not tell us what to do. He tells me to live righteously, but that only seems to help clarify a few major decision points in life — don't get drunk, don't have an affair, don't cheat on my taxes, and don't gossip or tell lies.

Now What?!

Put simply, God's requirements seem so demanding in light of the resources He offers for knowing what to do and how to do it. The burden of choice seems unfair. It is in the crucible of choice that many choose to either opt for what is comfortable and safe or choose to bludgeon others with their right to choose. In either case — avoidance of choice or assertion of choice — a hatred of God and others is inflamed. And in many cases, the choice to love, with the inherent confusion, risk, and uncertainty, is forsaken for the relative safety of self-protection.

Self-protection is the self-centered commitment to act without courage, compassion, boldness, and tenderness for the sake of the other. It is an intentional, though usually unconscious, disposition that offers the other everything or anything but the heart. Self-protection can be dressed either in codependent maneuvering that lacks self-identity, freedom of choice, and strength, or in counter-dependent distancing that alienates through self-assertion, demanding control, and intimidation. In either case, in extreme or even in subtle form, there is a failure to offer both a tender and a strong heart. The result will be an absence of bold love.

LIFE ISN'T FAIR!

If the context of choice is one that deepens our commitment to opt for finding life on our own, the context of perceived injustice fuels our hatred as well. A client who had been sexually violated by her brother, uncle, father, grandfather, pastor, several teachers, and dozens of boyfriends put words to one of those points where hatred of God is common: "I cannot figure God out. He seems to rain blessings on those who hate Him and send storms against those who love Him. If there is justice, it seems to come only to those who don't need it."

How many people have uttered those words in angry confusion? Habakkuk, the prophet, laid his angry complaint before God:

> How long, O LORD, must I call for help,
>> but you do not listen?
> Or cry out to you, "Violence!"
>> but you do not save?
> Why do you make me look at injustice?
>> Why do you tolerate wrong?
> Destruction and violence are before me;
>> there is strife, and conflict abounds.
> Therefore the law is paralyzed,
>> and justice never prevails.
> The wicked hem in the righteous,
>> so that justice is perverted. (Habakkuk 1:2-4)

These words express the heart of any honest person who looks at the travesty of life and God's seeming inactivity. The psalmist said, "Surely God is good to Israel, to those who are pure in heart. But as for me, my feet had almost slipped; I had nearly lost my foothold. For I envied the arrogant when I saw the prosperity of the wicked. They have no struggles; their bodies are healthy and strong. They are free from the burdens common to man; they are not plagued by human ills" (Psalm 73:1-5).

Facing Injustice
Injustice—the unequal distribution of sorrow and happiness—is the steamy cauldron that stirs up the hateful stew of envy, contempt, and bitterness. How could God permit my body and

soul to be sexually abused by my respected Christian father and then give my close friend a father who is crude and self-centered, but who loves her and is respectful and kind to her? The plaintive cry of so many wounded hearts I have worked with is the same: "Where is God when life is cruel and unfair?"

God does not seem to dispense the (temporal) blessings of joy and happiness according to character or faithfulness. A woman who has not worked on her character and has sex with her boyfriend ends up marrying him and over the years develops a happy home and a successful relationship with her family. Another woman who is chaste and consistent in her pursuit of godliness finds herself single, lonely, and close to the final alarm on her biological clock. It isn't fair!

A family has three healthy kids and little time to spend with their brood because they are avariciously pursuing the good life. Yet they have ample family time as they jet off on another exciting trip. Another family I know has three kids, one who is dying of a fatal disease. They have little time together as well. The father must work two jobs to pay the outrageous medical costs involved in dying without undue pain. The mother is almost always exhausted and struggles to emotionally nourish their other two children. It just isn't fair!

A man I know has faithfully worked to bring truth and life to the souls of his flock. He has chosen the hard route of service in a rural area where change in practice is viewed as irreverent and personal discipleship is seen as meddling. He has labored long and hard, seeing few results and knowing little joy. His oldest son is about to start college, and the father is unable to offer him a penny of support. The son is bitter, and the father is overwhelmed with the seeming foolishness of staying in a congregation that will not support him organizationally, spiritually, or financially. He told me about one of his friends who went to seminary with him then took a job in a large, suburban church. After about ten years of service, he was offered a high-paying job by one of the elders in the church. The offer was too good to refuse. He not only can continue some of his favorite ministries, but can do so without concern about supporting his family. It isn't fair!

The unfairness of life really does cause my feet to slip and my foothold to be lost for a time. Is my struggle simply due to the fact that life is unfair? Is it just that God could allot His earthly blessings more equitably and limit the suffering? Let me state an obvious point: It is not life's or God's seeming unfairness that is so difficult to bear (though it is painful), it is the unbearable fact that in light of the radical injustice, God calls us to love, to turn the cheek, to offer our coats, and to carry the burden of our abusers one more mile. The law of love is not mitigated by the abuser's failure, irrespective of the damage perpetrated. God seems to have now joined ranks not only with those who choose not to intervene to halt the injustice but, even worse, to be on the side of the Persecutor, the Abuser, the Evil One.

The disciples felt the same confusion and incredulity toward Jesus when He told them to forgive their abusers (Luke 17:3-4). They were stunned when Jesus told them to forgive the one who hurt them not once or several times, but seven times seventy. In response to His outrageous command, they said, "Increase our faith" (verse 5). The Lord was not impressed by their desire for more faith. He heard their cry for more faith as a means of dodging His words. He answered, "If you have faith as small as a mustard seed, you can say to this mulberry tree, 'Be uprooted and planted in the sea,' and it will obey you" (verse 6). His position was clear: Even the smallest amount of faith is sufficient to forgive if a person wants to forgive and bear the inherent risks of loving in a fallen world. The issue is never capacity, but whether one desires to forgive. I have worked with abused men and women who hear the words of Christ and quit in rage. The law of love is too exacting and unrelenting; therefore, why bother and why try when failure and even greater abuse are the end results?

Consider the inequality of blessing, the success of the wicked, and the tragic damage experienced by innocent people in light of the unrelenting demands of the law of God to love. These alternately mock the apparent foolishness of living for God one moment and the next sing a siren song of desire that beckons the weary pilgrim to seek secular balm to heal the wounds of an unjust world and the demands of a cruel God. The options offered in the secular world span the gamut from the outright immoral ("have an affair") to the unbiblical ("take care of number one") to the questionable ("learn to love yourself first") to the legitimate but ineffective ("take a day off," or "why not take up a new sport?"). The theme that enables all the options to be sold in one store is the crushing reality of injustice. *If God will not act on my (or others') behalf, then I will step in to make up for His lack.*

The approach may be different (an affair versus taking a vacation; one is clearly wrong and the other is a legitimate option), but if the energy involved is to escape from the tragic reality of living in a fallen world, then both lead to the same end—*finding life through soothing the soul rather than from struggling with God.*

And who wants to struggle with God as one looks at the blight of injustice? There are days when I talk to a young child who was physically and emotionally bloodied and torn into pieces by a man's sexual and power lust, and I want out. I want relief. I frankly don't care how I find it, but I want wings to fly above the countryside littered with crushed souls.

One morning, I read in the paper about a traffic accident that occurred in our community. An aunt driving with her two nieces was struck by a drunk truck driver. The girls' father, a volunteer medic, was minutes behind the accident and stopped to help. He did not know his family was in the crushed car. He opened the car door and his youngest daughter fell into his arms — dead. His other daughter died on the way to the hospital.

I read the story and I screamed. My tears were angry and cruel. I audibly shouted, "Good job, God. Damn you." The rest of the day I battled with lustful thoughts—an insatiable desire to eat, a smug attitude toward those who were confident of God's love, and a distant and protective possessiveness toward those who were suffering. I wanted to ease their pain (and mine) by striking dead their Egyptian abusers and leading them through the desert to the Promised Land.

My desire for relief and respite from the wounds of a

fallen world and the demands of God was not, at this point, a hunger for a perfect, restored relationship with God, the One who loved me so much He died for me. Rather, it was the rageful grasping for soothing and solace in response to God's unrelenting demands and cruel inactivity. There is a subtle difference to be noted. One can long for wings to fly away because of a passion for God's presence, a longing for His fellowship, and a heart for His touch. One can also passionately desire a vehicle to fly above suffering due to a hatred of the God who hears the cries of His children and does not seem to act.

It is possible to face injustice and suffering and work for its demise as a response to the gospel. The consequence of my injustice has been paid for by His death and resurrection; therefore, I long to see others who are unjust come to taste the humbling delight of His kindness. Or injustice can be fought as a screaming protest to God's silent inactivity. In fact, the subtlety between the two options may be profound. Both may be involved in working with abused and battered women, protesting against abortion clinics, nourishing children who have been sexually assaulted, and boycotting stores that sell pornography.

The difference may not be easily noted, but in time the energy of hatred versus gratitude will be sensed in those who receive their strength and kindness. One will serve with humble, quiet grace and the other with angry, demanding assertion. One fights for a General who has already won, and the other for a revolution that is in question. One hates injustice, and the other hates the God who has not dealt with injustice according to our timetable. The latter enters the fray with a frenetic, scrambling energy that is busily in control; the former with a centeredness that is strong and passionate (such as Jesus' display of wrath in the temple), but that is never inconsistent with a deep concern for the one with whom the battle for justice and love is fought.

Struggling with God
In the face of injustice—which is daily and monstrous—one either learns to aggressively ask the hateful question, "Where

is God?" or ask, "Who is God, that He bears His own sorrow as the unjust succeed and the just suffer?" The enraged assertion attacks injustice with furious self-will; the struggling question waits honestly in trusting silence for God's perspective. This kind of trust is not a passive, other-worldly asceticism that smothers present groanings beneath a pious futuristic hope. Rather, it is a passionate, pregnant confidence in a God who will enfold an honest struggler in strong arms of comfort and love.

In summary, it is the daily horrors of living in an uncertain and unjust world that fuel our hatred toward God and deepen our passionate desire to take life into our own hands. It seems utterly unimaginable that in a world where your child may be playing in the neighborhood one day and lying in the morgue the next, a victim of a drunk driver, that God expects us to choose life and love over self-protection and self-centeredness. Our desire and efforts to love are blocked by our hatred of a God whose response to injustice seems inadequate—a hatred that is either overt and bellowing or subtle and seething.

The Christian who acknowledges that a part of his heart still rages against God is in conflict—a deep, internal war between love and hatred. Our regenerate hearts are built to cling to what is good and to hate evil (Romans 12:9), to hate all that is wicked (Psalm 45:7), and to enjoy what is lovely (Philippians 4:8). Christians are compelled to seek justice and extend love. It is as natural to our reborn souls as breathing. But the flesh, that disposition to hate God, does battle with our spirit deep within our being. I hate injustice and I want the Evil One to pay; I ignore my harm of others and I believe I deserve a break from God's law.

When will the hatred we feel toward others be transformed into utter compassion, and the fury we feel toward God be transfigured into glorious praise? The answer, in part, is when we are silenced by our own sin and stunned by God's response to our hatred.

CHAPTER THREE

STUNNED INTO SILENCE:
The Liberating Insult of Grace

❖

T he hatred in our hearts is most often quiet and dormant. It is like a genetic disease that appears only under careful scrutiny. Let me again state an obvious point: Hatred of God and others is usually labeled as something more palatable to our human sensibilities. For that reason (and many others), the good news of the gospel seems mildly pleasant, and often irrelevant.

If our sin is a mere failure to conform — simply a mistake to do what is right — forgiveness is really the granting of an opportunity to try again. In that light, it is like forgetting to finish one's homework. We deserve a low grade, and grace becomes merely the privilege of doing it over to get a higher mark. Such a view of grace might generate appreciation, but it would never drive us to worship. If, in fact, sin is not only a failure to hit the mark of God's perfection, but also a deep, insidious energy that desires to eradicate from our existence an affronting God who demands perfection, then forgiveness becomes breathtaking, incredible, and wonderfully insulting.

How does the gospel alter our hearts, especially for

someone who has had orthodox familiarity with the gospel for eons without ever being deeply changed? How do we embrace the truth so that our hateful hearts are overwhelmed by gratitude? The answer, in part, is to be silenced by the gravity of our condition.

Silence is required for deep change to occur. Once we are silent, it is possible for us to look into God's eyes and discover His response. We anticipate fury, yet what we find is fondness; we expect, at least, cool indifference in light of our disregard and anger, yet what we discover is passionate joy at our return to a relationship with Him.

God's disruptive and scandalous response to our hatred transforms fury into gratitude and deadness into life. The silence that deeply changes our heart is the hush that comes when we are caught in our hatred and found to be without excuse. The experience of being captured by eyes that searingly penetrate to the depths of our hurt and fury intensifies our shame and terror at first. Over time, however, the experience of being seized by God's strong and tender sorrow (in the light of what we deserve) stuns us beyond words and opens our heart to freeing gratitude. Consider first what it means to be silent before God.

STUNNED INTO SILENCE

Silence can be so deafening that no other sound can be heard. A silent man may not be quiet in heart; in fact, turbulent waters may be roaring in the midst of seeming stillness. Such was the still noise between my wife and me moments before I was to speak at a major Christian conference.

We were at a seminar attended by over 300 counselors and people-helpers who had come to hear several from our ministry speak on the issues of counseling. I was aware of the distance between us, but I had only about thirty minutes to shower, dress, and take one final look at my notes. I finally broke the silence by asking Rebecca if there was anything wrong. The torrent that she unleashed startled me with dumbfounded amazement. In the next few minutes she poured out what seemed to be a hundred years of hurt, fury, loss, and betrayal. Most of it was directed against me for failing to be as involved with her as I seemed to be with other people.

Earlier in the conference, I had talked and prayed with a number of participants, many of whom were past students, trainees, and clients. For whatever reason, the time was very intense and deeply personal. Many of the participants expressed their affection and gratitude, and a few spoke to my wife about the way God had used me in their lives. Each interaction added more details about my involvement with others and, in contrast, how little I had pursued similar issues in her soul.

Finally, after a number of intense interactions, Rebecca dissolved under the weight of her loneliness and my inattentiveness. The floodgates of twelve years of marriage poured through, and I was silent. She was not being rational. She was certainly not being sensitive to the fact that I was soon to spend three hours lecturing. Worst of all, she was wrong, or so I thought. I loved her. I sacrificed for her. I was a good husband. She had no right to spew her anger in my direction. My silence was quiet rage—the silence of withdrawal, the retreat of wounded fury.

The furious silence soon changed to another kind of ill-productive silence—the quiet of self-hatred. During my lecture, I could not face my wife's eyes. She was not enraged or distant, but every time I glanced her way, I could see the etching of sorrow in her look. I could not bear the pain; I looked away. When we were back in the room, I busied myself with mundane activities. Even though my back was turned, I could feel her presence and I wanted to flee. Instead of physically escaping, I burrowed myself in self-condemnation. I was a lousy husband; I failed my wife; I should not be in the ministry.

When I finally talked, my voice sounded hollow and strained. It was best to try again tomorrow. We attempted to sleep. I will never forget how wide the chasm spanned between our two backs. I wanted to turn over, but it felt like an enormous weight rested on my body that kept me from turning toward her. I pondered what I would say, and the content sounded superficial. I wanted to say, "I'm sorry for failing you for twelve years; I'll do better tomorrow." It seemed ridiculous. How does one ask forgiveness for harm that goes back a decade? Wasn't it better to hope that tomorrow would bring a better day and to cut the losses and trust that we could get on better footing? The silence of self-condemnation, despair, and/or frail hope is a subterfuge that pretends the symptoms are due to stress when the problem is cancer.

At first, my silence was shock ("What is she saying?"), then shame ("Does she love me?"), then rage ("How could she be saying this to me?"), and finally, hollow self-contempt for being such a lousy husband ("Why should I try? I'll just fail"). The sequence from shock to self-contempt did nothing to change my heart or alter the framework of our marriage. Neither would a process of taking care of myself by affirming my value as a worthwhile person. A silence was required—a stillness that would allow all self-centered maneuvering to be heard and all foolish efforts to solve the problem to be spotted.

Such rare stillness will likely not happen, in most cases, by simply reading words in a book or effortfully trying to become silent by meditative exercise. The silence of being caught is an existential moment that can be prayed for (Psalm 139:23-24) and prepared for (1 Corinthians 11:31, 2 Corinthians 13:5), but it cannot be summoned like a butler called to come to our service.

Such a moment was planned (from the foundation of the earth) to arrive later during the week of that conference. One afternoon, a good friend asked if Rebecca and I might meet with her after one of the evening sessions. Our friend, a spry and wonderfully wise woman young in her seventies, began our half-hour meeting (which lasted four hours) by saying, "I am shaking with fear. I don't know how to counsel, but I fear for your marriage." She spoke with boldness, as a woman who had wept and prayed for us. What occurred that night is too personal and too wonderful to describe. It seems trite to state that I saw my wife's pain, my sin, and the mercy of God, but that is precisely what occurred.

At one point, I described why I had been so busy and blamed my lack of communication on my wife's natural quietness. At that point, our friend asked, "Do you know the name _____ _____?" He was the founder of a major Christian ministry, used of God in countless lives. I knew his name, ministry, and sterling reputation. I admitted to being a silent admirer of his for years. She said, "Let me tell you a story about him." She proceeded to add countless details about his rich walk with God, his integrity, and his faith. She told me stories about his unique trust in God's provision that allowed him to take profound risks on the basis of a deep, abiding confidence in the goodness of God. Soon, I was anticipating that I was going to be called to mimic this man's life and vision. I felt deflated and pressured; I could never match up to his stature. In fact, she was preparing my heart for a Nathanic twist in the story line.

After regaling this man's life, her voice grew somber and reflective: "I've known him for decades. And his life has torn me to pieces. I've seen God use him mightily in the lives of others, and I've also watched what has happened to his wife, children, and friends as he has pursued his calling. He is a godly man, but his family is relationally starved. It has taken years for them to shake off the effects of his driven perfectionism and relentless involvement with others. Dan, I fear you may build Christ into the lives of others and neglect those you are most uniquely called to love."

I was dumbfounded. I was being compared to a great Christian leader (how honoring), but in the area where he was most deserving of condemnation. I was overwhelmed. My eyes were open to my arrogance, defensiveness, drivenness, and failure to love. Our friend had lovingly, delicately, and wisely painted me into a corner; I was unable to maneuver by her or offer other explanations for my sin.

Silence will not begin until that persistent inner voice justifying our failure to love is muted. Unfortunately, my inner voices enjoy talking at great length, and they find me to be a wonderful listener. How I was silenced by my friend's words is beyond my understanding, but without the stark silence,

I would have likely continued to make small changes that amounted to pressured efforts to prove I was not such a bad guy.

Stillness Is Not Immune to Sin
Lest I be misunderstood, be clear that a silent heart is not immune from the effects of others' sin. I grew progressively silent in the light of what I saw in my heart, but if I had been asked about where I felt failed by my wife, I could have spoken of deep hurt. The key is that the silence that dawns in light of seeing your own sin does not discount the damage of others' sin. It simply puts it, for a time, in the background, where it waits to be addressed when your own heart is less disposed to judge and rage at another's failure. The psalmist proclaims, "Be still, and know that I am God" (46:10). One form of stillness arises when we are caught in our sin and painted into a corner where we cannot escape the reality of what we deserve.

The Apostle Paul does the same kind of paint job in the first three chapters of the book of Romans. Paul builds his case from the premise that we are all excuse makers. We believe that if our hearts were known, we would be found innocent. It seems so reasonable. Our thoughts run along this course, "If you only understood the unbelievably tough decisions I am called to make every day, you would not hold me accountable to make any more. Indeed, if you truly understood how hard I've labored to make any godly and honoring decision, you would get off my back. Even more, if you only understood how much I've been hurt, neglected, and abused, you would know that God requires little (or next to nothing) from me."

A sexually abused woman once told me, "When God did not intervene to stop the abuser, He lost any right to require me to do anything. He owes me; I owe Him nothing." Her words are stark and brutal, but I believe she reflects the core posture of the heart that struggles with God. She simply had the angry courage to put words to the battle to understand God's goodness, His response to injustice, and the burden of fulfilling the royal law of love.

Paul argues that all excuses must first be silenced if the

gospel is to have power in one's life. He states, "Now we know that whatever the law says, it says to those who are under the law, so that every mouth may be silenced and the whole world held accountable to God" (Romans 3:19). How does the law silence the heart? It actually seems to increase fury. Paul says sinful passions were "aroused by the law" (Romans 7:5). The law of God—His standards and demands for perfection—are impartial to our circumstances and our struggles. His holiness is unrelenting; His demands are huge. Under the law, our hope for success is crushed, but most people prefer the hope of perfection attained through their good intentions or modest efforts. The presumption of innocence is impossible to forsake, unless His gleaming, spotless holiness is comprehended as a reality that I will one day face without the benefit of any shading excuse or explanation.

But most still wonder how God could hold them accountable to a standard as high as His own holiness and perfection, especially when He seems to have done such a poor job protecting their hearts from the ravages of a fallen world. For most, the exacting demands of the law might invoke silence, but it is similar to the silent withdrawal of a small child who knows another word spoken will bring the slap of an angry parent. That silence is full of terror and barely hidden rage. Clearly, this kind of cowering before the law does not lead to looking into the eyes of God. It may spark conformity and better performance, but it will not increase gratitude and passion for the gospel.

SURPRISE ENCOUNTERS

What is the kind of silence that brings about a lengthy look into the eyes of God? It is the silence evoked by surprise. Few words could be more important for an understanding of the gospel than surprise. There are few experiences in life that have the power to shed us of our burdensome struggles like surprise.

Our family delights in the exquisite joy of the artful surprise. It is not enough to hide, jump out, and shout "Boo!" I returned home from work and was full of myself and my troublesome world. I climbed the stairs and went to my bedroom closet. I opened the door and reached for a hanger. I parted the clothes in front of me to hang up my jacket, and one of my daughters was quietly standing eye to eye inches from my face. I was so surprised that it did not even register. It was (at least for her) a delightful, delayed response. I gasped and stumbled back. It was the quintessential scare; she did not speak a word. I never anticipated her presence. It was so inconceivable and jolting that I lost my thoughts, burdensome as they were, in an instant.

I believe a surprise encounter with God's presence is worlds more startling. When one stands face to face with God, the presumption of innocence and the self-justifying demand for change is stripped away. God, in His kindness, draws us into battle with Himself—a fight to the death that is fearful and wonderful, a battle that calls forth and reveals our rage against Him. Think about God's disruptive method of provoking silence.

Job, during a gruesome experience of suffering, said with pompous confidence, "Oh, that I had someone to hear me! I sign now my defense—let the Almighty answer me; let my accuser put his indictment in writing. Surely I would wear it on my shoulder, I would put it on like a crown. I would give him an account of my every step; like a prince I would approach him" (Job 31:35-37). Job called on God to answer him. He shouted in fury, "Let the Almighty answer me." Job assumed that God would not only listen, but be constrained by his plight to respond.

His arrogance became even more clear when he assumed that God would not only agree, but would not contend with him. He said, "I would find out what he would answer me, and consider what he would say. Would he oppose me with great power? No, he would not press charges against me. There an upright man could present his case before him, and I would be delivered forever from my judge" (Job 23:5-7). Job was soon to be astonished and silenced. Because Job guessed wrong.

God did oppose him with great power. With unparalleled

intimidation, God instructed Job "to brace yourself like a man" (Job 40:7) and pummeled him with relentlessly probing questions that exposed the fury behind his demands. Job presumed an audience with God would clear his name and move God to act justly and relieve his suffering. What he discovered was that "no plan of yours [God's] can be thwarted" (Job 42:2). Job was overwhelmed by his suffering and loss but he turned his (seemingly) justified rage against God. "Why don't You act on my behalf?" "Why do You let me suffer for apparently no reason?" God acts utterly independent of our wounds and rage. *How dare He?*

He dares, in fact, to tear us away from all presumptions of logic, fairness, safety, and normalcy. In so many ways, He is like an emergency room physician, who at first is unconcerned with establishing rapport and a good bedside manner. His commitment is to keep the patient alive, to curtail all the immediate threats to life, and to build the first step in a recovery that will be full and wonderful. He is a scepter who burns brighter than any flaming bush and cuts deeper than any jagged knife. He will have His way and invites us to join Him in the mystery of relationship.

In her book *Pilgrim at Tinker Creek*, Annie Dillard paints a frightening, and yet thoroughly comforting, picture of God's otherness:

> There is not a guarantee in the world. Oh your needs
> are guaranteed, your needs are absolutely guaranteed
> by the most stringent of warranties, in the plainest,
> truest words: knock; seek; ask. But you must read the
> fine print. "Not as the world giveth, give I unto you."
> That's the catch. If you can catch it it will catch you up,
> aloft, up to any gap at all, and you'll come back, for
> you will come back, transformed in a way you may not
> have bargained for—dribbling and crazed. The waters
> of separation, however lightly sprinkled, leave indelible
> stains. Did you think, before you were caught, that
> you needed, say, life? Do you think you will keep your
> life, or anything else you love? But no. Your needs are

all met. But not as the world giveth. You see the needs of your own spirit met whenever you have asked, and you have learned that the outrageous guarantee holds. You see the creatures die, and you know you will die. And one day it occurs to you that you must not need life. Obviously. And then you're gone. You have finally understood that you're dealing with a maniac.[1]

Many Christians will undoubtedly be put off, if not offended, by the use of the term *maniac* to describe God. But honesty requires us to admit that that's how He seems. Talk to Job. His God struck a bargain with Satan to see how faithful Job would be. Job is found to be without sin in the normal sense of the word, but out of an imperfect heart he develops a malignant, slow-growing, self-justified rage at God. God, then, intervenes in a violent storm and exposes Job by His pointed, probing, sarcastic power. Then Job repents. Why? Because he sees God, after having spit in His face.

Silence, in its life-changing power, comes to those who see the darkness of their own heart in light of the holy standards of God. Even more, they see the reflection of their hatred in the still tender eyes of God. The miracle of grace — really, the wonder of God's character — produces the miracle of our change. A sight of God's holiness without a hint of His mercy will lead to either hopeless despair or to something even more awful, a pharisaical presumption of ability to "do His will." On the other hand, a mouthful of mercy without a somber taste of holiness seems to move us to a brazen familiarity with deity that twists Him into everyone's favorite uncle. Such intimacy is sloppy and undignified, and it eventually leads us to paint God with colors of our own making. The Bible portrays God in ways that ought to stun us.

But it takes a while to cut through the evidence of pointless cruelty to the beauty of His love. After all, what kind of God would have agreed to such a deal with His enemy? It is beyond our understanding. Even more so, what kind of God would put up with Job's foolishness? It is utterly beyond our comprehension. What kind of God would show Job His presence, bring him to his knees, then recoup every loss by double? It is so above our ken that words cannot express the mystery of His purpose, other than to say as Job, "My ears had heard of you but now my eyes have seen you. Therefore I despise myself and repent in dust and ashes" (Job 42:5-6). God, in contrast to our sensibilities and desires, seems crazy. *It is the sudden and utterly disconcerting loss of our presumptive, arrogant notions about life and God that silence our fugitive thoughts.*

Job was silenced by the enormity of his foolishness. He conceded, "Surely I spoke of things I did not understand, things too wonderful for me to know" (Job 42:3). Asaph, the psalmist who struggled over the plight of the righteous and the benefits of the wicked, came to a point of silence in the same manner. He stated, "When my heart was grieved and my spirit embittered, I was senseless and ignorant; I was a brute beast before you" (Psalm 73:21-22). *Silence, a quieting of our relentless, pulsating fury toward God, occurs when that fury is at full boil and we meet the God we think we despise. We then find that He is all we feared, but infinitely more kind than we could have ever imagined.*

THE GASP OF JOY

Godly silence always yields stunned joy. It is our raw foolishness in the face of God's unyielding power, His relentless purpose, and His glorious presence that silences us. His unnerving goodness stuns us. He simply does not respond to my hatred as I fear He will, as I have experienced in countless other relationships before, and as I know He should! His discipline, though painful, eventually yields a harvest of joy. His exposure of my sin, though penetrating and shame-inducing, leads to an embrace that is sweeter than meringue.

Our experience with hating people and having them know it does not prepare us for meeting God. I've hated — or perhaps a more palatable term, disliked — people before. They don't like me, and I don't like them. One person in particular comes to mind. She is a jealous, insecure, flesh-eating gossip who is pleasant to my face and ruthless behind my back. Worst of all, she is petty and judgmental of my wife. She was once in our home and, for more than an hour, talked about what she would do to make our house more homey. Anyone who has walked through our home knows my wife is a master of creating a tastefully elegant and simple environment. Our "guest" talked endlessly about her own decorating plans and never gave my wife the first hint of a compliment.

In the few other interactions we've had with her, she deflects all concerns in our life to similar experiences in her own. She is pervasively blind and defensive to her effect on others. I don't like being around her; she knows it. I know she knows it, and we continue to circle each other in a dance of dislike. I don't turn my back to her, and she watches me with keen intensity. In our few encounters, there is a polite, superficial distance, but one time I accidently put her on the spot and there was a low growl and the baring of teeth. Her response was a warning not to tangle with her—keep your distance and I will keep mine. I heeded her warning and took a wider path to avoid her lair.

What do enemies naturally do when one is caught by the other? The way of the world is fight or flight. If I cannot find an adequate path to flee from your attack, if face will be lost if I turn and run, then I will attack with all the fury and vengeance of a wounded, cornered animal. What do we expect of God when our attempt to put Him in the corner ("You've failed me, and now You expect me to be perfect") is reversed and we are found naked and silent as a brute beast? Our path is blocked, and to fight is absurd. What will He do now that we are without word, excuse, or demand? The answer is odd. God does not grant us a wide berth; He does not avoid our shame. He relentlessly pursues with passion.

MORTAL COMBAT

There is no better picture of God's style of relentless, intrusive goodness than the life of Jacob. Recall several key facts about Jacob. As his name implies, he was a supplanter, a deceiver, a con artist with immense talent. He sold his brother a bowl of soup for his birthright and managed deceitfully to obtain his father's final blessing. He fled to his mother's relatives, where he further perfected his shrewd financial and manipulative talents.

At one point, his success drew the ire of his father-in-law, so he decided it was time to return to the home of his father. To do so, he knew he would likely pass through the land of his brother, who vowed to kill him. The night before he was to meet his enemy, his brother, he found himself in another encounter:

> That night Jacob got up and took his two wives, his two maidservants and his eleven sons and crossed the ford of the Jabbok. After he had sent them across the stream, he sent over all his possessions. So Jacob was left alone, and a man wrestled with him till daybreak. When the man saw that he could not overpower him, he touched the socket of Jacob's hip so that his hip was wrenched as he wrestled with the man. Then the man said, "Let me go, for it is daybreak."
>
> But Jacob replied, "I will not let you go unless you bless me."
>
> The man asked him, "What is your name?"
>
> "Jacob," he answered.
>
> Then the man said, "Your name will no longer be Jacob, but Israel, because you have struggled with God and with men and have overcome."
>
> Jacob said, "Please tell me your name."
>
> But he replied, "Why do you ask my name?" Then he blessed him there.
>
> So Jacob called the place Peniel, saying, "It is because I saw God face to face, and yet my life was spared."
>
> The sun rose above him as he passed Peniel, and he was limping because of his hip. (Genesis 32:22-31)

The force of this narrative is almost impossible to contain. The story describes a fight between Jacob and God. Listen to the words again: God and Jacob wrestled all night long.

The deceiver, the shrewd businessman, the committed, self-centered manipulator rolled on the ground for hours with God. Jacob pitted sinew against God's muscle, man's sweat mixed with God's, man's blood commingled with the blood of God. And somehow God could not prevail. The text says, "He [God] could not overpower him." How is that to be understood? There are, of course, many interpretations, but one view is that God will not snuff out the smoldering candle or crush the broken reed. His fury comes against those who arrogantly and indifferently ignore Him, not against those who deceive and destroy but nevertheless seek His blessing. *Anyone who seeks truth — irresistibly drawn to the One who is truth — will inevitably be arm to arm, flesh to flesh in mortal conflict with the Blesser whose exercise of power will never contradict His kindness.*

The text also indicates, without question, the supremacy of the power of the "man." At the point where Jacob strove to his utmost limit and appeared to take the match to a draw, the "man" merely touched Jacob's hip and he was broken — from that point on he walked with a limp. The "man" was apparently toying with Jacob. After the decisive victory, his foe was free to depart, but Jacob would not let go without a blessing.

Now compare the two points in life where Jacob sought after blessing. When Jacob sought Isaac's blessing, Jacob was articulate and smooth; with the "man," Jacob was desperate and broken. With the first blessing, Jacob became a stranger and alien to his own family. With the second, Jacob, the supplanter — the one who grasped after others to get what he wanted — gained a new name, *Israel*, meaning the one who struggles with God. *Worldly deception leads to loneliness, but godly desperation to a new name and a changed heart.*

Jacob named the place Peniel, implying he knew he had wrestled with God. He had seen the face of God and was spared. It appears he was less awed by the blessing than by the mere fact that he was alive after seeing God. The writers of Scripture knew what it was to encounter God face to face. It was fatal (Exodus 33:20-23, Judges 13:22). God is too holy and too pure for sinful man to observe without being destroyed. Yet Jacob, hardly a representative of moral virtue, saw the manifestation of God and lived.

What are we to learn about our God? Millennia later, the text is still almost too hot to handle. I fear drawing any conclusion. The text, however, is to be taken seriously. God seems to honor struggle. His nation's name, Israel, implies He wants His people to strip down to the flesh and do battle with Him. He blesses even the one who fights against Him—as long as the fight is with Him, for the sake of knowing Him and being known by Him. In my fury and hatred against God, I still suspect that God will destroy me. In fact, He should. His plan, instead, is merely to cripple me—to mark me with His awesome handiwork of brokenness, weakness, and poverty. The creator God, who dwells in majesty and glory, walks with the marks of shame in His hands and side, and invites me to bear the same honor. It is in this context that I understand the message of the gospel.

Let me set the scene: I hate God and put Him in the corner. In His goodness, He turns around and exposes my foolish rage as puny and impotent. I am now in the corner. I am silent and, at some level, ashamed and terrified, watching to see what He will do. He moves toward me and a cosmic fight ensues that is, on my part, as ridiculous as a little boy attempting to sink a battleship with a single stream of water from a squirt gun. What happens next is so absurd that I fear to put words to it. He lets me be His equal. He restrains Himself and draws out the battle.

God exposed Jacob's arrogance and fighting fury, and then humbled him, deepened his desire, blessed him, renamed his soul, arranged for his future, and then left him to limp toward his brother whom he had earlier betrayed. The same is true when I fight with God; the battle ends and I am a broken winner, a glorious loser, a man whose name and destiny is changed, though I will never again be able to run and deceive as I once did.

God's response to my rage stuns me. He silences me, engages me in mortal combat, then blesses me. What is the blessing? Jacob saw one element of the gift—he survived after seeing the face of God. Our blessing in Christ Jesus is the same and more—wonderfully more. We have met God, and He has not destroyed us. In the Cross we encounter God, in both His fury and mercy. In order to better comprehend God's scandalous response to my hatred, we will briefly consider both elements found in the Cross—God's fury against sin and His mercy toward our condition.

THE WRATH OF GOD

The fury of God is against sin. He despises sin and cannot bear it in His presence (Isaiah 59:2). Make no mistake. God is ruthless and brutal against sin. His exposure of Job was not merely a lesson in humility. His wrestling with Jacob was not merely good drama. In both cases, it was a battle for the soul—a life-and-death exercise in earnest.

God wars against sin, doing battle with the sinner and against the Evil One who continually seeks to lead foolish people into the deception of sin's relief. God has purposed to destroy the Evil One and eventually every manifestation of evil, including every sinner who is not wrapped in the arms of His beloved Son. He loves beauty so fully that anything that compromises His likeness must be changed or destroyed. What most of us view as the brutal, harsh cuts of a mugger are the sweet transforming trimmings of a Gardener who prunes away disease and dead limbs in order to enhance the beauty of the plant's verdant, green glory.

In order to talk about the love of God—His merciful gift of forgiveness—one must be deeply sincere, almost driven, to face the darkness, the foul blight, the oozing stain of sin. This is not a terribly popular thought, an even less attractive exercise. Why, when so many suffer from severe self-contempt, poor self-images, and profound relational emptiness, would anyone, especially a psychologist, encourage wounded strugglers to ponder their wickedness? It sounds cruel, but it can be life giving. How?

The answer is as complex as the convoluted, fallen human soul, but it can be addressed in simple terms: *Mercy is persistently meaningful only to the degree I am silenced by the enor-*

mity of my refusal to love God and others with my whole heart, soul, strength, and mind. To the degree I comprehend what I deserve (and that understanding ought to be deepening every day and in every interaction with other human beings), I will be wholly overwhelmed by the direction God's wrath proceeds in His holy hatred. John Stott remarked in his book *The Cross of Christ*, "As Brunner put it, 'where the idea of the wrath of God is ignored, there also will be no understanding of the central conception of the Gospel: the uniqueness of the revelation in the Mediator'. Similarly, 'only he who knows the greatness of wrath will be mastered by the greatness of mercy.'"[2]

The thought that the Cross is not merely the revelation of God's love, but is first the expression of His holy fury is foreign to our ears. We have heard so much about God's love that His wrath seems alien and exaggerated. We are free to define the vague higher power of modern culture in any way we choose, provided our definition allows no room for God as Judge.

If the Cross is merely a sign — a bloody proof of His love — then it is little different than the extravagant expenditures of advertisers who spend millions to sell a product for $19.99. It is just too much, for too little. Leave out the reality of wrath and the Cross is a caricature of sentimental love. If one brings to bear the reality of what our sin deserves — separation from life and love — Jesus' sacrifice on the Cross becomes the mystical intersection of two powerful, turbulent rivers — wrath and mercy.

THE MERCY OF GOD

The mystery is great. How can God be both furious about our sin and passionately disposed to do us good? In his book *The Mediator*, Emil Brunner states, "The cross is the only place where the loving, forgiving, merciful God is revealed in such a way that we perceive that his holiness and his love are equally infinite."[3] John Calvin puts it even more forcefully: "For in a manner which cannot be expressed, God, at the very time when he loved us, was hostile to us until reconciled in Christ."[4] Jesus Christ, the one innocent, perfect God-man, reconciled us to God the Father through drinking the bitter cup of God's furious, foaming wrath (Psalm 75:8, Matthew 26:42). He stood naked and ashamed before the violent curse of God, as my propitiation, my justification, so that I will never face God eye to eye in His unrestrained fury toward sin (Galatians 3:13).

Job, Jacob, and I have the same privilege — as arrogant and deceitful people, we can wrestle with God, knowing that we will not be destroyed; Someone else went through that in our place. That means I will never be sent away into exile. I will never again be a stranger to the promises of God. I will never be stripped naked and shamed by His furious eyes. In my darkest rage and most insolent self-justification, I will not be punished — disciplined, perhaps, but never condemned. My blessing goes beyond the stunning fact that I have encountered God and I am alive. It is not only the fact that I am now no longer God's enemy, but that I am His son, His friend. Paul seemed barely able to constrain himself as he said,

> Hope does not disappoint us, because God has poured out his love into our hearts by the Holy Spirit, whom he has given us.
> You see, at just the right time, when we were still powerless, Christ died for the ungodly. Very rarely will anyone die for a righteous man, though for a good man someone might possibly dare to die. But God demonstrates his own love for us in this: While we were still sinners, Christ died for us.
> Since we have now been justified by his blood, how much more shall we be saved from God's wrath through him! For if, when we were God's enemies, we were reconciled to him through the death of his Son, how much more, having been reconciled, shall we be saved through his life! (Romans 5:5-10)

It is a fact more amazing than life. God adopted me at the cost of His Son's life and at the cost of His own sorrow. The immense emotion involved in those few words is more than any human being can comprehend.

As I wrote the last sentence, my two-year-old son, Andrew, toddled into my office and said, "Ho, Ho, Ho, Chrissmuss soon." I love him so dearly. There are times I have held him as he drifted off to sweet sleep, and I have wept. I almost could not bear the thought that sleep was a shroud that would separate us for a few hours. He is my son, my boy, my delight. If another person's life depended on giving up my son, I'd rather see the other person perish than inflict my son or my soul with earthly separation.

In his book *The Crucified God*, Jürgen Moltmann expressed the loss for the Father and for the Son: "The Son suffers dying, the Father suffers the death of the Son. The grief of the Father here is just as important as the death of the Son. The Fatherlessness of the Son is matched by the Sonlessness of the Father."[5] The loss for God the Father, God the Son, and God the Holy Spirit is the annihilation of intimacy and joy. For a time, the Godhead was at war with Itself. The cost is beyond compare.

What does God get in return? He gets adopted children who are petty, petulant, spoiled, demanding, argumentative, mistrusting, angry, critical, and an irritant to everyone but God. The trade of the One for the many does not seem a wise deal. God isn't a terribly shrewd businessman. Nevertheless, our God bought us with an infinite price and intends on seeing us crowned with His very glory. Is it any wonder that Paul shouts at the top of his lungs, "I pray that you, being rooted and established in love, may have power, together with all the saints, to grasp how wide and long and high and deep is the love of Christ, and to know this love that surpasses knowledge—that you may be filled to the measure of all the fullness of God" (Ephesians 3:17-19). Paul prays that I will know the unknowable love and be so full of God that I achieve dimensions of being that reflect the boundlessness of God.

THE TRIUMPH OF THE CROSS

What is the impact of the blessing that I will not be destroyed, that I am privileged to be in His presence with His presence existing in me? If judged by the standards of holiness, the impact is negligible. Compared to the perfect holiness of God's character, my own sanctification in this life is hardly discernible. The scandal of the Cross is that it is so foolish. God, the infinite Creator, becomes a perfect sacrifice for the sake of a twisted human soul. He not only dies, but does so as a public spectacle of shame.

The separation of God from God is heard in the awful cry of dereliction, "My God, My God, why have you forsaken me?" (Matthew 27:46). At that moment, as the Son became sin, the Father turned His eyes away in the agony of hatred and love, full of sorrow and joy. It was the most inconceivable moment in the history of being. In the moment of tragic defeat, our foolish God revealed the wonder of His wisdom, passion, and might.

The change in me is, at least for now, minimal, but the consequence of the Cross was cosmic. The effect was to destroy the power of the Evil One. The Cross was not only our open door to life, but it was the final nail that sealed the Evil One's fate. Paul rejoiced: "When you were dead in your sins and in the uncircumcision of your sinful nature, God made you alive with Christ. He forgave us all our sins, having canceled the written code, with its regulations, that was against us and that stood opposed to us; he took it away, nailing it to the cross. And having disarmed the powers and authorities, he made a public spectacle of them, triumphing over them by the cross" (Colossians 2:13-15).

The victory of the Cross is the triumph of God. It is the grand paradox. In the most humiliating, inconceivable loss imaginable, God, in fact, triumphs over His enemy and shames the Evil One.

Whatever change occurs in me by my absorption of the implications of Christ's death and resurrection, the final act of the play is already scripted. I can relax. Although God's holiness and His law are relentlessly demanding and I cannot, at any moment, live righteously enough in my own holiness to please Him, He provides a way of escape through offering His Son as a covering for my sin. Now, when I am caught in my sin, He embraces me, the sinner, as His own son. He sees me wrapped in the righteousness of His Son and loves the me I am and the me I will become. I can rejoice.

THE THRILL OF SALVATION

Even if I have known little or no love in life, as a Christian I am face to face and flesh to flesh intertwined with love incarnate. Love is before me, like a wall, like a deep cut on my hand. It is unforgettable; it is inflamed within me; it is a shrill, silent, noisy, still voice that captures my deepest and most superficial thoughts.

What is the effect of salvation? He simply has put a small, deeply disturbing fire in the fabric of my being that cannot be extinguished or modulated. The irradiance spreads every time I try to contain it. The heat breathes down my neck every time I'd prefer to suffer in the cold. In simple terms, I am possessed by a God who will neither tolerate tepid indifference nor lukewarm piety. He wants my heart, and in fact He has it.

I both love and hate Him for making His home in the sinews of my soul. I am constrained by His presence to love, or at least to anguish over my failure to love, and then to humble myself by putting on those fine robes, the gleaming ring, and the well-fitted sandals. Why does He not make me pay? It would be so much easier if I could just suffer a few years in penance; but alas, He not only rejoices at my return, but He invites the whole neighborhood to celebrate with us. He charms me and compels me without force or pressure to rejoice, to be grateful for His wild and wonderful imposition. I can no more escape Him or His call than I can refuse, at least for long, to breathe or to stop my heart from beating.

Frederick Buechner's words in his book *The Magnificent Defeat* capture the wonder of our salvation:

There is little that we can point to in our lives as deserving anything but God's wrath. Our best moments have been mostly grotesque parodies. Our best loves have been almost always blurred with selfishness and deceit. But there is something to which we can point. Not anything that we ever did or were, but something that was done for us by another. Not our own lives, but the life of one who died in our behalf and yet is still alive. This is our only glory and our only hope. And the sound that it makes is the sound of excitement and gladness and laughter that floats through the night air from a great banquet.[6]

This is the framework for offering forgiveness and reconciliation to others. God in Christ models for us a wild, reckless, passionate pursuit of the offender by the offended for the sake of the most shame-free party known to man. If one has been forgiven much, then one will learn to boldly pursue through every possible means the one who has done him harm. The path will not be like any other journey. It is a path marked by quiet repentance, stunned joy, and passionate celebration. It is a path that leads both forgiver and forgiven into the heart of God.

NOTES
1. Annie Dillard, *Pilgrim at Tinker Creek* (New York: Harper and Row Publishers, 1974), pages 269-270.
2. John Stott, *The Cross of Christ* (Downers Grove, IL: InterVarsity Press, 1986), page 109.
3. Emil Brunner, *The Mediator*, Olive Wyon trans. (Philadelphia, PA: Westminster Press, 1947), page 470.
4. John Calvin, *Institutes of the Christian Religion* (1559), vol. 2, Henry Beveridge trans. (Grand Rapids, MI: Wm. B. Eerdmans, 1972), page 454.
5. Jürgen Moltmann, *The Crucified God* (New York: Harper and Row Publishers, 1974), page 243.
6. Frederick Buechner, *The Magnificent Defeat* (New York: Harper and Row Publishers, 1966), page 89.

CHAPTER FOUR

FACING A WAR OF HEARTS:
How Do We Harm Each Other?

I s the path of love really so difficult that it requires a battle to death with the Almighty of the universe? Is life so full of wounds and troubles that forgiveness must be a central reality in all relationships? Or is forgiveness rather like an emergency tool kit one must pull out on the rare occasion of a severe relational breakdown?

The answer is intimately related to the fact that we live east of Eden. We live outside the garden, and all around us a war of enormous proportion is being waged against our souls—a war of abuse that pits us against the lion who seeks to damage and devour our lives. In one sense, every relationship, including the most intimate in design and/or practice and the most superficial and functionary, are used by the forces of evil to allure us away from the conviction that God is good and reigns righteously supreme.

The realities of life, if faced in the stark, naked light of day, do not immediately reveal His goodness. His perfect character cannot be easily seen in the shards of a sin-broken world. The question about His goodness must be approached in the light of the awe and wonder one finds in being forgiven through the atonement of the Cross. His goodness shines bright in the light of His redemptive love.

If God's goodness is looked for primarily in turns of fortune—a car screeches to a halt a few inches from your child, a check comes in the mail at the right moment from an unknown friend, a diagnosis of malignancy is found to be incorrect—then the verdict on His heart toward us will always be pending on the arrival of a new set of facts. We will, then, become either a judge ("How can God be good, if He let my son die?!") or a bargainer ("God, I'll know You are good if You bring my husband back to me"). God does not seem to show His goodness to those who peer through the lens of a skeptical examiner or a demanding negotiator. The Evil One uses the pain and confusion of a fallen world to shadow doubt over God's goodness. As long as the laughter of being forgiven is silenced by the somber tones of doubt and anger, God's goodness will be shrouded in the darkness of this world. Forgiveness is the light that penetrates the dark and frees the somber, shamed heart to leap with love.

One reason we are so easily blinded to the vital importance of forgiveness is our penchant to deny that we are in a war. The Evil One wants us to question God. He desires, even more, for us to ignore the need to grapple with God or the world in which we live. *We will see the importance of forgiveness as a central category in relating to others to the extent that we see every relationship enmeshed in a war that leads to a taste of heaven or hell.* If we understand the battle we are engaged in and the nature of the wounds we experience, forgiveness is seen as the foundation for comprehending the goodness of God and the only hope for restored relationships with others. The premise of this chapter is that forgiveness becomes more necessary to the degree the damage of living in a fallen world is faced.

What is the nature of the war that pervades every relationship? In simple terms, the war is a battle with sin. Every relationship is strained by the burden of sin. If carefully examined, every relationship has ample reason to fold under the constant weight of harm.

The damage usually is incidental and bland. For example,

I called my wife from the phone of an expensive, five-star Italian restaurant. I was exhausted from my flight and my teaching schedule, and I had looked forward for days to this gluttinous reprieve from my labor. The phone call was equally anticipated. I had not talked to her for two days, and I was lonely, hungry, and excited about the momentary opportunity to sneak back into the garden — that is, a talk with my wife and a meal of choice veal and chocolate cake.

We chatted pleasantly for a few minutes sharing news and small hors d'oeuvres of endearment. When I saw my party be seated, I excused myself and told her where I was and the reason for my departure. Her comment was terse: "I hope you don't overeat again. Did you know Jim has lost almost fifty-five pounds on his diet?" I could have screamed. In one "helpful" instant, I felt my blood thicken and my appetite increase ten-fold.

Is this war? Or is it simply the normal tensions and insensitivities that occasionally dot the sky like harmless clouds on a warm, pleasant day? At the moment, it felt like a real battle, against real forces of harm. I don't believe my wife is against me or desires at a fundamental level to hurt me, though I felt wounded by her words. The battle began with my wife's comment, which may (or may not) be true and properly timed, but it seemed to be part of a war that is far deeper and more expansive than her words.

What is the war that we fight, and what wounds are the price of engagement in the battle? Most Christians agree that life is, and involves, a struggle. The metaphor of war is not unfamiliar or denied, but many would differ on the nature of what is involved in the battle.

WHAT IS WAR?

The sounds of war are never far away. The low rumble of artillery and the ear-shattering wail of jet fighters overhead are a common, daily intrusion for those with ears to hear. The blood of soldiers is flowing daily in what is truly the mother of all wars — the fight between good and evil, the war between

God and the prince of darkness.

I just looked out my window, and saw our sixteen-year-old neighbor, David, driving his car slowly and thoughtfully toward his driveway. He waves at my youngest daughter and son, who are playing in the yard. The scene is idyllic. A kind adolescent interacting with my children. Where is the war? It may exist, but not in my neighborhood. Perhaps in the inner city or in a third-world ghetto, but not in suburbia, and certainly not in most homes.

Unfortunately, the metaphor of war seems like a television cliché that has lost its punch because most lives are utterly disconnected from the carnage of a true war. Christians seem to see the war of God against evil in terms that are limited to moral issues — pre- or extramarital sex, pornography, abortion, and secular humanism. Other Christians who see the war in terms of social injustice view the battle in light of poverty, class struggles, racial prejudice, and sexism.

I utterly agree with both perspectives, although few who battle one war seem to accord the other much validity. But notice that in both perspectives, the fight is not perceived as an issue of the heart or in context of relationships. Both externalize the war in terms of an "ism" (capitalism, secular humanism), which is a philosophical system of living, or a group of faceless, nameless enemies who oppose life (abortionists, freedom of choice activists, or bigots). Again, I should not be read as minimizing the war against philosophical tenets or social, political, economic, or religious groups that deny the gospel. But if this is the only real battle, then the war is not only extremely far from where many live, it is largely irrelevant to the lives of Christians who are called to arm themselves with the armor of God.

A Supernatural War

There is a war, and it seems that many Christians are not only on the back lines, but also uninformed as to the nature of the battle. The war is against the powers of the prince of darkness. There are many who may read the last sentence and, in a knowing and perhaps condescending manner, agree the real war is against the forces of evil. Paul says, "For our struggle is not against flesh and blood, but against the rulers, against the authorities, against the powers of this dark world and against the spiritual forces of evil in the heavenly realms" (Ephesians 6:12).

There are many who believe the real war is exclusively supernatural; therefore, when a person struggles from depression, disease, or destructive social ills, the only legitimate focus is to do battle with demons through the work of deliverance. Deliverance ministries abound and offer Christians the opportunity to be freed from almost any manifestation of sin, struggle, or spiritual battle through binding the effects of the demonic and removing their presence and deleterious effects. The consequence of this is to remove the battle to a sphere of existence that is alien to the daily, ordinary, normal struggles of most people.

If the war is seen as an "ism" or a faceless group, then the average person is disconnected from the fight. If the battle is doing or receiving "deliverance," then most people do not need to be rescued from the immediate attack of Satanic forces or are not "gifted" to fight directly with the powers of evil. Again, I would be misread if I were seen as categorically castigating all deliverance approaches to life's problems. My concern is that few seem to know the battle that rages around them even in enjoyable moments and pleasant interactions, and few seem to be aware of the wounds that result from their daily engagements.

The real war is supernatural and is against the forces of evil arrayed against God and His people. The commander-in-chief of the evil forces is the prince of darkness, and his cohorts include legions of rebellious angels who hate God. But the war doesn't rage "out there" in heavenly realms far removed from the daily grind of life. The powers of darkness work for the destruction of good through all ideologies, social structures, institutions, and events. To put it most simply, the Evil One works through the basic building block of all ideologies, social structures, institutions, and events—namely, people. In other words, he works through the dynamics of one person relating to another, attempting to accomplish his destructive goals.

Through one human being relating to another philosophical and societal structures take their shape. The terrain of the eternal war is the battleground of relationships. The battles may be of immediate and enormous consequence, like the choice to have an abortion rather than face the shame of an angry father's stare, or more long-term and seemingly insignificant, like the choice to chew on a spicy piece of gossip about a coworker. In either case, no one makes a moral, ethical, or social decision without engaging in a contest of supernatural proportions.

The battle is not ultimately against flesh and blood, but it is fought with flesh and blood against powers and principalities that show themselves in the normal relational entanglements of life. The rumblings of the battle are always with us, and the consequences of war are impossible to escape. Our eyes need to be open to the war we are engaged in and the wounds that require forgiveness.

THE NATURE OF THE WAR

The war fought against us is diabolic—that is, subtle, slow, ordinary, and unsurprising. Seldom are the forces of evil so obvious as demon possession or the traumatic onslaught of Job's troubles. The war against us is disguised behind the humdrum monotony and imperceptible abuses of daily living, so that a call to arms is ignored as silly adventuring or the paranoid delusions of negativism. The battle is usually hidden, but it is made up of apparently insignificant and occasionally severe wounds. Let me illustrate.

During one seminar break, which lasted approximately fifteen to twenty minutes, I was lectured by a fellow professional therapist on a theory of counseling I studied in graduate school. I asked him what he was hoping to accomplish by his lecture, and he said, "Your training is obviously deficient since I've heard you lecture for two hours and you never addressed the importance of cognitive-behavioral change." I thanked him for his admonition, and the next person approached. A pleasant, matronly woman took my hand and said, "Young man, you would be a far more powerful speaker if you would button your collar and try to look more professional." Her pleasant voice purred with condescension. She patted my hand and said, "God be with you." She departed, and a young man asked me for a minute of my time. He informed me that I was too assured of myself and insisted that it would be better for my audience if I were to charge nothing for my seminar and humbly take a love-offering.

At that point, I excused myself, wandered to the men's room, and occupied an empty stall for no other reason than to escape from Christians. Over a few minutes' break, I felt discouraged, hurt, angry, and nihilistic. The comments may have been offered with the most sincere and benevolent motivation, but I felt like a victim of a hit-and-run accident. I wondered if I was wearing a bull's-eye on the back of my shirt with the request, "Kick me." And all this occurred with fellow saints — brother and sisters who share the same Father, hope, and promise.

It is imperative to know that a great deal of the harm that will come our way in the war against the Evil One will be at the hands of fellow Christians — so-called "friendly fire." In fact, I would suggest that it is unusual for those in ministry to be attacked by the "unbeliever." The typical agent of war will be those who share the name of Christ who direct their missiles against those who are on the same side. The Evil One is at his finest when he uses the damage of friendly fire to inflict abuse. Satan, however, is not picky; he will be delighted to use any person or situation to achieve his destructive ends. It is imperative to understand something of his *modus operandi*. The better we understand the nature of abuse from friendly or unfriendly fire, the better we will understand the necessity of forgiveness. Satan has countless battle plans that he hopes will work to destroy the heart of God's people.

The Evil One seems to do his greatest damage through subtle or overt assaults against the dignity and beauty of the soul. The primary method is through any form of abuse that involves either a desire to destroy and/or a desire to use. Jesus spoke about these two strong passions when He said, "You have heard that it was said to the people long ago, 'Do not murder, and anyone who murders will be subject to judgment.' But I tell you that anyone who is angry with his brother will be subject to judgment. . . . You have heard that it was said, 'Do not commit adultery.' But I tell you that anyone who looks at a woman lustfully has already committed adultery with her in his heart" (Matthew 5:21-22,27-28). The Lord described two core kinds of harm involved in this world war—murder and anger, and adultery and consuming lust.

MURDER AND ANGER

The first form of harm comes from those who use anger to attack us. Few face the threat or reality of physical attack (although the numbers are growing), but all of us endure emotional assaults that range from frustration to anger to rage in countless daily encounters. The events often seem trivial. A surly waitress in a greasy restaurant is expected. It usually does not surprise or upset us. And often the assault is as subtle as the turned-up eyes of a friend who thinks our thought was foolish. The fact is, we face anger daily, and unless it is unexpected or blatantly overt, we tend to relegate the experience to "that's the way it is." To some degree, we all ignore countless daily insults.

At a recent seminar, I asked some folks who were talking in a church lobby if they could speak more quietly, because they were disturbing the presentation. One man glared with cool disdain and retorted, "You can ask, but this is our church, not yours." I smiled and walked away, cursing my odd calling of involvement with Christians. In moments, however, I forgot the interaction and returned to my responsibilities. The event was lost until I went to bed that night, closed my eyes, and began to drift off to sleep. In the semi-comatose stage of pre-sleep, I was suddenly jolted awake in the presence of his cold, hateful eyes. I felt haunted. I did my best to trivialize their appearance and chided myself for being so weird and oversensitive, but nothing seemed to ease the power of his stare. I am not sure why his voice, words, and eyes affected me so deeply, but it was clear that all my efforts to minimize the experience did not work. Minimizing an assault rarely, if ever, enables us to deal with the anger of others.

It would be too dramatic to say that all experiences of others' anger are damaging. Nevertheless, the bombardment of anger at us from an angry culture is at times overwhelming. Sometimes, even a small word coated with irritation, contempt, haughtiness, or anger can sink deep into our souls and set off a profound series of chain reactions. It is imperative to understand the role anger plays in what Jesus calls "murder."

A Desire for More

In every person there is a passionate, driving desire for more. At first, the desire for more is usually thought of in extremely superficial terms, such as money, cars, houses, or simply pleasure. In time, our material desires give way to something that is less superficial, like more time for our families, better health, and more harmonious relationships with others. Even deeper desires may eventually rise to the surface in the form of a more equitable and just world and an end to hunger and suffering. But at the core, mankind longs for the ultimate "more" — a perfect relationship with the One whose bright presence dispels all darkness, sin, disease, and sorrow and who draws us to dine with Him forever.

The dilemma is that our longings for material joy are almost always partially blocked; our desires for better health and deeper relationships are never entirely possible; and the illusion of world peace seems no more attainable than the gold at the end of the rainbow. Our passion for more is usually stymied. The world simply does not bend to the desires that roar or whimper inside us. Our desires — from picking the quickest line in the bank to the overwhelming hope that our children will walk righteously with the Lord — are rarely satisfied in a way that relieves the ache of incompleteness. During the few times that all seems well and the delight of the moment caresses our weary soul, one need only recall that the vision of transfiguration will pass and the trek down the mountain will end in facing another brutal scene of the fall.

Our heart seems to rage against the ache. Our typical response to the heartbreak and sorrow of disappointment is murderous rage. James stated our propensity in these words, "You want something but don't get it. You kill and covet" (James 4:2).

It is a strong phrase, "You kill." I fear that most of us do not consider our actions as ever murderous. It seems we usually see our unkind words, cool stare, or purposeful withholding of love as simply not being as kind as we should be. In fact, compared to actual rape, murder, and mayhem, our occasional moments of relational failure seem as insignificant as a quarter compared to the national debt.

A Desire for Vengeance

James chose a word that reflects the energy inside of us, even if our behavior is civil and the appearance of our offense inconsequential. Murder is the desire to take vengeance *now*. It is a passion to be like God and bring judgment down on those who have stood in our way to gain satisfaction.

One man told me that he chose his career as a lawyer as a means to live out his crusade against all pretenders and fakes. His father was a pompous, arrogant businessman who used his position of power to humiliate those he came in contact with—his peers, neighbors, and family. The man wanted his father to pay. He was brimming over with the furious, blind tempest of vengeance, and in his case, the practice of law provided a vehicle for well-paid and societally sanctioned murder. He couldn't prosecute his father, nor could he take the risk to speak a disagreeable word to him. But he could make other cruel men pay.

The same is true, to some degree, for us all. We want someone to pay. The desire for immediate vengeance is usually not a conscious, moment-by-moment desire, but when a significant loss, insult, or injury occurs, we often feel an energy of anger that far supersedes the event itself. In most cases, the energy of murder goes back further than the present event to memories of past harm that are unresolved.

If it is true for us, then it is true for our parents, our spouses, our children, our neighbors, our business associates, the members of our church. All relationships struggle with the presence of undealt-with and often hidden anger. That is not to say, however, that all relationships are in appearance or in fact on the border of collapse. I enjoy a wonderful relationship with my wife, children, parents, partners in ministry, and friends. I consider myself to be a man who has been enormously blessed. I am deeply loved and respected by a number of people who offer me exquisite foretastes of what will one day be my main course. The fact is, however, that even in the best relationships, disappointment is an ongoing reality and, consequently, so is the potential for anger.

Unless a person is glorified, there is always a remnant of murderous anger that silently but potently intrudes into the day-to-day interactions of his best relationships. We know, intuitively and experientially, for example, that our parents (at times) felt anger toward us. We know we were sources of embarrassment, pain, and disappointment to them. The fact that we were (and occasionally still are) the object of their wrath ought not surprise anyone who believes that sin is both an ongoing and a destructive reality in the life of every person.

Again, listen to the Lord Jesus' words: "'Do not murder, and anyone who murders will be subject to judgment.' But I tell you that anyone who is angry with his brother will be subject to judgment" (Matthew 5:21-22). Unless His words are to be ignored or trivialized, we are required to face the fact that even the best parents occasionally respond with anger that Jesus calls murderous.

I am aware many read these words as an overstatement of the truth. Many parents, perhaps even the majority, are good parents. I consider myself to be a good parent. But I have no doubt that my children will one day be able to report bursts of anger, cruel words, icy stares, unjust questioning of their character, and many other signs of murderous anger. The realities of existence require us to say that—no matter how insightful, strong, and caring a parent might be—no parent can keep his or her anger entirely hidden from the soul of the child. The result will be to some degree a fragmentation of the child's sense of self. Anger murders. It cuts into the soul like a sharp knife and leaves a jagged wound. The wound may be no more traumatic than a paper cut, or it may come close to destroying vitality in the heart.

Emotional and Physical Abuse

If the damage is significant with loving parents, who being sinful still know how to give good gifts to their children, how much more is it true when a parent does not attempt to deal with or at least hide their murderous rage? It is a tragic fact that many parents abuse their children. Murderous rage often shows itself in emotional and physical abuse. Emotional abuse is a form of verbal or nonverbal murder. Even more so, it tears at the intactness and integrity of a child's heart. Instead of a knife wound, emotional and physical abuse is similar to the murder and then cannibalistic devouring of the worth and beauty of a child.

Emotional abuse involves either the profound omission of involvement or the equally destructive commission of shaming a child. A parent who abandons a child is emotionally abusive; a parent who betrays a child's trust by failing to protect them against harm has emotionally abandoned the child. On the other hand, emotional abuse may involve active, aggressive patterns of shaming a child. A child who is mocked for a physical or learning disability or a child who is humiliated by being called demeaning names has been emotionally abused.

A child may grow up in a world where emotional abuse is the common language of the home. An older child may regularly humiliate a younger child with impunity. The younger child then bears the active shaming of the older child and the passive abandonment of the parents. In that case, the emotional abuse is so normal that any other form of involvement may seem odd, and even dangerous. The ripple effect is perverse. The child is accustomed to being lonely and hurt, and may choose to find another smaller or younger person to harm.

The rage is then cycled into someone else's life who, of course, will abuse someone else. This is even more true when the murderous rage includes physical violence.

Physical abuse involves any physical discipline or contact that is either (1) severe and unusual (such as being slapped in the face, burned with cigarettes, spanked until the child cries); (2) capriciously administered without context (meaning the discipline comes out of the blue without explanation or opportunity to change); or (3) perpetrated with a mood of contempt or fury (emotional abuse is almost always part of physical abuse). Physical abuse generates enormous dread and fury. It is not uncommon for the severe merging of terrible anxiety and anger to be hidden under a thick glacier. The cool, in control, distant demeanor of an adult who was physically abused as a child often hides a violent and frightening rage that is held in check by the absence of emotion or longing.

Many physically abused adults are able to report the horrific violence perpetrated against them in a manner that is no different than someone talking about the undesirable presence of rain in the forecast. The result is often a deep chasm in relationships. The icy distance is made up of molecules of hatred that are too cold to touch. Hatred of one sort, again, gives birth to a new order of hate—the cycle of physical cruelty spawns another cycle of cold, civil cruelty. The means of murder may be different, but the energy is the same.

The major elements of murder-anger are seen in emotional or physical abuse. It is imperative, however, to recognize that the constituent elements of emotional abuse (*abandonment and shame*) and physical abuse (*cruelty, inconsistency, and rage*) are found in countless other forms of "murderous abuse" perpetrated, to some degree, by all those with whom we are in relationship.

One of the best illustrations of "normal" murder found in countless relationships is gossip. Proverbs tells us, "The words of a gossip are like choice morsels; they go down to a man's inmost parts" (26:22); and "He who covers over an offense promotes love; but whoever repeats the matter separates close friends" (17:9). Gossip is delicious; it sinks to the depths of our being. It is a tantalizing thrill to repeat words that simultaneously deepen our position of power in an inner ring while we exclude someone else from being part of the group—a double pleasure. The thrusts of our verbal sword cut deep and have the power to kill reputations, destroy ministries, and sever friendships.

Few need to be convinced that the children's nursery rhyme, "Sticks and stones may break my bones, but words will never hurt me," is an enormous lie. Words are often like packages that, when opened, contain a bomb that explodes in the face of the other.

I spoke to a friend I had not talked with in a few months. I asked him, "How are you doing?" He responded, "Fine. Frankly, it's hard to catch you up since you've not been involved in my life for some time." I felt stung by his words. He didn't scream; he was matter-of-fact and casual. But his inner self brimmed with angry accusation. I certainly did not feel invited to a discussion that explored what might really have been going on in each of our hearts and lives.

Angry words spoken without a deep desire for reconciliation have the power to cut to the very heart and create internal bleeding that is unseen, but deeply felt (Proverbs 12:18). Murder-anger attempts to destroy those who stand in our way. It kills those who represent memories of the past. It makes someone pay for the terrible ache of betrayal and abandonment, and cruelty and shame.

Destructive anger is not the only harm that is perpetrated against us. It is, unfortunately, not the only abuse that requires the work of forgiveness to heal. The Lord spoke about another form of abuse—the destructive power of lust.

ADULTERY AND LUST

The second form of harm comes from those whose lust to avoid emptiness and find satisfaction causes them to use other people as food for their empty souls. The lust is adulterous in that it is a desire to find satisfaction illegitimately, apart from God and His righteous path.

God has blessed us with much to enjoy on this earth—everything from full bellies to rich relationships that ease the ache in our souls. Our desire, or lust, to embrace all good things is perfectly legitimate because we are created to long deeply for fulfillment, ultimately through union with God. But destructive lust has a different flavor. It is a strong craving to possess the life and soul of another in order to simultaneously fill an emptiness in oneself and destroy the fullness in another. Destructive lust is the intersection of desire and destruction, and emptiness and vengeance. A person whose heart is fueled by such lust not only sucks life out of a host in order to dim the intensity of his loneliness, but also relishes mastery and power over someone or something. Lust is obvious in the sexual realm, but its presence is a pulsating rhythm in other dimensions of life.

I talked to a woman whose lust to bear a child was a craving that consumed her thoughts and soul. The desire to be a mother, though deeply legitimate, became a distorted obsession that shaped her life. Her compulsion spawned chronic daydreams of cuddling with a child in the warm bliss of maternal intimacy. She acknowledged she never received that kind of love from her mother or any equivalent, including her husband. She was bound and determined to be full, and the baby was the designated object that would bring fullness of life.

There was an even darker component to her lust. She was aging. She felt the graying intrusion of her forties staring her in the face, and she desperately wanted to rob mortality of its sting. A baby would make her eternally young. She already had four children; she knew that children tend to accelerate the aging process, but her heart hoped that a young baby would transport her to the ecstasy of her youth.

The object of one's lust might reflect an obvious desire to alleviate emptiness, but it also reflects an angry fist that is shaken in the face of the chronic sadness of life. Destructive lust is fueled by a determination to make life more palatable and perfect than it can possibly be in a fallen world.

The damage of lust, sexual or otherwise, is ever present.

Not everyone is an adulterer (in the technical sense), nor is everyone the victim of someone's adulterous sin. We are assaulted daily, however, by the lustful misuse of others, and unless it is unexpected or blatantly overt, we again tend to brush it off with the resignation of "that's life."

It would be too dramatic to say that all experiences of others' lusts are obviously damaging. Nevertheless, the bombardment of lust from a narcissistic culture can be overwhelming. At times, the quiet demands of others to be supportive or noncritical can drain and immobilize us and silence our sense of what is right or loving. We all face the constant requirements of others to be for them what no one but God can be. Consequently, we all experience being used by others. It is imperative to understand the role this lust plays in what Jesus calls "adultery."

Adultery, or sexual immorality, is condemned. But something more than immorality is condemned by Jesus. In the first part of the passage in Matthew, Jesus reveals that murder is energized by the desire to destroy—to murder through the power of anger. In the second part, He exposes the energy behind immorality to be a desire to use and possess—to steal and consume through the power of lust. Anger, for the most part, is far more obvious in its expression and its consequences. Lust, on the other hand, is potentially so private and subtle that it is difficult to discern until it slithers from under the rock into the bright daylight. The subtle nature of the lust that seeks to adulterously possess what is not ours to enjoy requires careful definition.

Lustful Fantasies

The lust Jesus spoke about is fantasies, which include, but likely go far beyond, sexual thoughts and feelings. But sexual fantasies are a useful means of understanding the nature of lust. Lustful sexual fantasies involve seeing arousing stimuli and then transcribing it onto our favorite scenes of arousal, seduction, and consummation. A key element to many fantasies is the desire to be captured or to conquer the interest and passions of an attractive counterpart. The word *capture* is likely closer to feminine fantasies, and the term *conquest* may describe the more typical male fantasy.

Sometimes it is not so cut and dried, of course. Many women lust for the opportunity to so overwhelm a male that it is, in fact, a conquest. And many men long for the passive role of being the object of an aggressive woman's passion, so that it could be said that those men desire to be captured. In any case, the theme of most sexually lustful fantasies is capture or conquest, which leads to a consuming, soul-filling arousal that transports the soul to another plane of existence.

This is the key. Lustful fantasies are an effort to escape the humdrum daily grind of cleaning up Play-Doh and washing the 1,000th diaper. It may also be the means to flee from the terror of making a presentation to the board of elders. Fantasies are private magic carpets that serve to deliver the soul from boredom, anxiety, anger, loneliness, and rage to a "better" world that offers momentary relief and satisfaction.

Lust is the effort to possess another in order to steal enough passion to be lifted out of our current struggles into a world that feels (for an instant) like the Garden of Eden. If anger is the desire to make someone pay for blocking our return to the garden, then lust is our effort to push our way back into the garden.

A Desire for Union

Let me put it more graphically. Lust, in part, is a desire for union—that is, a desire to be absorbed into another. It is an odd conjunction of desire that seeks to be both very full of one's self and simultaneously lost in the warmth and strength of another. An orgasm is a paradigm of this apparent contradiction. An orgasm is a release of tension; the tension intensifies both a sense of desire and a sense of oneself; the eventual relief dispels the tension in a constriction of excitement that brings a loss of oneself in the wash of well-being.

Our hearts desperately long for Eden. We want fullness of self that removes the stark, brittle light of self-consciousness. Our hearts, in other words, live for an experience of worship that fills our beings with a joy that is so deeply in awe of the other that we are barely aware of ourselves. Sexual immorality, or adulterous lust, provides a tragic counterfeit of a loss of self that also enhances the self. It inevitably leads to even more empty, self-consuming despair.

Lust is the fallen desire for union gone mad. Lust may be sexual, but it may also be directed toward a person or object in a nonsexual manner. Lust may be directed toward a person, object, position, or state. Many lust after being happy (state); others lust after reputation (position), antiques (objects), or people. *In any case, destructive lust involves the heart of a thief whose passion is to be satisfied, not the heart of a lover whose desire is to give.*

The current "disease" labeled "codependency" provides an excellent paradigm of nonsexual lust. The person who lives for approval and involvement with another is often willing to sacrifice life and limb to "possess" the heart of another. The energy behind possessive love is lust—that is, the desire to find a host who will provide a vital energy that appears to be missing in the codependent.

The codependent is usually aware of an emptiness, an ennui, a boredom, a soullessness that seems strangely relieved in the presence of the beloved. The fullness experienced in a smile from the beloved is often enough warmth to endure the literal or figurative blows of rage that icily strip the codependent of any remaining shreds of dignity. It is not unusual for codependents to bind themselves to the stark task of trying to draw blood out of a stone. The frustration of emptiness seems to lead to even greater sacrifice and commitment to serve the object of their desire. In turn, the object of their desire usually intensifies his rage to disentangle the threads of sticky, absorptive enmeshment.

This process looks like a dance of death, where codependents ask their partners to provide intimacy, while subtly inviting an avalanche of hatred to be unleashed. The person who is the object of the codependent's needy lust often feels alternately prized and then violated in the heat of the absorptive passion. The whirlwind of desire and destruction sabotages the self and intensifies self-protective despair.

When satisfaction is not forthcoming (of course, it never is fully), lust will inevitably turn darker and meaner. A private fantasy of sexual gratification with an attractive object of desire will likely not suffice over time. A more intense, more consuming desire to be captured or conquer will take over. It may not be enough to be merely wanted by an attractive man or woman; the "wanting" will likely descend into darker control and subjugation. Soon the fury of emptiness will be conjoined with the desire for absorption, and perversion will be born.

Lust almost always becomes perverse. Perversion is the wedding of lust and rage. The soul is never satisfied with the taste of pleasure; it demands to be satiated. When unrequited hunger mingles with the fury of wanting someone to pay for the pain of emptiness we are forced to experience, a tumultuous interplay of violence and passion is fused that simultaneously seeks to use and destroy.

In sexual terms, lust may be experienced at first as pleasurable and satisfying. Fantasies will almost always move from the private to the relational—from thought to deed. The fantasy may be innocent and the deed righteous. That would be the case when the lust is really a passionate desire to give pleasure to and experience union with the one to whom a covenantal, God-honoring life commitment has been made—that is, one's husband or wife. All other sexual lusts will devalue the soul and, in fact, intensify the emptiness. In turn, these lusts deepen both the hunger and the fury—leading to a desire to quench the emptiness through sexual violation.

We live in an age where sexual violation is the norm. I recently flipped through a magazine that advertised school buses. As I skimmed the pages of this odd journal, I was startled to see a bikini-clad woman pointing toward a huge, yellow, quite unattractive school bus. What in the world did a bikini-clad woman have to do with a bus? Nothing, other than that every other reader did the very same thing I did—stopped turning pages and stared in disbelief and mild interest. Is it any wonder sex sells?

The power of lust does not stop with advertising. It moves

in and through the fabric of every relationship. A girl is chosen by the boy to go to the dance because she is physically attractive. What happens to the girl whose breasts are not as big or whose thighs are too big? She stays at home. Sexual energy can be the basis a person is chosen for marriage, a job, or a position of ministry. Tragically, lust can lead to even more severe violations. The incidences of sexual abuse; date rape; sexual violations by pastors, counselors, physicians, lawyers, and mentors; marital rape; and coercive sexual involvement in dating relationships are at incomprehensibly high levels. It seems as if it is not possible to grow up in our culture without being sexually violated in some way.

Nonsexual Lust

In nonsexual terms, the outcome of lust is some form of misuse, absorption, and devaluation. One example of this is a corporation that requires a young man to give the cream of his life to the "work" that is more than a career; it is a way of life. He is rewarded, applauded, and sent off on privileged trips. The only price for his success is more time, more energy, more soul taken from all other endeavors in order to keep the job. After years, it is apparent his value to the company has decreased and other young men and women, just like he used to be, are waiting in the wings for his territory. A reorganization occurs, and he is reassigned to a job that everyone knows is impossible. The only option is early retirement—a loss of income, status, benefits, and a reason to live. The same scenario, in one form or another, occurs in churches, Christian organizations, families, and friendships.

I worked in one church where I enjoyed a congenial mentoring friendship with the senior pastor. After finishing a game of tennis, we sat and talked about our lives and ministries. He was supportive, but honest about a number of concerns he saw in my ministry style. Our interaction went well, and we departed for a quick shower and meal before a conjoint elders and staff meeting. An hour later, the pastor opened the meeting, after prayer, with the agenda of terminating my employment. I was stunned. I would have been fired that night if several elders had not spoken on my behalf. I felt betrayed. I was used and then discarded when the differences between us required dialogue.

There are many who can report being the refuse of someone's disappointed or furious lust. I've worked with many wives who were discarded by their husbands after the husbands found younger women more exciting. I have equally seen husbands shunned by wives whose lust was directed toward ministry, bridge clubs, and hassle-free avoidance.

The effect of being the object of destructive anger is fragmentation—the loss of intactness. The effect of being used, violated, and discarded is a loss of a sense of boundaries. It is as if one's sense of self merges with the other in a sick union, and it is difficult to discern what is right and wrong, good and bad, legitimate and illegitimate.

For example, a woman who had lived most of her life to avoid her mother's anger found a sense of peace and satisfaction in being her mother's confidante, friend, counselor, and surrogate spouse. She succumbed to her mother's demands and desires, and felt exhausted and inadequate to be enough. In countless ways, she allowed herself to be used and taken up in her mother's desires. After a significant illness, her mother's cruelty, lust for control over her daughter, and hatred of anyone who failed her became overwhelming.

The daughter finally refused to be used any longer, and her mother sank into a furious, morbid depression. The attending physician even said, "If you don't do something your mother will die." She told me, "I feel like an orange that has been crushed, squeezed dry, and tossed away." She found it difficult to trust her sense of right and wrong when her mother's depression was implicitly blamed on her. She was, at times, confused when her mother would be kind and then enraged. At first, she felt like she should apologize for being too critical, and when the fury descended, she felt at fault for being too selfish. A lengthy history of being absorbed by someone will make it difficult to trust one's intuition and the quiet stirring of God's Spirit. No wonder Jesus condemned the passion of consuming lust.

HOPE FOR THE BATTLE

So far we've looked at two fundamental forms of damage that
are perpetrated against us — and certainly by us — as we relate in
a war-torn world. A day does not go by in which we escape being
murderously attacked or adulterously absorbed. The assaults
may not even be noticed, but their cumulative wounds produce
exhaustion and discouragement. The assaults that are denied or
ignored do not seem to require forgiveness. On the other hand,
the events of tragic, overwhelming assault (sexual abuse, rape,
divorce, betrayal, gossip, etc.) seem too great a wound to forgive.
And yet a life of love, joy, and purpose will not occur without
forgiveness that permeates every fiber of our relationships.

Given the damage that is done, what is our attitude to be
toward evil in the world, or more pointedly toward ourselves
and others? Many Christians, unfortunately, cower under the
weight of the Fall. The burden is too overwhelming, and the
task too great. If the realities of life were the only basis for
determining whether the war could be won, we would truly
appear to be defeated. But we are not called to engage in the
battle according to the world's perspective or with the fallen
order's weapons.

Paul, as an example, was no stranger to the terrible sadness
of living with the effects of the Fall, especially in the lives of
other Christians. He fought the battle to establish their hearts in
love and did so with the kind of weapons that assured victory.
Paul said,

> By the meekness and gentleness of Christ, I appeal to
> you — I, Paul, who am "timid" when face to face with
> you, but "bold" when away! I beg you that when I
> come I may not have to be as bold as I expect to be
> toward some people who think that we live by the
> standards of this world. For though we live in the
> world, we do not wage war as the world does. The
> weapons we fight with are not the weapons of the
> world. On the contrary, they have divine power to
> demolish strongholds. (2 Corinthians 10:1-4)

The energy of life that comes from being forgiven leads to a boldness to pursue and free the offender who is encumbered by destructive, deadening hatred and lust. We are warriors — warriors of love, warriors who despise evil, warriors who demolish and destroy that which is inconsistent with the beauty, justice, and love of God.

To better comprehend the high calling of fighting the war on God's side, we need to understand more of what it means to have a divine Commander-in-Chief whose battle plans have been drawn since the foundation of the world. In the next chapter, Tremper will describe our divine Warrior.

CHAPTER FIVE

OUR DIVINE WARRIOR:
Hope for Triumph in Battle

❖

Our everyday experience screams at us that we are engaged in warfare. All of us know the bloody conflict described in the last few chapters. We struggle against others (friend and foe alike), against ourselves, and most tragically, against God.

Does it surprise us to discover that the Bible describes our lives in terms of warfare? It shouldn't. If we have any understanding of the Bible at all, we know that it speaks directly to our life's experience — our joys, our doubts, our gloom, our terror. But the Bible does much more than simply confirm our experience: It gives us insight into it and imparts to our everyday struggles a cosmic and redemptive significance.

Most readers of the Bible fail to recognize the incredible pervasiveness of these themes. Virtually every book of the Bible — Old and New Testaments — and almost every page tells us about God's warring activity.

IMAGES OF GOD

The Bible is God's own revelation to us, the people whom He loves with such intense personal passion. God paints a rich, lively portrait of Himself to us in its pages. What is startling about the Bible is that it never speaks of God in the abstract, sterile language of much contemporary theology. It always talks about God in relationship with His people. And so we find that we learn as much about ourselves as we do about God.

The Bible also avoids arid philosophical or specifically theological language. God describes Himself in the context of concrete and emotionally rich relationship. God is a warrior, committed to leading and protecting His troops until victory is won. And He is so much more. If we take a moment to reflect on how the Bible pictures God, these images flash vividly through our minds and evoke deep feelings in our hearts.

God Is Our Father, We Are His Children

Perhaps it was no different at any other time, but my generation, the baby-boomer generation, relates to this image perhaps better than any other. I think it is in part because we felt ambivalent about our own fathers. Ours was the time of the "generation gap." Children felt distant from their fathers, and as adults, we struggle with an absence of intimacy and the straitjacket of unyielding authority. In the vacuum of intimacy and protective strength, many of us desperately pursued a relationship with God the Father.

The image tells us that God is an absolute authority above us, but an authority who cares for us as His own and in the most intimate way. People who have had abusive fathers may at first experience God as equally demanding and abusive, feeling repulsion at His discipline and suspicion toward His kindness. But over time, His fatherly strength and care can become a harbor of rest. Though for some of us, our earthly model distorts the divine reality, nonetheless we know what fatherhood should be from what we lack.

God Is Our Mother, We Are His Children

In this day of debate over the sexes, the church often stands against feminism, and indeed forms of it are godless and damaging. However, the Church must be careful about its tendency to overreact in an opposite direction. I don't know how many people I've talked to who actually think God is male! This is a preposterous idea. God is not a sexual being, but chooses to communicate to us about His incomprehensible character using picture images that are familiar to us. The father image comes readily to mind, but too many Christians ignore the mother image.

God is our loving Mother (Psalm 131, Isaiah 66:13). God reveals Himself to be like a nursing mother who will satisfy, comfort, and play with her child. Her arms are a haven of rest and security. God our Mother is compassionate, merciful, and caring toward us. Other feminine images are used of God in order to tell us that He is wise beyond belief (Proverbs 8-9).

God Is a King, We Are His Subjects

The parent metaphors have a note of precious intimacy. The royal image reminds us that God is far above us (Psalms 47, 93, 95-98). It reminds us that He is in control, not just of our lives, but of the entire cosmos. We learn that, while we are on intimate terms with God, we need to approach Him with the utmost respect. After all, He holds the threads of our life in His all-powerful hand.

God Is Our Husband, We Are His Wife

Once again the emphasis is on affection and love. As a matter of fact, the intimacy is intensified here. Implied in the metaphor is a level of intimacy that is illustrated in sexual foreplay and intercourse. Ezekiel compares God to a man who saves the life of an abandoned child, the offspring of despicable, God-hating people; nourishes her until puberty; and then draws her into a union of holy matrimony, consummated by sexual intercourse (Ezekiel 16:1-14).

In her beauty, God's wife hands over her sexual favors to every person who passes by whether or not they show interest. God also compares Himself to Hosea, a man married to a harlot, who longs to "allure her; . . . lead her into the desert and speak tenderly to her" (Hosea 2:14).

We feel close to our parents, but there is no one with

whom we should feel more open and vulnerable than our spouse. Even those with a bad marriage can understand this image. They know what they yearn for, and the Bible tells them that God is like that and not like the disagreeable or sinful person who is their husband or wife. The image of God being a betrayed, heartbroken, and forlorn spouse is shocking. Our divine Lover actually endures enormous abuse from His chosen bride as she turns to others to find what only her true Spouse can provide. Those with bad marriages, and any who are honest about the loneliness even in good marriages, will be taken back by God's painful struggle with the same problems they face.

God Is a Shepherd, We Are His Sheep

As we meditate on His image, we encounter the first nonhuman analogy for the relationship between God and man (Psalm 23). The relationship between the Shepherd and His sheep is an excellent one to communicate the complete and utter dependence we have on God. If a shepherd abandons his flock, the sheep don't know what to do and are prey to all kinds of life-threatening danger. So the shepherd imagery tells us that God is not only our Protector, but also our Guide in life.

The list could go on. The Bible bombards us with rich images that give us scintillating glimpses of God's ultimately incomprehensible nature. We come to know Him more intimately through meditating upon these relationship pictures. And we have just scratched the surface of the meaning of the five images that we've mentioned. All the images of God with which the Scriptures present us are immeasurably deep, unable to be exhaustively understood. Books upon books could be written about any one of them.

GOD THE WARRIOR

In this chapter we are going to investigate one image, that which pictures God as a powerful warrior and we, His people, as His trusting soldiers. Before we begin, though, we must realize one other important truth about the Bible.

As Christians who have grown up with the Bible in our culture, we sometimes treat it as a book that fell out of heaven whole. We have to remind ourselves constantly that God used a number of different authors living over a 1,600-year period (circa 1500 BC to AD 100). Over this lengthy period of time, God slowly unfolded His plan of salvation and relationship with His people.

As we keep this in mind, we see that God's people have been at war with the Enemy since the Fall (Genesis 3). The Fall showed clearly that God had an enemy, and ever since that time, all people are on one or the other side of the battle. As Saint Augustine put it, an individual is either in the City of God or the city of man. In Genesis, we see God's curse on the serpent clearly delineates the two sides: "I will put enmity between you and the woman, and between your offspring and hers; he will crush your head, and you will strike his heel" (Genesis 3:15). From this point and for the rest of history, there is vicious conflict between God and Satan, and between those who follow God and those who reject Him. Think of Cain and Abel, the line of Lamech and the line of Seth, Moses and the Egyptians, the Israelites and the Philistines, David and Goliath, and Elijah and Ahab. The list could go on and continues to this very day.

THE PHASES OF BATTLE

As we look at this virulent battle from the Bible's point of view, we can see that it falls into five different phases. Since we are involved in this biblical warfare ourselves every day, understanding the phases of the war will help us see our place in God's unfolding battle strategy, where we fit into the biblical drama that unfolds in a powerful way beginning with the Fall and ending with the consummation.

Phase One: God Fights for Israel

"The LORD is a warrior; the LORD is his name" (Exodus 15:3). This phrase is part of a song that Moses sung as he rested on the far side of the Red Sea. Around him were the tens of thousands of weaponless Israelites who had narrowly escaped death under the wheels of Egyptian chariots. Out in the middle of the Red Sea floated the bloated bodies of Egyptian warriors — testimony of God's judging power and might, testimony to God's warring nature.

Starting with the Fall and spanning the whole Old Testament, God protects His people from the harm their enemies desperately desire to inflict on them. And to do so, the divine Warrior works through violent means. For example, God fought for the people of Israel as they entered the Promised Land and encountered the formidable and ancient city of Jericho. God Himself appeared to Joshua before the battle dressed for the conflict and with a drawn sword to give him instructions on how to take the city (Joshua 5:13-15, 6:1-5). One of the most memorable events of Old Testament history is how God, the divine Warrior, caused the walls of Jericho to fall so that the Israelites could totally destroy the city (Joshua 6).

A second example is somewhat different from the norm. It is a fight between two individuals, David and Goliath, but this episode vividly illustrates what it means to have God as a warrior who protects His people (1 Samuel 17). The contest is incredibly unfair! David is an inexperienced shepherd; Goliath is a mega-warrior. Goliath is huge, a champion of his people. David has no armor; Goliath is armed to the teeth with the most recent weapons technology. But as David stands before Goliath, he expresses the confidence of a person who knows he is God's warrior:

> "You come against me with sword and spear and javelin, but I come against you in the name of the LORD Almighty, the God of the armies of Israel, whom you have defied. This day the LORD will hand you over to me, and I'll strike you down and cut off your head. Today I will give the carcasses of the Philistine army to the birds of the air and the beasts of the earth, and the whole world will know that there is a God in Israel. All those gathered here will know that it is not by

sword or spear that the LORD saves; for the battle is the LORD's, and he will give all of you into our hands."
(1 Samuel 17:45-47)

David fights with all the resources at his disposal, but he knows that his victory is not due to his own strength or skill, but due to God who gives him the victory.

This is the central theme of Old Testament holy war: God is present with His people as a warrior. Time and again, God showed Himself willing and able to fight for His people. He does not hesitate to enter the battle and use creation itself as His weapons — hail, rain, floods, the sun and moon, earthquakes, and rivers. All are His servants when He fights for His people's salvation.

Phase Two: God Fights Against Israel

At first glance, phase two may seem to contradict the point of phase one. How can God fight against Israel if He is present with His people as a warrior on their behalf?

Quite simply, the Old Testament reminds us that God did not give His people a carte blanche for victory no matter what their lifestyle was like. As a matter of fact, He issued some pretty stern warnings to them if they should ever turn their backs on Him, including this one:

> The LORD will cause you to be defeated before your enemies. You will come at them from one direction but flee from them in seven, and you will become a thing of horror to all the kingdoms on earth. Your carcasses will be food for all the birds of the air and the beasts of the earth, and there will be no one to frighten them away. (Deuteronomy 28:25-26)

God promised to protect His obedient people (Jericho), but He also threatened to defeat them if they disobeyed (Ai) (Joshua 7).

Unfortunately, there are all too many examples of this in the Old Testament (1 Samuel 4-5), but perhaps the most heartrending is the destruction of Jerusalem and the Babylonian exile. As we read the book of Lamentations, we experience with the author the utter confusion and sorrow mixed with anger behind his cries:

> The Lord is like an enemy;
>   he has swallowed up Israel.
> He has swallowed up all her palaces
>   and destroyed her strongholds.
> He has multiplied mourning and lamentation
>   for the Daughter of Judah. (2:5)

God fought against His own people and, in the case of the exile, almost brought them to complete annihilation.

God is for us far more, at times, than we would prefer. He is committed to removing all vestiges of sin from our soul when we wish He'd be satisfied with a clean new outfit. His interest in us far exceeds our concerns. Our perspective is usually limited to achieving a better life, and His desire for us is radical conformity to His Son's perfect character. No wonder He seems like an enemy when His discipline begins to grind off our arrogance in order to perfect His beauty.

God wars against us like a surgeon who uses a knife to cut out a malignant tumor. The knife cuts through flesh and muscle. It draws blood and causes terrible pain. But the purpose is redemptive. He is destroying disease and ugliness that, left unattended, would eventually destroy the whole organism. God's sometimes ruthless discipline is directed toward those He loves, not toward those who are outside the claim of His blood.

Phase Three: Hope for the Future
Thankfully, the Old Testament does not end on such a dismal and soul-destroying note. It is true that the post-exilic return to Israel is small, and even such a great event as the rebuilding of the temple is greeted by the profound sadness of those who knew the glory of the first temple (Haggai 2:3).

Nonetheless, the Old Testament concludes with incredible

optimism about the future. The people of God are oppressed and suffering in the present, but their situation is going to change. The evil nations of the world are powerful, but their arrogance has a divine limit placed on them. God is coming in power against them as a warrior. Against the four horrifying hybrid beasts that represent successive evil kingdoms, the exilic prophet Daniel tells us of a warrior "like a son of man, coming with the clouds of heaven. He approached the Ancient of Days and was led into his presence. He was given authority, glory and sovereign power; all peoples, nations and men of every language worshiped him. His dominion is an everlasting dominion that will not pass away, and his kingdom is one that will never be destroyed" (Daniel 7:13-14).

Zechariah, a post-exile prophet, concludes on a similar note:

> A day of the LORD is coming when your plunder will be divided among you.
>
> I will gather all the nations to Jerusalem to fight against it; the city will be captured, the houses ransacked, and the women raped. Half of the city will go into exile, but the rest of the people will not be taken from the city.
>
> Then the LORD will go and fight against those nations, as he fights in the day of battle. (Zechariah 14:1-3)

In these passages and others like them, the Old Testament looks forward to a day of divine violence when God will make all things right again. The thought of God destroying their enemies put joy into the hearts of His people.

Phase Four: Jesus Christ—The Divine Warrior

The last voice of the Old Testament period was the optimistic cry of the prophets who looked into the future and saw God's decisive intervention as a great and powerful deliverer. The first voice of the New Testament is that of John the Baptist with an unmistakably similar message:

"The ax is already at the root of the trees, and every tree that does not produce good fruit will be cut down and thrown into the fire.

"I baptize you with water for repentance. But after me will come one who is more powerful than I, whose sandals I am not fit to carry. He will baptize you with the Holy Spirit and with fire. His winnowing fork is in his hand, and he will clear his threshing floor, gathering his wheat into the barn and burning up the chaff with unquenchable fire." (Matthew 3:10-12)

John looked forward to a violent intervention by God. And he thought it would happen very soon!

When Jesus came out to the Jordan River to be baptized, John immediately recognized Him as the One he had been anticipating with such incredible fervency. From that point forward, Jesus increased in reputation and ministry while John decreased to the point of being thrown in prison. However, notice what happens after some time elapses. He hears that Jesus is preaching the gospel, healing the sick, and exorcising demons—and he begins to doubt! He doubts that he baptized the right man (Matthew 11:1-19).

Since John was in jail at the time, he sent two of his servants to visit Jesus and "check Him out." They ask Him the question that was burning in John's mind, "Are you the one who was to come, or should we expect someone else?" (verse 3).

Jesus does not respond with a simple yes. Rather, He takes these two messengers with Him to witness more sermons, healings, and exorcisms. Then He sends them back to John to report what they have seen.

What is Jesus telling John by His actions? He is telling him that He is indeed the One that he expected. He is the divine Warrior. But that is not all. He is also informing him that He did not come to wage war against Israel's flesh-and-blood enemies (at that time, the Romans), but rather He came to fight an even more serious enemy—the Devil himself.

Much in the New Testament reflects this war between Jesus and the Devil, but the Cross is its climax. Paul speaks of the Cross in distinctively militaristic language: "He forgave us all our sins, having canceled the written code, with its regulations, that was against us and that stood opposed to us; he took it away, nailing it to the cross. And having disarmed the powers and authorities, he made a public spectacle of them, triumphing over them by the cross" (Colossians 2:13-15).

It is nearly impossible to wrap words around the wonder of this event. Death on a cross was considered to be an ignoble, shameful death, reserved for the most despicable criminals. The Cross appeared to be the Evil One's most successful, glorious moment. He'd destroyed God; he'd disrupted the one relationship — the Trinity — that seemed to be independent of his control. The satisfaction in the heart of the Devil as he shamed glory must have been beyond measure.

But the Cross, like a brilliant conundrum, was, in fact, the height of glory. What appeared to be the death of God, the shaming of the prized only begotten Son of the Most High, and the dissolution of the Trinity was actually the most glorious interplay of justice and mercy, worked out in perfect harmony by all members of the Godhead. It was the powerless disarming the strong, and the shameful shaming the proud.

This is the heart of the gospel, and it is based on a tremendous irony. God won the greatest war of all — the war against the Devil himself — not by killing, but by dying. When Jesus died on the cross, He incisively defeated Satan and all of his evil hordes.

Phase Five: The Coming Day of Christ

Was John the Baptist wrong? He expected a violent deliverer to come crashing down on the enemies of God's people, but instead he saw Jesus offering them salvation. On the surface, it looks like John made a horrible mistake.

But he didn't. Before He died, Jesus told His disciples that He would return in the future with a full display of power:

"At that time, the sign of the Son of Man will appear in the sky, and all the nations of the earth will mourn. They will see the Son of Man coming on the clouds of the sky, with power and great glory. And he will send his angels with a loud trumpet call, and they will gather his elect from the four winds, from the one end of the heavens to the other." (Matthew 24:30-31)

Jesus' speech intentionally reminds us of Daniel's vision referred to earlier. It appears that John the Baptist got it right after all. Jesus is the divine Warrior who will bring judgment not only upon spiritual enemies, but upon human ones as well. Like many of the prophets, John simply did not know the "times and circumstances" of the fulfillment of the message he was given (1 Peter 1:10-12). He did not know that Christ's appearance had two parts, a first and a second coming.

Much of the Old Testament looks forward to Christ's second coming, describing it as the final and ultimate Day of the Lord. Previously, we saw how Zechariah looked forward to a day on which God would exercise His revenge on His enemies and would restore His people. Isaiah, too, described the longed-for day when "he will swallow up death for all time" and "will wipe away the tears from all faces" (Isaiah 25:8). The Second Coming of Christ is that horrible and glorious day — a day His people hope for and His enemies dread.

This "Day of the Lord" is called the "Day of Christ" in the New Testament (1 Corinthians 1:8, 2 Corinthians 1:14, Philippians 1:6). It is most fully described in the book of Revelation. Revelation 19:11-16 gives us a taste of the nature of the end times:

I saw heaven standing open and there before me was a white horse, whose rider is called Faithful and True. With justice he judges and makes war. His eyes are like blazing fire, and on his head are many crowns. He has a name written on him that no one knows but he himself. He is dressed in a robe dipped in blood, and his name is the Word of God. The armies of heaven were following him, riding on white horses and dressed in fine linen, white and clean. Out of his mouth comes a sharp sword with which to strike down the nations. "He will rule them with an iron scepter." He treads on the winepress of the fury of the wrath of God Almighty. On his robe and on his thigh he has this name written: KING OF KINGS AND LORD OF LORDS.

Thus, in this last and climactic fifth phase, Jesus Christ will return to earth as a glorious Warrior who will once and for all bring all evil—spiritual and human—to a violent end.

THE CHRISTIAN WARRIOR TODAY

The Scriptures thus confirm our everyday experience that our lives are a battle. But precisely how are we engaged in this warfare? Where do we as twentieth-century Christians fit into God's unfolding battle strategy?

It is clear from examining the Scriptures that we live in what we called phase four, but we yearn eagerly for phase five. That is, we fight now against the spiritual forces of evil, yet we look forward to the day when the battle will be brought to an ultimate and complete conclusion. We live in the period after Jesus Christ won the victory on the cross, but before the mop-up operations are completed at the Second Coming.

Many parts of the New Testament give us direction in our battle against evil in the world, but perhaps no other passage of Scripture surpasses Ephesians 6:10-18 for describing the Christian's holy war:

Finally, be strong in the Lord and in his mighty power. Put on the full armor of God so that you can take your stand against the devil's schemes. For our struggle is not against flesh and blood, but against the rulers, against the authorities, against the powers of this dark world and against the spiritual forces of evil in the heavenly realms. Therefore put on the full armor of God, so that when the day of evil comes, you may be able to stand your ground, and after you have done everything, to stand. Stand firm then, with the belt of truth buckled around your waist, with the breastplate of righteousness in place, and with your feet fitted with the readiness that comes from the gospel of peace. In addition to all this, take up the shield of faith, with which you can extinguish all the flaming arrows of the evil one. Take the helmet of salvation and the sword of the Spirit, which is the word of God. And pray in the Spirit on all occasions with all kinds of prayers and requests. With this in mind, be alert and always keep on praying for all the saints.

Many Christians neglect reading this passage on the background of the Old Testament theme of the divine Warrior, and our neglect might cause us to lose hope during the fury of the battle. When my boys were small, sometimes we would wrestle. They loved beating on their father until the tide turned and the old man suddenly experienced a surge of energy and overthrew all three attackers. The swing from victory to defeat brought a cry of consternation: "Dad, let us up! Let's quit! Let's play something else!"

The same is true when we stand dressed to the nines in our well-starched armor, Bible under our arm, ready to pounce on a problem. When the mud and blood begin to mingle together in an unearthly hue, it is important to know that God is still the divine Warrior who has already secured victory, no matter how tragically defeating this particular battle may appear.

We are to fight, like Israel was to fight. But, also like Israel, we need to recognize that we will have victory only as we allow God to use us. We are not to be passive; we are to "stand firm." But our strength to do this comes only as we put on the "armor of God."

Who is the enemy Paul is talking about in Ephesians 6? The ultimate enemy of the Christian revealed in this passage is Satan and his demonic powers. Our struggle against Satan encompasses three fronts, and we should not underestimate our enemy's strength. To do so leads to the temptation to fight our battles on our own strength, and our own strength will lead to our quick and easy defeat. When we realize that we have no power in ourselves to fight the battles of life, we are driven to Jesus, our divine Warrior. He is the One who provides us with the spiritual weapons we need to fight—truth, righteousness, the gospel of peace, faith, salvation, the Spirit, and prayer.

THE BATTLE FRONTS

Front One: Standing Firm Against Evil

This front is the focus of much of this book. Most Christians don't need to be convinced that there is much sin and evil in the world. Wickedness emanates from institutions and people (unfortunately from Christians as well as nonChristians), from ourselves (as we'll discover in the third front), as well as from others. The following is just the tip of the iceberg.

Many Christians from Roman times to today have suffered at the hands of a wicked government. Christian martyrs through the ages testify to the potential wickedness of political institutions. One of many contemporary situations is the plight of a Ugandan Christian named Kefa Sempangi. Dan and I went to seminary with Kefa and heard his account firsthand. He has since published a book, *A Distant Grief,* in which he remembers his near death at the hands of one of then-president Idi Amin's death squads and his subsequent flight to the Netherlands and the United States. But even after his return to Uganda in the post-Amin era, his life as a minister and a politician has been beset by further persecutions.

The medical industry, the heart of so much mercy and healing, is also one of the perpetuators of the abortion industry and, as such, is an institution, like all other human institutions, tainted by the hand of the Evil One. One woman confided in me that as a teenager she turned to her doctor for help when she discovered she was pregnant. The doctor advised her that she needed an abortion and calmed her fears with the assurance that there was nothing wrong with the procedure. She has struggled with guilt-induced insomnia ever since.

My wife and I will never forget the call we got from the Yale University student clinic where we went to find out whether she was pregnant with our second child. The nurse told her, "You're pregnant," but before we had time to rejoice, the nurse asked my wife if she wanted an abortion. In this world torn by conflict, the human institution most dedicated to preserving human life finds itself destroying it.

Many, indeed all, other human institutions are similarly affected by the conflict between the divine and the demonic. Both Dan and I, as well as our children, have been active in sports through the years. We have derived enjoyment and healthier bodies because of it. But we can both testify that on some levels there is a sports ethos that allows, and even encourages, the use of pain-deadening and muscle-enhancing drugs, which are ultimately life threatening. My wife and I both sport bad knees, the direct result of coaches insisting that we start playing too soon after a minor injury. They were more interested in winning than in health!

Even the church as an institution is the source of much pain and evil. It doesn't take the obvious cases like the Spanish Inquisition to illustrate this point. We have all experienced the hardness of a dysfunctional church family at some point in our Christian life. One of the saddest moments of my life was when I was up for ordination. This denomination had a liberal tendency, but I didn't know much better since I was still a young Christian at the time. It was the denomination in which I grew up, and I felt attached to it. However, I was wise enough to go to an evangelical seminary because I knew I had to be taught by people who respected the Bible as God's Word, something not true of this certain denomination's seminaries.

About a year into my work, the ordination council called me to a meeting and told me that they would not ordain me because I attended this evangelical seminary and because I held certain biblical doctrines. Perhaps what hurt me more than anything was the conversation I had with another person my age while I was waiting for the committee to meet with me. This man ridiculed me for my trust in the Bible and then proceeded to deny every doctrine I considered essential to Christianity — the historicity of Jesus and His bodily resurrection, the role of the Holy Spirit, the trustworthiness of

Scripture, and the Second Coming. He, too, was meeting with the church council that day, but for a reason different than my own. He was being ordained on Sunday, and they were setting up the service for him! I felt like someone kicked me in the face.

These are just a few of the examples of societal forces and institutions that are the source of evil against which we should battle. But we all know that institutions are not abstract entities that exist independent of human involvement. Institutions are made up of people. We are really talking about a spiritual battle with real people on either side.

Front Two: The Fight to Win Souls

Opinions may differ, but I cringe every time I hear someone say, "I won a soul for Christ." Perhaps it's the arrogant voice that usually goes along with the claim.

But I have to admit that there is some truth to this old Christian expression. When we share the gospel with others, we are involved in warfare, just as real as, and indeed with longer lasting implications than, the battle of the Israelites against Jericho.

A careful study of the entire Bible indicates that evangelism replaces warfare as we move from the Old to the New Testament. That is, in the Old Testament, the predominant way of relating to the outsider (the non-Israelite) was to fight with real weapons. In the New Testament, the way we are to relate to the nonChristian is defined by Jesus in the Great Commission: "Therefore go and make disciples of all nations, baptizing them in the name of the Father and of the Son and of the Holy Spirit, and teaching them to obey everything I have commanded you" (Matthew 28:19-20).

And doesn't experience teach us that evangelism is often like a war? Some of our experiences are more explicitly warlike than others. As Dan mentioned in the preface, he and I have been close friends a very long time, even before we became Christians. I became a Christian the summer before we went to college together in 1970. We were roommates, and I became acquainted with some other Christians soon after arriving. We would all share the gospel with Dan, and he would battle us, mainly through mocking ridicule. Looking back on it twenty years later, I realize that as young and naive Christians, we gave him plenty to make fun of! But at the time, it was a real struggle, because Dan knew exactly what to say in order to embarrass us. We were encouraged, though, in the struggle because we all saw how God was softening Dan's heart to receive His promise of salvation.

This example is a personal and, in retrospect, lighthearted one. But there are plenty of Christians who can tell horrifying stories of real abuse as a result of evangelism. The reason for this is that when we share the gospel with a stranger or friend, we are not just involved in a quiet clash of ideas with another rational human being. We are sharing the news of sin and redemption with someone who is on Satan's side, whether that person is conscious of it or not.

If a person is not devoted to Christ, there is only one other alternative—they are devoted to Christ's Enemy. That is why Paul talks about baptism as a symbol of death. It is warfare. If a person becomes a Christian, he dies to the old man and puts on the new by "having been buried with him [Christ] in baptism and raised with him through your faith in the power of God, who raised him from the dead" (Colossians 2:12).

Front Three: The New Man Versus the Old Man
Jesus instructed us to take the beam out of our own eye before we take the speck out of our brother's (Matthew 7:5). In this way, He told us that the battle is not only against others, it is also within ourselves. Facing the deeply embedded evil of our own hearts is where the most bitter fighting occurs. It's like a civil war. Your enemy, your old self, is a dearly beloved friend you really don't want to kill.

Paul perceptively shared the struggle that went on in his own heart, knowing it's the struggle we all go through:

So I find this law at work: When I want to do good, evil is right there with me. For in my inner being I delight in God's law; but I see another law at work in the members of my body, waging war against the law of my mind and making me a prisoner of the law of sin at work within my members. What a wretched man I am! (Romans 7:21-24)

Once we become Christians, we are no longer in Satan's army; we are in Christ's. We fight for the gospel, taking on Satan, our former commander-in-chief. However, there is a part of us that still acts like we are part of this world, rather than pilgrims looking forward to the realities of heaven. The Bible names this tendency the "old man" (Ephesians 4:22, Colossians 3:9) and tells us to cast it off and put on the "new." Theologians call this the process of "sanctification," but it's just another way of saying that Christians should become more like Christ every day.

Whatever you call it, our Christian growth is a battle against Satan in our own hearts. This front, for most of us, is the hardest. It's not easy to fight evil in another person. It may be tough for some of us to share the gospel with others. But it's grueling to face the dark, cold reality that we have to battle against our own vicious and destructive thoughts, emotions, and actions.

This is because deep down we really enjoy our sin and find any way we can to justify it in our eyes. I am not often emotionally down, but when I am depressed I need to have a scapegoat—God has given me too much work, my wife is ignoring me, my children are brats, my Little League team is uncommitted. I would much rather be happy than depressed, but at times like this, I would rather be depressed than to think that I have over-committed myself to writing projects, been cold toward my wife, not disciplined my children sufficiently, and not taught my Little Leaguers how to hit or field.

As we engage in battle on this final front, we must remember that it is ultimately God against whom we struggle. It is not merely the new us that takes on the old us in our own power. And this is the reason why the battle always goes to the advantage of the new man; it is God who fights for us. The battle of the cosmos—the struggle between God and Satan—is waged in our very hearts, and the message of the Bible is absolutely clear: Nothing can stand before God in defiance and survive.

SPIRITUAL WEAPONS

I think by now it's pretty clear that the Bible confirms our experience that life is a battle. This is why God has revealed so much throughout its pages about His nature as a warrior and our participation in His army.

However, it is extremely important to remember that the warfare has shifted as we move from the Old to the New Testament period from a physical to a spiritual battle. It is one we must fight with spiritual weapons, not physical ones.

The teachings of Jesus do not allow us to hit an abortionist or bomb a clinic. We are not permitted to kidnap a potential convert and force him to listen to the gospel. And we shouldn't whip ourselves (physically as some monks did in the Middle Ages) to discourage our sinning. Our weapons are prayer, faith, and bold love.

Prayer

Most of us think of prayer as a retreat from the action, not as an offensive weapon with which we attack the Enemy. After all, when we want to pray, we usually seek out a quiet spot. We also hear and use the expression "let me pray about it" when we are not sure we want to do something we are asked to do.

In reaction against this, we must cultivate a mindset that sees prayer as a powerful tool by which we can foil Satan's schemes and destroy his handiwork. We are to see prayer as our principal means of communication with our divine war Commander.

In the war between Iraq and the allied forces who came to the aid of Kuwait, one of the largest of many discrepancies between the two sides was in the area of communication. The Allies were in constant touch with each other and knew the enemy positions through the use of highly sophisticated technology. On the other side, the front lines of the Iraqi armies knew very little about their enemy's positions and could not even communicate with their commanders in Baghdad. The result was a completely lopsided victory for the Allies.

We need to use prayer to ask our spiritual war Commander to open our eyes to the conflict so we may see where the Enemy is located, and then to provide us with the strength to carry on the battle.

The curses of the psalms are a model of using prayer as a weapon. The psalmist made some very strong statements as he spoke to God about his enemies:

> Pour out your wrath on them;
>> let your fierce anger overtake them.
> May their place be deserted;
>> let there be no one to dwell in their tents.
> Charge them with crime upon crime;
>> do not let them share in your salvation.
>> (Psalm 69:24-25,27)

While these psalms are models to us for prayer, they must be wisely used in the knowledge that the object of our warfare has shifted from flesh and blood enemies to spiritual ones. Our weapons must be spiritual, too. One concrete way the Christian can use prayer as a weapon against an abuser is to pray for his repentance.

Faith

The second weapon of spiritual warfare is faith, a deep trust in the One who is our Commander-in-Chief, Jesus Christ. Faith is multifaceted. One of many ways to think of faith is as a willingness to let go, to relax in the presence of Someone who is good. A small child squeals with anticipation as her father lifts her above his head and gently tosses her into the air, catching her as she tumbles toward the ground. The child could scream and cry at being lifted and turn her little body into a stone-like, inflexible dead weight. Such a response indicates a lack of trust. Faith may not take away all our fear or doubt, but it will enable us to know, at some deep level, that our Father is good and His purpose is consistent with His character.

Faith, then, is an assertion of trust, even when our circumstances point in a direction that seems to call into question God's goodness. Faith is vision of what cannot be seen, a knowing of something that is beyond verifiable human knowledge. It is an assent to the inner witness of the Spirit that continues to keep a flame alive in us after all our efforts to snuff it out have failed. Fundamentally, we know that He is capable and willing to bring the battle to a successful completion. Indeed, the Scriptures tell us that He has already accomplished the victory on the cross, and we have a preview of the final day in the book of Revelation.

One of the many lessons of the Viet Nam War was the disastrous consequences of a lack of trust between soldiers and their commanding officers. Soldiers often did not trust the abilities of their officers, and there were even alarming reports that soldiers would put a bullet in the back of their officers during battles.

A firm trust in God is incredibly important if we are to endure the day-to-day battles of life. We need to know that God is there in His power to encourage us to face the angry boss at work, our unrepentant spouse, or our disobedient children.

Bold Love
Last, bold love is a weapon fit for the spiritual battle. Not much needs to be said here because, after all, the whole book describes it. But here I want to emphasize that the spiritual nature of our weapons does not mean that they are intangible. We are not to be passive. We are not called to love people, even those who hurt us, from a distance, but we are required to move into their lives to open the door to their repentance.

JESUS CHRIST: LOVE WARRIOR

The Bible calls us to the life of a warrior in a world of conflict. But God does not send us out to fight on our own or even to pool our resources with other Christians. No, He sent His Son to first win the battle. He defeated evil by dying on the cross. He shows us that the way of victory is through love and sacrifice, not hate and greed. He gives us confidence to face abuse today because "our present sufferings are not worth comparing with the glory that will be revealed in us" when He comes to rescue us for the last time (Romans 8:18).

Jesus Christ, the warring Lamb of God, is the model of bold love that the Bible gives us to emulate. But how can we really do this? We are human, fearful, and selfish. Thankfully, learning to love and forgive is a process. In the next chapter, Dan will describe the qualities that grow in a soldier's heart as he or she learns to trust the divine Warrior who triumphs in battle.

PART TWO

Strategy for the
War of Love

❖

CHAPTER SIX

RÉSUMÉ OF A WARRIOR:
Qualifications of the Heart

Any endeavor as demanding and significant as the battle to forgive requires preparation and time to develop. There is an assumption held by many Christians that at conversion, once the Spirit of God indwells their being, they will be able to do all that is required — love, forgive, serve, witness, pray, disciple, etc. It is true that at conversion we are free to serve God and others with a new heart, but it is beyond comprehension to believe that we are instantly capable of doing so. The heart of a believer will be able to love and forgive in a way that is different when compared to her life prior to conversion, although if measured by certain behavioral standards, the believer may be more clumsy and inelegant in her effort to love than she might have appeared prior to conversion.

For example, a woman who prior to conversion might have ignored her husband's drinking may now see his bouts with alcohol from a more honest and serious standpoint. In the past she might have quietly endured his destructive behavior, whereas now she may argue, complain, and vocalize her concerns, and thus be labeled as judgmental and pushy. In fact, her conversion may lead to an increase in boldness and spiritual perception that erupts in new struggles with hurt and anger. Chances are her definition of love will expand and it will require more of her than ignoring her husband's alcoholism as she did in the past.

Coming to know Christ may not immediately increase what most people call "love." Whenever someone strives to love with the love of God, they enter into an endeavor that has more possibility of failure than any other enterprise in life. Simply said, God's standards of love are always higher than ours; therefore, all efforts to love biblically will inevitably lead to a sense of our incompleteness and self-centeredness. God calls us to love, but love is developed over a lifetime of struggling to comprehend the personality of God who pursues us with relentless passion.

Growth is always developmental—that is, progressively learned, building block by block, slowly over time. The process is a journey, a pilgrimage through the unknown valleys of trial, tempest, and turmoil. In one sense, there is very little preparation involved prior to beginning the journey. The Lord simply asks the ill-prepared pilgrim to walk by faith in the understanding that He will provide. On the other hand, the journey is in itself a preparation where each experience is cumulatively used to prepare our hearts for the next turn in the path. He promises we will never be given more than we are prepared to handle (1 Corinthians 10:13), although at any one point, we might be tempted to differ.

A day after I wrote these words, I learned that my father was diagnosed with inoperable lung cancer. No words can describe my sense of horror, emptiness, rage, and heartache in hearing his oncologist say, "Your father is fatally ill. He will likely not live beyond a year to two years." An hour after learning the news, I walked into a delicatessen to pick up a cake for my son's third birthday party and I saw happy people talking, drinking coffee, and buying tasty treats. I wanted to scream, "My father is dying!" The only reason for not shouting was my inability to say those words out loud. I felt mute. When I tried to tell my wife what I was feeling, I was speechless.

Most of the day I spent in silence.

That night I was scheduled to be on a nationally syndicated radio show to talk about the struggles caused by sexual abuse. I could have backed out of the program, but it seemed fitting and right to go on. At another point, given different circumstances, I might have chosen another course of action, but I wanted to add my voice to the host of others who are saying, "The Evil One might win another battle, but he will not win the war." I wanted, in my own small way, to taunt the Evil One with the words, "O Death, where is your sting?"

I still wonder, other than by God's kindness, how I was able to enter into the battle of others' struggles that night. I don't believe I could have chosen that course a few years ago, even with His supernatural intervention. I would not have been prepared to enter into another's wounded heart when my own heart felt such emptiness and pain. There are still many moments when I choose to hide in my own pain. There are, however, a few times when I again choose to walk into the battle even though my own strength seems inadequate to lift a sword.

What are the qualities of soul that must be learned over time to enable us to speak when we feel there are no words to offer? What turns in the preparatory process must be passed in order to enter the hearts of others when our own wounds seem to cry louder than the righteousness of God? Four central qualities are required — courage, conviction, calling, and cunning. Each will be progressively deepened as we choose the path of our divine Warrior.

THE QUALITIES OF THE SOUL

Courage: A Willingness to Sacrifice for a Better Day

We will not be free to love until the cliché "this is not our home" becomes real. It is sewn into the fabric of our being that we will courageously defend whatever is most dear to our hearts — a woman will, at all costs, protect her young; a man will defend against intruders who attempt to harm his family or home. In a similar way, we will take heroic risks to protect whatever is the treasure of our heart, be it a child, a home, a country, a philosophy, God.

It seems that most of my life is sacrificed protecting and enhancing a home that is supposedly not my home. I still read self-help books on parenting, hoping someone will finally tell me how to parent correctly so that my children and I can avoid the sorrow of life. I often listen to sermons with the same energy ("tell me how to make this life work better"). The root desire behind our propensity to find concrete, manageable steps for living the Christian life often boils down to a demand to find order, predictability, and consistency in a world where there is little to none. How would you answer the questions, "Do I live for heaven?" or "Do I live demanding that life be like heaven?" Your answers will determine what you will spend your life fighting for.

What most of us spend the energy of our lives warring against is reality — the fact that life is awful and the truth that this world is not our home. I am surprised when the effects of a fallen world impinge on my life. I know people die. I know tragedies occur. I am aware that people have affairs and marriages end. But for some reason, I am stunned when a good friend dies or a child of parents I know is diagnosed with a fatal disease. I am shocked when someone I've worked with in a ministry context has an affair and leaves his wife. Though I face sin and its debris every day, I somehow assume that when I leave my office, I can drive away from sin's sorrow.

When I see the debris of the storm in my friends, family, and my mirror, I am forced to see that the ravages of sin are inescapable. If I am surprised by sin in my life or in others, I am operating according to a tragic assumption about life. *If I do not anticipate the regularity and tragedy of sin, I unavoidably come to believe this world is my home.* It may be near impossible to release the lie, "This is my home; I deserve life, love, and liberty," but no one will choose a path of sacrificial, courageous love if this life is either all there is or is nearly as good as the next. One will choose the better only if the present is faced as it is — not worth living for, but worth dying to change.

Paul reflected that truth in these words in Philippians

1:21-24: "For to me, to live is Christ and to die is gain. If I am to go on living in the body, this will mean fruitful labor for me. Yet what shall I choose? I do not know! I am torn between the two: I desire to depart and be with Christ, which is better by far; but it is more necessary for you that I remain in the body."

His words still sound alien to me, and certainly sound foreign to a culture bent on self-discovery, self-healing, and self-enhancement. Paul was clear about his options and knew precisely which one was better and why he chose to remain with the less desirable alternative. He did not live with the assumption that life, in itself, offered much beyond what it holds for the next.

The "much" this life does hold, however, is not what most of us would consider desirable. The greatest gift this life offers is the joy of forming Christ in others. Paul further states in verse 25, "I know that I will remain, and I will continue with all of you for your progress and joy in the faith." There is a power-ful connection between Paul's two sentences. To the degree that this life holds the possibility of "getting something," we will labor and flounder to achieve what only heaven can offer. On the other hand, to the degree that this life is viewed as a place of pilgrimage—a place where it is never honorable or right to build a lasting foundation—I am released to live and love through seeing my life used to advance your progress and joy in Christ.

The writer of the book of Hebrews offers us a perspective on deepening this reality in our life. When talking about people of faith, he states, "All these people were still living by faith when they died. They did not receive the things promised; they only saw them and welcomed them from a distance. And they admitted that they were aliens and strangers on earth. . . . They were longing for a better country—a heavenly one. Therefore, God is not ashamed to be called their God" (Hebrews 11:13,16). There are several key words involved in the process—*welcoming, admitting,* and *longing.*

Welcoming from afar. People who see a better home ahead are able to welcome what is not currently enjoyed. Think of the oddity of welcoming something that has not arrived. Not long ago, I was waiting for an important piece of mail to arrive. Every day that it did not come, I felt more irritated with the postman. It was not his fault or problem, but I found myself less disposed to speak kindly to him. The idea of welcoming something from afar that we desperately desire to arrive is possible only if our heart is busy in preparation for the arrival.

The greater the anticipation of the arrival, the more active we will be in preparing a room for the homecoming. An expectant mother who cleans and paints the nursery is a poignant image of the one who welcomes from afar. Are we pregnant with hope of His return? Do we prepare our heart daily for His advent? If we do not anticipate His return, then we will either be lulled into thinking that what we currently enjoy in this life is enough or lapse into fury for this life not being enough.

Admitting emptiness. Anticipation deepens our awareness of disappointment. The saints who waited for the Lord's first coming "admitted" they were aliens and strangers. They did not deny the sorrow of anticipatory emptiness. The flip side of waiting with keen excitement is intense sadness when the beloved fails to come. The proverb says, "Hope deferred makes the heart sick" (Proverbs 13:12).

We are to live with the ongoing cycle of anticipation/sorrow. If we "admit" our deep desire is not fully met, then we can embrace the reality of a sojourner who has not yet found rest and peace. It is not "abnormal" to be empty, sad, and lonely at the deepest place in our souls that was fashioned for eternity—to be dissatisfied with the empty provisions of this world, sad over the destruction of beauty, lonely for the companionship of lost friendships. It is not only not abnormal, but wrong to be otherwise.

Longing for home. If left at the last sentence, I would imagine most readers would dismiss the thought as despairing. However, there is another key word in the passage—*longing* for a better country. The cycle of anticipation/sorrow is anything but morbid because of the passion of longing. Longing is the succulent smell that draws us out of our lethargy and despair, and sweetly offers a small, seductive taste of what our

heart anticipates in banquet proportion. The process of antici-
pation/sorrow/passion draws us to wait for His day, and frees
us to see our day as not our own. It releases a willingness in us
to courageously sacrifice our life for another, knowing whatever loss is experienced is incomprehensibly small compared
to what beckons from afar.

For example, a good friend, John, recently put a stop to
a tragic and destructive relationship with his father. For over
three decades, his father, a violent and cruel alcoholic, would
physically or emotionally tear his son to shreds. After the son
married, the father's rage turned against the new daughter-in-
law. For years, every family occasion involved an undermining
of her cooking, housekeeping, and parenting. John chose to
ignore the abuse and berated his wife for being so sensitive.
When the viciousness went beyond his capacity to deny, he
would counsel his wife to turn the other cheek and be a witness
to his family by forgiving their sin.

Sadly, it took years, but eventually John came to see his
perseverance and long-sufferance as cowardliness. He had
tuned out his father's abusive words. He had not anguished
and wrestled with what it meant to protect his wife and,
indeed, love his father. As John faced the sorrow of being an
orphan with parents and a man without a home in this world,
he repented of trying to make this life a permanent place of
rest. Facing the extent of his cowardliness and the damage he
caused his wife freed him to begin to live with courage.

Courage comes only to the degree that the allure of heaven
breaks the seduction of vanity fair. As clarity about my status
as an alien and stranger deepens, I am free to develop greater
clarity about the reason for my existence and to behave
accordingly.

Calling: Living Out the Offense of the Gospel

One of the simplest and most confounding questions a human
being can ask is, "What am I living for?" The answers we offer
can be initially evaluated as either honorable or self-serving.
A man who is living solely for the joy of acquisition and
power is self-serving; another man who is living for the

betterment of his family and their future is more honorable in his expenditure of time and money. *It is possible, however, to live for apparently noble purposes without bearing the offense of the Cross.*

One can be appropriately moral and sensitive to others for no other reason than that it makes life more simple and easier to bear. A moral life, however, is intended to be more than pragmatic. A life of covenantal loyalty is designed to bear witness to the world that it is insane to live in rebellion. In that sense, all goodness, although perhaps pragmatically reasonable, is prophetic and intentionally disruptive to any who believe that life can be lived with cavalier disregard of God. All true morality and sensitivity bears the foolishness of the Cross; therefore, it offends and invites the foolish heart to return to truth.

The gospel offends. It strikes at the heart of man's arrogance and rage. It demands a response of brokenness — or evokes mockery and contempt. The gospel does not settle for good, moral living; it requires radical transformation of the heart. In that sense, *the calling of every Christian is to prophetically live out a disruptive goodness that embraces foolishness before the wise and weakness before the strong.* To do otherwise — to live merely for another paycheck or summer vacation — is to live for legitimate desires that never attain the dignity and honor of our highest calling.

Paul describes the unique calling of every Christian:

> Thanks be to God, who always leads us in triumphal procession in Christ and through us spreads everywhere the fragrance of the knowledge of him. For we are to God the aroma of Christ among those who are being saved and those who are perishing. To the one we are the smell of death; to the other, the fragrance of life. And who is equal to such a task? (2 Corinthians 2:14-16)

The passage depicts an ancient Near Eastern king who is victorious in battle and ties the defeated warriors to a long rope behind his chariot. The slaves are now indentured to serve the victorious king in his army. It is not unusual for the servant-warriors to be called to fight against the very people of whom they were once a part. Their weapons and knowledge of the enemy are now useful for service to the victorious king. The king triumphantly leads the vanquished foe through the city to the praise of his people. The smell of victory excites adoration for the victorious king, and the smell of defeat crushes those who hate his success.

In the same way, we are the King's prisoners, conquered by His victory on the cross. He has triumphed over the Evil One, and we have been claimed as His bond-servants. Our lives are now the aroma of His victory—to those who long for truth and beauty, a fragrance of life, and to those who despise being enslaved by good, a stench of death. Our lives either attract or repel, invite or offend.

Our calling is to be servant-warriors unto righteousness. We are not free men or women, but people bought with a price and called to fight on the side of good. *Our central calling is to provoke through smell.* It is through us that the fragrance of the knowledge of God slips through the hard, encrusted walls of denial and hatred in others, and beckons the soul to relinquish its fortress to God.

Our mission is to confound the world through the aroma of weakness and foolishness (1 Corinthians 1:27-30). We appear foolish because our weapons are immaterial (Ephesians 6:10-19) and our strategies apparently absurd, including trumpet blowing (Joshua 6:12-20), singing in front of the enemy (2 Chronicles 20:17-24), and sending troops home so that our numbers are not seen as the cause of our victory (Judges 7:2-4).

Our foolishness is lived out by calling all people to repentance—and then, deepened repentance—believing that God's Spirit can wonderfully alter the very structure of hatred and rebellion in the human heart. In one sense, our greatest foolishness is witnessed in our belief that Jesus Christ, very God of God, was a man, a human being, who came to overthrow the structures of evil in the world and in our hearts in order to deliver us from bondage to an unseen, subtle Enemy and from the deserved judgment of the unseen Holy God.

We are, indeed, an odd army, a motley crew, an unlikely fragrance whose weapon and strategy is to live out what it means to be forgiven through love. Nothing is more odd to a self-centered world than sacrificial love; nothing is more incomprehensible to the fallen heart than withholding revenge and offering the other cheek and carrying the burden of the abuser an extra mile.

Recall the story of my friend John. He believed, to the depths of his heart, that he was living out love and forgiveness. When he faced his cowardliness, he also saw how deeply enslaved he was to his family. He was not a bond-servant of Christ. He was enmeshed in a wicked family. He counseled forgiveness and practiced denial; he thought he was loving, but instead he was protecting himself. His great calling in life was to keep the family balanced and stable. He was the "helper" — the supportive, reasoned voice that calmed the waters after one of his father's tornado rages.

In simple terms, it is not possible to serve God and any form of mammon. Mammon is any false god that gains an allegiance only the true God deserves. John was a warrior fighting to keep reality from impinging on and destroying his family. In that sense, though he was a Christian, he did not live out the foolishness of the gospel. Embracing the offense of the gospel would have involved forsaking what seemed so reasonable — his well-defined role in the family. It would have meant shifting allegiance from his family to another Master.

Called into slavery. The life purpose for every believer is to live out the gospel — be it in our families, jobs, or places of recreation. We can developmentally grow in understanding our calling only to the degree that we embrace our status as slaves of a new Master. Paul states that slavery is not an option; it is a fact of being a human being. We are either slaves of righteousness or unrighteousness (Romans 6:15-23). There might be a choice as to direction, but those are the only two options. Our option is between walking in His triumphal procession and attempting to orchestrate our own victory march. The one appears shameful and demanding; the other looks glorious and free. What most of us do is volunteer for His army and then hope we are never called to serve in a war. We want the best of both worlds — God as our King and our will as the rule. Fortunately, no one can ride two horses for long. A point of division in the path will occur when one form of slavery must be chosen over the other.

God in His gracious but severe kindness replenishes our opportunity to follow in His triumphal train every time we choose to pursue slavery to unrighteousness. It is a seemingly endless piano lesson until the piece is technically played with soul-birthing passion. The joyful privilege of being on His side will one day be more overwhelming than our missed notes and lifeless fingers, to a point where the wonder of being God's fragrance — a picture of His beauty and wonder — stirs our hearts to play music unheard in any great concert hall. At the point our souls are free to play, sing, cry, and worship at the honor of bearing His smell, we will stand in awe of our power to attract and repel, to be used of God to enter the souls of others with shattering truth and glorious hope.

Few things caused Paul to exclaim, "Who is equal to such a task?" (2 Corinthians 2:16). He was reflecting on the awesome task of causing some people to be drawn to God and the equally overwhelming sorrow of causing others to be repulsed. It is something like the burden that every military officer faces when he sends troops to war — some will live, and others will die. Who is equal to the task, knowing that every word and deed may cause a person to explore or impugn the gospel?

Called into battle. Our calling to battle will be embraced to the degree we face the horror and honor of fighting for our King. In every war, there are casualties. Without question, war reflects hell, and the stench of death is never far. The horror of war is that we will see death in our ranks. Casualties come when those we colabor with turn from the fight and betray, for a time or for an eternity, allegiance to our God. Some of my most painful moments in the ministry occurred in talking to friends who capsized their calling in the arms of a foreign lover. The lover may be another woman or man, another god, money, fame, or power. Our calling will include accepting, at a level that is beyond words, the sorrow of seeing our friends turn against God and us. But it will also involve the honor of bearing arms for the righteous King.

We are conquered slaves who ought not be trusted or equipped to fight on His side. We are so prone to revert back to allegiance to the enemy king. Nevertheless, the great King outfits us, blesses us with His very presence, and allows us to wear the insignia of heaven. His trust in us appears so foolish and His pardon so unreasonable, but He continues to honor us with the standing as His son or daughter and the opportunity to fight on His side without condemnation or disgust for our failures.

Conviction: Joining God's Hatred of Arrogance
Courage prompts us to face the inevitability of war; calling propels us to the front lines of battle; and conviction intensifies our passion about the enemy to be fought. When we go to war, what are we to feel about our enemy?

For obvious reasons, it is easy for me to compare our enemy to cancer. Cancer, like sin, feeds on the healthy cells of the body. It sucks the life-giving nutrients away and destroys the body from the inside out. It is silent, malignant, and subtle. It may not even be diagnosed until the body is almost destroyed. In time, it ravages beauty and saps hope and joy. It brings death and sorrow.

I tremble as I write. I almost cannot put the words on my screen. How do I feel about my father's enemy, cancer? If I were a warrior and my father's enemy were to come into my presence, I would kill it. I long to wrap my hands around its neck and squeeze the life out of that which has sucked the life out of so many.

Is that God's attitude toward His enemy? We often hear the biblical-sounding phrase, "God hates the sin, but loves the sinner." The dilemma is that sin cannot be abstracted from the sinner. Without the blood of Christ, what is sent to hell — the sin or the sinner? Hell is not a housing project for abstractions, but a place where sinners are left to live out the consequences of their unpardoned sin.

For example, how is it possible to hate adultery without hating the adulterer? What is adultery? Is it merely sexual infidelity—sexual relations with the wrong person? Or is it a profound breaking of a covenant of trust, which cancerously devours the soul and relationships? If it is the latter, then adultery is a big deal. Sin is cancer personified; sin involves rebellious behavior, but it is more than a measurable, objective violation of the standards of God.

Many will agree sin is more than an abstraction or a mere behavior to be condemned; it is a force, a malevolent energy in the soul that blights and destroys. So what of the question, "Doesn't God love the adulterer, the gossip, the denier, the enabler, and so forth?" Doesn't He hate the sin, but love the sinner?

The answer is both yes and no. Indeed God loves the sinner, but He also hates the sinner. In Proverbs 3:32, we read, "The LORD detests a perverse man." The passage does not divide the man from his actions. Proverbs 6:16-19 ties both the person and his behaviors together:

> There are six things the LORD hates,
>   seven that are detestable to him:
>   haughty eyes,
>   a lying tongue,
>   hands that shed innocent blood,
>   a heart that devises wicked schemes,
>   feet that are quick to rush into evil,
>   a false witness who pours out lies
>   and a man who stirs up dissension among
>   brothers.

We are to join God in His hatred of both the sinner and the sin, beginning with the sinner with whom we are best acquainted—ourself. The marvel of grace is that we are all inflicted with the same cancer as those we are called to love. We are called to be ophthalmologists—eye doctors who see a disease in the eye of another and are so committed to removing that speck of cancer that we knowingly undergo the same surgery to remove the mass in our own eye in order to remove the disease in the other. The covering of grace enables us to know our disease is still rampant, but we will never die. Therefore, with a piercing hatred of our sin, we are called to announce tenderly and strongly the prospect of a cure to others. This kind of engagement with other sinners involves a hatred of whatever will destroy life and beauty.

Proverbs further says, "To fear the LORD is to hate evil; I hate pride and arrogance, evil behavior and perverse speech" (8:13). Most Christians I speak to find it inconceivable that they are required to hate. Normally we are encouraged to think of God not as a stern, angry father who beats us when we are bad, but as a warm, caring grandfather who does not want us to sin because He knows it will hurt us, but when we violate His will, He loves us anyway. God is love and wants us to love just as He loves.

Yet ask most Christians, "Does God hate cancer?" The answer is usually yes. Ask, "Does God hate arrogance and pride?" The answer is often a blank stare. If He hates the internal working of sin, not just the external manifestation of sin, then in a sense, He hates me because I am, at times, haughty and arrogant.

Is God stern and angry, or warm and kind? In a sense, He is both. He is a father who delights in His child, so He therefore disciplines His child with a rebuke (Proverbs 3:11-12). Another contemporary image is the oncologist. He is a cancer specialist who will do anything to destroy that which destroys. He will surgically cut away flesh; He will burn out cells through radiation; and He will poison them with chemotherapy. The treatment is, at times, brutal and appears cruel, but the result is profoundly life-enhancing and lovely. Discipline, though it often feels like a judgment that exiles and abandons us, is a labor of love that beautifies the heart through the disruptive touch of a severe mercy.

God despises the evil that works in me, that is me, and that is not me. Just as cancer is alien to the way I was built to be, so are arrogance, haughtiness, and perversity. Does God love me? Yes! He knows precisely what I might become if the cancerous cells are destroyed and my body and soul bear the loveliness of His Son. Does He hate what I have become, what I am now? Absolutely yes! Therefore, the full weight of His glory will be predisposed to destroy the internal malignancy that robs me of my soul, others of my beauty, and God of His glory.

Let me take you back to the story of John. Once he aligned himself behind the train of his victorious God, a huge battle began. He no longer was willing to ignore his father's abuse of his wife. He stepped in and put limits on what his father was free to say to his wife. He began to directly address his father's arrogant attacks and perverse speech in the moment. Several times, his father ordered John and his family to leave the house unless he apologized. Rather than apologize, John and his family departed.

John began to see his father as more than someone with an anger problem or as more than an alcoholic or a deeply troubled man. He finally saw his father as wickedly committed to destroying all those who stood in the path he perceived would lead to self-fulfillment. His father was an arrogant man whom God hates. He was a man John was to hate as well — and hate to such a degree that his cancer would be destroyed, so that he might live.

The intriguing phenomena is that as John came to hate his father's arrogance and perversity, he began to see and hate his own. He began to see that his father's sin, though more obviously damaging, was in essence no different than the fearful arrogance that originally blinded him to his wife's tears. As he refused to explain away his father's cancer, he was less willing to excuse his own. Jesus reflects that process when He said to "first take the plank out of your own eye, and then you will see clearly to remove the speck from your brother's eye" (Matthew 7:5).

We are called to fight in the war, hating evil and clinging to what is good (Romans 12:9). Our hatred of evil in others will deepen our hatred of what is ugly within us and, in turn, deepen our wonder of a God who forgives much. Our increased hatred and wonder will, over time, increase our wisdom in dealing with evil.

Cunning: The Wisdom of a Snake, The Innocence of a Dove

Courage prompts us to face the inevitability of war; calling propels us to the front lines of battle; conviction energizes our resolve to fight; and cunning enables us to get close enough to our enemy to destroy his power and offer the opportunity for surrender. If hatred is viewed as an impossibility for Christians, try telling Christians it is not only acceptable, but necessary, to be crafty and cunning in dealing with sinners.

When our Lord sent His disciples out for their inaugural evangelism campaign, He told them to "be as shrewd as snakes and as innocent as doves" (Matthew 10:16). The allusion seems to be to Satan and the Spirit of God. It is an odd, if not outlandish, comparison. Only the Lord Himself could make such a statement without it being viewed as blasphemous. We are to be as clever and cunning as the Devil and as good-hearted and -intentioned as God.

An excellent example of this passage is the prophet Nathan. God told him to rebuke King David for the sin of murder and adultery. It was well understood during that day that no one should make a king unhappy. You will recall in another passage that King Artaxerxes noticed that Nehemiah was sad (Nehemiah 2:2). Nehemiah was terrified because the consequence for disturbing a king was death. Imagine, then, how Nathan felt about not only bringing a few sad feelings David's way, but in fact, being the agent to expose his shame of murder and adultery.

Nathan told David a story. He told about the evil deeds of a cruel and enormously rich land owner who stole another farmer's only lamb. The story moved David, and he called for judgment on the man. Nathan, at that point, said, "You are the man!" (2 Samuel 12:7). Nathan tricked David into pointing the finger at himself. Nathan, through cunning and wisdom, gave David enough rope to hang himself and also escaped a dangerous mission with his own neck.

The methodology will likely be different in every situation, but the principle is the same: Be wise and use the situation to the best advantage in order to achieve God's larger purpose. Jesus commends this type of manipulative shrewdness. The dishonest servant is honored because he cuts a deal with those who owe money to the master. He knows he will gain favor in the eyes of his peers and be granted honor after the master fires him. The Lord recognizes this when He tells the disciples that "the people of this world are more shrewd in dealing with their own kind than are the people of the light. I tell you, use worldly wealth to gain friends for yourselves, so that when it is gone, you will be welcomed into eternal dwellings" (Luke 16:8-9).

Manipulative shrewdness. A shrewd attack occurs whenever a Christian borrows capital from the bank of the world (at good interest rates) and then uses the money to establish businesses that undermine the economic system of the world. For example, a professor at the seminary I attended was a card-carrying member of the American Civil Liberties Union (ACLU). The ACLU has never been known as a bastion of conservative thought, but its charter involves defending the weak and downtrodden. In many regards, its goals are consonant with Jesus' commitment to justice. In practice, the ACLU's ideology is often a narrowly defined application of leftist thinking. The professor, however, used its commitment to pluralism and fairness to hold it accountable to occasionally defend conservative Christians who were unjustly treated because of their values.

Another crafty Christian exposed her husband's outrageous attacks by giggling. For years, she bore his contemptuous barbs by withdrawing into a sullen funk. Occasionally, she would lash out, rant and rave, then descend into a deeper depression, but the effect merely added fodder to his smoldering rage. The battle lines were drawn, and it was trench warfare. The wicked equilibrium was shattered when she began to see the sinfulness of her sullen funk. The process was far messier and more deeply personal than I can imply by words, but her good, redeemed heart was eventually pierced by the reality that seemingly reasonable behaviors, given her verbally abusive husband, were actually fueled by her own rage.

Over time, she began to experience deep sadness over her sin and the sin of her husband. Redemptive sorrow eventually increased restorative passion, and she began to deal with his accusations without contempt for herself or for him. At times, she wept, but the tears were not coated with an angry heaviness that required a response from her husband. They were tears of pain that were gentle and open. At other times, his puffed-up cheeks and reddened face reminded her of a blowfish, and she could not help but giggle. In both cases, her tender, non-punitive passion infuriated him worlds more than her depressive funk. At least her funks could be patronized and blamed on a deficiency in her. Her passion, on the other hand, invited him to deal with his sin, and for that, he hated her with a new passion that dwarfed his past dislike of her. His hardness and cruelty became clearer to his friends and church, and eventually he was compelled to look at his life.

The reason for craftiness and surprise is simple: The fallen human heart is continually attempting to predict and control. As long as a person can be categorized and explained, his actions can be anticipated and dismissed. "You know ol' Frank. He's a religious fanatic. Did you really expect him to go to the office party?" It is a sad thing that Christians are often so highly predictable.

Craftiness. Craftiness, which is innocent with the pure desire of seeing God's glory reign supreme, is required to cut through defenses and open the enemy's fortress door. Frontal attacks are obvious and may be easily deflected; surprise attacks may open the door to the heart by breaking down the expected categories of response. Dressing the troops in red coats and sending them out to battle in regimented lines is not only arrogant, but foolish.

Our craftiness shows itself, fundamentally, in *choosing to do good to those who have done us harm.* It is alerting the enemy to our capacity, willingness, and resolve to use power and then offering peace — certainly, not offering peace at any cost nor conditions of peace that lead to the potential of damaging others. Rather, cunning is *an outmaneuvering of the enemy for the purpose of rendering him powerless, in order to offer him the opportunity for restoration.*

My friend John grew in courage, calling, and conviction as he dealt with his wicked father, but it took years for him to learn to fight with cunning. John was honest and direct. His father took his words and used them against him. John wrote his father letters, but the father showed his other children lines from the letter taken out of context, making John look harsh and unloving. Soon, John gave up in despair and exhaustion. After talking with John, it became clear that he had chosen to harden his heart and kill his desire for his father's restoration. In so doing, he cut off all contact and retreated to his own castle, building his walls so thick his father could never get near.

We chatted a month before his father's birthday. I asked John if there was anything he could give his father that reflected a heart of cunning and innocence. Nothing became immediately clear, but a few weeks after our talk, he noticed that the play *Phantom of the Opera* was playing in his parents' city. His father loved plays, especially dramatic musicals. The play is about a man, hideously scarred since birth, who hid his shame and hatred behind a mask of brilliant competence and cruel rage. The Phantom wanted love and recognition, but he wanted revenge even more. Someone had to pay for his pain and humiliation. The play gives a dramatic picture of how sacrificial love can transform hatred and shame. It is a story that might deeply touch his father.

John acted immediately. He purchased tickets for his mother and father. He found a musical score and sent it to his father with a note saying, "Music may inspire. Words may provoke. But drama is the passion of God. Happy birthday, Dad. Have a great night." I told John I thought his gift was a redemptive Trojan horse. The results of the evening are not in yet. I cannot report wonderful news, other than that John is deeply growing in courage, calling, conviction, and now, greater cunning.

PREPARED FOR BATTLE

Are you ready for battle? No one should ever go into battle without the four crucial prerequisites. Who, then, will ever believe they are ready for war? Without question, I will never feel ready if being prepared is defined as having unruffled courage, perfect confidence about God's purpose for me, unwavering hatred of sin, and flawless wisdom about dealing with sin in others. *I am prepared for battle when my desire to love is simply stronger (even by a molecule) than my desire to snuff out the flame of mercy that God has graciously intruded into my heart.* I am prepared to go into battle, if I cannot do anything but go.

I often tell people I counsel, "If you can escape from loving your enemy, do so! — until, your heart finds that it must love, not out of obligation, but out of the inner calling that compels you to live out the gospel in the reckless, wild, foolish, mysterious, supernatural path of love."

Does that not justify the choice to reject bold love? I think not. A person who chooses to face how they have been made (and then remade) in the image of Christ, who is filled with the Holy Spirit, who is enticed by the smell of life, and who is given ground to repent without shame or mocking accusation will, over time, be drawn more to live out love. The desire will never be complete, the motive pure, nor the expression perfect, but over time, our heart's passion will succumb to the winsome mercy of God.

The war is not over until the Lord returns. Only then are we free to lay aside our weapons and beat them into plowshares. Until then, we are to surprise the enemy by doing him good. But what does that look like? We need to take a detailed look at what it means to live out courage, calling, conviction, and cunning as we boldly love and forgive those who have done us harm.

CHAPTER SEVEN

HUNGERING FOR RESTORATION:
A Passionate Hope for Beauty

❖

As I pointed out in chapter 1, most of us have been badly misinformed about the nature and appearance of forgiveness in relationships. We have been bludgeoned with many twisted versions of "forgive and forget" and "turn the other cheek" that God never intended.

Recall the story of the woman who was crushed by her pastor's advice when she expressed her pain and anger over the irresponsibility and deceit of other Christians who had recruited her daughter into a rock band without involving the parents in the decision, and still others who had bilked her and her husband out of their hard-won retirement funds. Her pastor rebuked her for her bitterness and admonished her to put the tragic events behind her and get on with the business of serving God.

No doubt, this woman was angry and vengeful. But are anger and a desire for vengeance *ipso facto* proof that she was unforgiving and ungodly? Two common misunderstandings need to be clarified before we move into the topic of what it means to forgive: (1) Forgiving another occurs once and for all—once done, always done; and (2) forgiving another releases (forgets) all hurt, anger, and desire for vengeance.

FORGIVENESS IS NOT AN EVENT

It is commonly assumed that forgiving another is a one-time event. It is viewed as a climactic releasing of bitterness and hatred, and a return to a state of kindness and compassion. Forgiveness is often talked about in the past tense, "I was so hurt by my father that it took years before I forgave him," rather than being viewed as an ongoing work of the Spirit of God.

It seems that many experience one major moment when a transition takes place from holding on to bitterness to releasing the rage. This moment is often viewed as the point when forgiveness occurred; therefore, it is now finished and resolved. Forgiving another may often have an actual moment of climactic transition, similar to conversion when a person goes from death to life, but it is naive to believe forgiving another for any one failure or for a lifetime of harm is ever entirely finished. The fact seems to be that as any harm is more fully faced, then it requires the deepening of forgiveness to overcome. To forgive another is always an ongoing, deepening, quickening process, rather than a once-and-for-all event.

FORGIVENESS IS NOT FORGETTING

Another common perspective taught about forgiveness is to "forgive and forget." The concept comes from two major passages, Psalm 25:7 and Jeremiah 31:34. The psalmist asks God not to remember the sins of his youth, but instead to recall His mercy and love. In the Jeremiah passage, God says, "For I will forgive their wickedness and will remember their sins no more." Christians are told to be like God, who does not remember sin but forgives wickedness.

For most believers, the proof of forgiveness is an absence of hurt or anger. It is assumed that if you still feel the bitter, cold December winds of betrayal when you see the friend who told the lies about you, then you've not forgiven him. And if you still feel anger and want the other to pay for taking advantage and using you for his own wicked pleasure, then you've not forgiven him. The proof is in the emotional pudding. Strong emotions are evidence that you have failed to forgive.

In many situations, this simple formula is true. A person who feels life-dominating hurt and anger is rarely forgiving. A forgiving heart will not be chronically bound in morbid despair or vitriolic hatred. It will not feel chained to the past, unable to move into the present and future. But is it accurate to say that all hurt, anger, and desire for vengeance is proof of a failure to forgive? Before addressing that question, we need to look more closely at a few problems with the notion of "forgive and forget."

There are several grave problems with the idea that God is "forgetful." First, God does remember sin. We are told that we will all one day appear before God and receive our rewards based on "the things done while in the body, whether good or bad" (2 Corinthians 5:10). It is apparent God does remember sin and righteousness, and uses the evidence to determine our due.

A second problem involves making a metaphor into a methodology. "God's forgetfulness" is a metaphor, or a word picture. Many seem to understand that the phrases which tell us our sins are removed "as far as the east is from the west" (Psalm 103:12) and hurled "into the depths the sea" (Micah 7:19) are metaphors, but God's loss of memory is somehow viewed as a fact. A metaphor is like a wonderfully broad-stroked impressionistic painting of a seascape. It is overstated and dramatic, full of life, but not intended to be taken as an overly precise and literal representation of the actual thing being painted. Imagine how absurd it would be if someone wanted to discover the actual place where the east is divided from the west in order to deposit the sins of another. In the same way, it is absurd to take the metaphor of forgetfulness and make it into a tangible requirement for forgiveness.

Then what is the meaning of the metaphor of forgetfulness? What does God's forgetfulness look like for us as we go about forgiving others? The Scriptures use many metaphors and stories to illustrate the meaning of forgiveness. A central theme is that an incomprehensible debt owed to the Master has been mercifully canceled. The canceled debt frees the debtor from eternal imprisonment, shame, and destitution. The only debt that remains is to offer others a taste of redemptive love (Matthew 6:9-15, 18:21-35). *To forgive another means to cancel the debt of what is owed in order to provide a door of opportunity for repentance and restoration of the broken relationship.*

There are many elements of forgiveness, including three aspects that will be highlighted in the next three chapters. Forgiveness involves *hungering for restoration, revoking revenge,* and *pursuing goodness.* If we are to understand what it means to forgive another person, we must be clearer what it means for God to express these three elements of mercy to us.

There are many things to be learned from God's forgiveness. First, we are not called to wipe away our memories or pretend the past is not a big deal. God recalls every sin, and each sin is viewed as worthy of eternal damnation. The debt incurred by even one transgression could not be repaid if one took 100,000 lifetimes to work out the debt. Forgiving another should never be on the basis of the size of the transgression or the seemingly small consequences of the sin.

Second, God is hurt by sin, and it draws forth passionate anger. God spoke of His hurt and anger over the sin of His children in deeply personal terms: "Is not Ephraim my dear son, the child in whom I delight? Though I often speak against him, I still remember him. Therefore my heart yearns for him; I have great compassion for him" (Jeremiah 31:20). God delights in His children, but sin breaks His heart.

The natural response to deep personal pain is to deaden one's heart to the sorrow. Instead, God says He will remember Ephraim, no matter how deep the anguish. Yet God is active and angry. It must be assumed that the presence of hurt and anger is not the final proof of a lack of forgiveness. In fact, an absence of strong feeling would imply a lack of heart involvement.

God speaks against Ephraim because He desires to see His child return to relationship. The verb *yearns* paints the picture even stronger than the word *desire.* He craves relationship. The word may be too strong for many, because it implies a deficiency in God. How is it possible for a completely independent and self-sufficient God to choose to desperately want relationships? The answer completely eludes me; I am left with a paradox. He is holy and utterly transcendent, yet equally humble and incarnately near. He passionately longs for His children to return to Him, and He remains holy far removed from sin.

The driving motive behind forgiveness is the hope of reconciliation. Reconciliation is a moment of glorious rest and beauty. Most have experienced moments of tension with a friend. Nothing is said, but the air is heavy with the unknown, unstated offense. The tension is felt, but is it real? Is it a byproduct of an overly sensitive, fertile imagination? A struggle in your friend unrelated to you? Or, as you fear, a signal that a great gulf is widening between you and your friend due to some actual or perceived failure on your part? What do you do? Ask? Confront? Ignore and be pleasant? Hope your friend brings it up first?

The tension is at times unbearable. It is a constipation of the soul that cries for relief. The longer the block lasts, the more intolerable the anguish. When the air is finally cleared and the block is unleashed and hearts are reconnected, there is enormous rest and joy. Reconciliation is restored peace, true shalom, or wholeness and health returned to something that was broken and diseased.

Reconciliation is a difficult concept for (at least) two reasons: (1) Many misunderstand reconciliation as a requirement for peace at any cost, and (2) many cannot imagine ever wanting a relationship with a person who has not changed. Let me offer a few thoughts about each issue.

RECONCILIATION REQUIRES REPENTANCE

Reconciliation is costly for both the offended and the offender. The offended forgives (cancels) the debt by not bringing immediate judgment and termination of the relationship, as might be reasonable and expected, given the offense. Instead, mercy is offered in order to invite the offender back into the relationship. The cost for the offended is in withholding judgment and instead offering the possibility of a restored relationship. The cost for the offender is repentance. *Biblical forgiveness is never unconditional and one-sided.* It is not letting others go off scot-free, "forgiven," and enabled to do harm again without any consequence. Instead, forgiveness is an *invitation* to reconciliation, not the blind, cheap granting of it.

Jesus says, "So watch yourselves. If your brother sins, rebuke him, and if he repents, forgive him. If he sins against you seven times in a day, and seven times comes back to you and says, 'I repent,' forgive him" (Luke 17:3-4). Jesus makes it clear that forgiveness is conditional. We are not to rebuke unless a sin has been committed, nor are we to forgive unless true repentance has occurred. This strikes many Christians as wrong. Are we not to forgive, irrespective of the other person's response? Didn't the Lord forgive those who crucified Him when He said, "Father, forgive them"?

An important question must be asked: When the Lord forgave those who crucified Him, did He grant to each of them, at that moment, a place of eternal intimacy with His Father? I don't think so. I believe He was freeing them from the immediate consequences of touching God for the purpose of destroying Him. They deserved the kind of immediate judgment that occurred when the Ark of the Covenant was touched in the Old Testament. Jesus was only forestalling their judgment in asking for them to be forgiven. The only redemptive forgiveness offered in that scene was to the thief who was crucified beside Jesus. The thief's response of repentance and faith granted him reconciliation and intimacy with the Father.

The point for us is crucial. Reconciliation is not to be withheld when repentance—that is, deep, heart-changing acknowledgment of sin and a radical redirection of life— takes place in the one being rebuked. Nor is reconciliation (the offer of restoration and peace) to be extended to someone who has not repented. *Forgiveness involves a heart that cancels the debt but does not lend new money until repentance occurs.* A forgiving heart opens the door to any who knock. But entry into the home (that is, the heart) does not occur until the muddy shoes and dirty coat have been taken off. The offender must repent if true intimacy and reconciliation are ever to take place. That means that cheap forgiveness — peace at any cost that sacrifices honesty, integrity, and passion — is not true forgiveness.

A FORGIVING HEART HUNGERS FOR REDEMPTION

The second issue involves the inconceivable thought of restoring or wanting to restore a relationship with someone who continues to perpetrate the same kind of harm that originally caused the rupture in the relationship. A woman asked me in a wide-eyed state of disbelief, "Are you saying I should want a relationship with a father who continues to leer at my breasts and make lewd comments?" My answer was yes and no. Is she to want relationship with him as he is? Of course not. Is she to hunger for relationship with him, deeply desiring him to become the man that God intended for him to be if he repented? The answer is yes. We are to hunger for what redemption and the work of repentance might do in our life and in the lives of those we love and those we hate.

A passionate desire for reconciliation with one transformed by God's grace will enable us to offer true forgiveness. Forgiveness that is offered without the deep desire for the offender to be restored to God and to the one who was harmed is, at best, antiseptic and mechanical and, at worst, hypocritical and self-righteous. *Forgiveness is far more than a business transaction; it is the sacrifice of a heartbroken Father who weeps over the loss of His child and longs to see the child restored to life and love and goodness.* Forgiveness always involves the strongest emotions of the soul. It always beats with a fervor for the offender and the relationship to be restored to beauty.

One man told me of the battle to restore a marriage he had broken through an extramarital affair. He said the hardest part of restoring the relationship was his wife's absence of hurt and anger. She was kind and condescending, pleasant and vacuous, forgiving and self-righteous. It appeared that her forgiveness had no purpose beyond "doing what's right," fulfilling an obligation rather than canceling a debt for the hope of heart-thrilling restoration. Though her forgiveness was robotic and passionless, all their friends marveled over her strong faith and balanced emotions. He longed for the passion of a soul that wrestled with the wrong done and then offered the same passionate embrace of forgiving love.

Many might balk at the idea of offering forgiveness with the motive of a deeply healed relationship. Some want to forgive so they won't have to live with negative feelings — bitterness, anger, hurt, and guilt. In a sense, that motivation is legitimate. The prodigal returned to the father so he would not be hungry. But the choice to forgive must have a greater power than merely removing negative consequences from our soul.

I told one woman, "Forgiveness is inviting the one who harmed you to a banquet of fine food and wine that you have prepared so that he might have a taste of life." Her face went pale and her voice turned to a growl: "I will forgive him, but I would never feed him or eat at the same table with that swine." Her anger was understandable, but her view of forgiveness did not include the desire to see the "swine" restored to God or to her. Therefore, her anger was vindictive and her heart was hard. *It is the hunger for reconciliation that tenderizes the heart toward the offender and toward the God who might work a miracle in his soul.*

I run a great risk of being misunderstood. I am not arguing that the abuse victim, the person who has been betrayed by an unfaithful spouse, or an employee who has been let go two months before retirement ought to warmly invite the betrayer over for a nice meal and a pleasant discussion. Before any action or plan of forgiveness is considered, we must first and foremost see if our heart wants the inner ache (in self, the other, and God) to be bound up and healed. Or do we only want the quick thrill of immediate vengeance?

I counseled a woman who had been barbarously and ritualistically abused by her father and mother. After many months of work, she began to explore her feelings toward her father. At one point, she asserted that she would, and could, never forgive her father for his evil cruelty. I asked her this question: "What would you do if God gave you the choice between pushing a button on your left, which when touched would utterly destroy your father at this minute, or a button on your right, which would lead to radical, deep repentance and the kind of change that would make him the father God intended him to be?" She sat stunned for a long time. Her shock turned to silent, teary rage. She glared at me for almost twenty minutes. After what felt like an eternity, she said, "You have put me in a terrible bind." I agreed.

Her next words were startling. She said, "If I push the button on the left, then I am saying I am as evil as he is. But if I push the button on the right, then I am admitting I really want him to be my father. And I am far more afraid of allowing my heart to feel desire and longing than I am of being evil." She had spent most of her life killing the desire for her dad to be a true father. The idea of pushing the button on the right, with its implications, was far more terrifying than pushing the button on the left.

DEVELOPING A HUNGER FOR RECONCILIATION

How does God work to create a desire for restoration with those who've harmed us? How does He alter our hearts to want communion with the person who used intimacy as the basis for betraying us? If it is impossible to truly forgive until our hearts are burdened with desire to see the abuser reconciled to God and us, then what must occur to deepen our understanding of forgiveness? In part, the answer is that He deepens our hunger for reconciliation by increasing our desire for beauty and perfection—ultimately, our hope for heaven. Hope plays a profound role in our desire for healing.

Facing the Fear of Hope
Janet's father is a cold and distant man. He is the head of the deacon board, the president of the civic association, and respected and loved as an honorable and trustworthy man. He has never once in his life told his daughter that she is lovely, bright, gifted, or a joy to his heart. He is not obviously abusive,

but his neglect and disengagement deeply damaged Janet.

At one point in our work together, after acknowledging his sins of omission perpetrated against her, she came face to face with a reality that was even more terrifying and unnerving than any of the past loneliness — the desire to forgive him. She was afraid that her desire to forgive would mean pretending that everything was fine. Even more terrifying was the thought that she might reengage the deadened desire for a father. "I know what I'm most afraid of and it has little to do with his wrongs," she said wistfully. "If I admit that I long for a father, I will feel a sorrow and loss I'm not sure I can bear." Her greatest terror was embracing a hunger that would likely never be satisfied this side of heaven, and her heart was steeled against the agony of a yearning she could neither deny nor embrace.

Many people refuse to acknowledge their desire for reconciliation with someone who hurt them, because of a terror of hope. Hope is a radically dangerous passion. Hope is anticipation. It is a vision of the future that guides how the present will be lived. All of us have experienced a time when anticipation that infused our lives with sunny vibrancy suddenly turned into a cold, wet rain.

The junior high girl hopes all summer long for a chance to go out with a certain desirable boy. He approaches her at the pool. Her heart is beating, and suddenly she feels light-headed and dry-mouthed. The conversation goes wonderfully, almost too well. She feels radiant, but then he mentions another girl's name with a bit too much interest and warmth. Soon the conversation turns to how well she knows this girl and if she would introduce him to her. For the rest of the summer, with a distant, contemptuous air, she avoids boys. To open her heart to feeling radiant and lovely after experiencing the bitter sting of disappointment and shame seems too great a risk.

Crushed hope is more than most people can bear. The writer of Proverbs said, "Hope deferred makes the heart sick, but a longing fulfilled is a tree of life" (13:12). The swell of hope is often dashed against the shoals of a cruel, fallen world. The result is a sickness of soul that is similar to nausea.

I recall after one surgery waiting with keen anticipation for the moment when I could eat solid food. The day arrived, and I was circumspect, eating only bland, white mush. I ate the right food, but I overate. That afternoon, I began to tumble in waves of nausea. I went up and then down, up forever and ever, and then fell to depths of bottomless sickness I did not think I would survive. I did survive, but I avoided eating solid foods for days for fear that I would go through the agony again. It is the same for many who experience the profound tumult of seeing hope vanish in the wake of disappointment.

Why should anyone hope for a restored relationship with someone who did terrible harm? Especially in light of the fact that many who did grievous harm are not believers, or unwilling to look at their own sin and repent? For example, Janet's cold father refuses any overture to look at his life or the damage done by his withdrawal from involvement. Why should Janet enter the sorrow of wanting what she will (likely) never enjoy? The answer is simple: *To deaden hope is to lose the hunger for heaven and the joy of one's own salvation.* Paul says that as we groan internally for what we long for, our expectancy for the day when all things will be made right is intensified (Romans 8:21).

Hope is as essential and basic to life as water. Hope may be dangerous and able to be denied, but it cannot be destroyed. It springs back because eternity draws the soul to anticipate the arrival of a day that will set everything right. The human soul might try to ignore hope or trivialize it by focusing on material gods or attainable relationships, but God is relentless in whispering to the heart, "Look beyond the moment." As we wait eagerly for His return our hearts are transformed, day by day, by the passion of what lies ahead. Passionate hope for that day deepens our passion for living and loving today in a way that brings the thrill of redemption into every moment.

Our Passion for Beauty

The author of Ecclesiastes wrote, "He has made everything beautiful in its time. He has also set eternity in the hearts of men" (3:11). Hope is rooted inside us because we have been created with the anticipation of His arrival. We await the day of beauty when everything will be restored and bear the mark of His glory. A current manifestation of our hope for heaven is our passion for beauty.

We are beings who crave beauty. Beauty is seen in any glimmer of truth and perfection. Anything that bears a molecule of God's integrity, wholeness, and completeness shines with the beauty of His glory. For example, we love the smell and gleaming sheen of a new car, yet we shudder when we drive by a junk car lot that is strewn with the disemboweled parts of a dying race. We love the sound of a lone flute quietly inviting us to worship, yet we squirm with embarrassed irritation when the soprano warbles out of tune. We love beauty. It is formed in us by the distant memory of Eden and the keen anticipation of heaven.

Beauty borrows its light from the glory of God. No piece of art can bear what we call beauty unless a light exists that gives meaning to its shape and color. In the same way, God, the maker of beauty, patiently pounds the clay, driving out all the air bubbles and shaping it in a form that not only serves a useful purpose, but also delights the eyes.

There is something inside us that is drawn to beauty and repulsed by ugliness. When beauty is defiled or tarnished, there is a loss, an anger, a sorrow—a desire to see it put right. I was barely a teenager when I first saw in person Michelangelo's Pieta. It is a marble statue of Mary holding in her lap the limp, dead body of Jesus. His face is at rest. Her face is full of sorrow. The beauty of the work moved me. It was so real. It drew me to another realm that both excited and terrified me. Years later when I was in college, unsaved and not terribly concerned or drawn to beauty, I read about a madman who took a hammer and attacked the statue. I burst into tears. I was furious and saddened at the pointless, wanton act of violence against beauty.

In every person there is a desire to create beauty, at least to preserve it; to redeem ugliness, or at least to see it destroyed. That is the nature of humankind—to want to create and join beauty. It is our link with heaven.

Embracing the Hope for Restored Beauty

The heart cannot help but hope, but it is reluctant to let hope press unrestrained toward its fulfillment — heaven. Instead, we live out our desire for beauty in pursuing fun times, good sex, a new car, a steady boyfriend, a few weeks of rest from labor. And all these desires are legitimate. The problem is that few see them in the light of what each ultimately inches toward. Each has the power to delight and please, but will lose its meaning unless it is seen in the light of a deeper anticipation.

What is the allure that draws us on? It is the hope of reconciliation, the removal of all barriers of bitterness and hatred. It is the keen desire to see weeds destroyed and goodness grow like a wild flower. The desire for beauty is seen every time we look at our desk and groan. The piles of debris look like a topographical map of the Rockies. Even if we are sloppy and undisciplined, occasionally we are energized to see chaos overcome and order wrestled from anarchy. We clean off our desk, or we go nuts until we do.

Our desire for order is a remnant of the garden and a reflection of our hunger to return. The hunger for heaven is entangled in our yearning for order, relief, rest, excitement, pleasure, and passion. Unfortunately, the hunger for heaven is ignored in the daily enterprise of cleaning our desk, taking a break, or watching a good movie. What can be done to increase our perspective? The answer, in part, is to enter deeply into our hunger for more and the disappointment of incompleteness.

Hunger and disappointment serve as internal witnesses against all efforts to make any part of our existence into a real piece of heaven. Our tendency is to satisfy our desire for beauty and restoration in some activity as mundane as keeping the car clean, the Day-Timer organized, and the grass green. Nothing is wrong with these activities, as long as each continually frustrates us with a failure that edges us beyond the mundane to something so mysterious and wonderful that all frustration, failure, and struggle is light, momentary affliction in comparison.

This is exceptionally true in the area of relationships. I must be sufficiently involved in at least a few lives to know the horror of sin and the wonder of the slow work of redemption.

If I taste both the horror and honor of being involved with people in the mysterious work of growth, I will be drawn to desire even greater change in my life in order to better facilitate the change in others. In turn, all change in our hearts leads to a clearer picture of what it will be like for sin to be destroyed and righteousness to live supreme. Imagine a world where every person is more interested in adding to your weight of glory than in the benefit that might accrue to them; where every tear is surrounded by the tears and strength of God and wiped away never to be felt again; and where natural enemies, the lion and the lamb, are at peace and dine together without fear or damage (Isaiah 11:6).

The image of the predator and the helpless victim living in harmony and peace is a perfect picture of reconciliation. It is the reversal of the fallen natural order where the strong preys on the weak. No longer will the predator take advantage of those who are smaller. The weak will be full of power and dignity, and the strong will be humbled and broken.

The hunger for this day is told and retold in countless stories. A classic example is Cinderella. The evil stepmother and sisters may go to the ball and leave Cinderella home to do their work, but somehow the magic of the universe will intervene to see her beauty enhanced and justice prevail. She not only makes it to the dance, but she is pursued and honored by the prince. The meek will inherit the earth.

It is for that joy that Paul tells Christians to be at peace with everyone:

> Live in harmony with one another. Do not be proud, but be willing to associate with people of low position. Do not be conceited.
>
> Do not repay anyone evil for evil. Be careful to do what is right in the eyes of everybody. If it is possible, as far as it depends on you, live at peace with everyone. (Romans 12:16-18)

Paul appears to be codependent when he tells us to do what is right in the eyes of everybody and to be at peace with everyone. Notice, however, that his words are conditioned by the phrase "If it is possible, as far as it depends on you." He is realistic. Not all relationships will work. As much as we might desire to see the lion and lamb live together, it may simply not occur soon. Paul is not naive about the tragedy of sin. He knows there will be tragic divisions and unnecessary heartache. But he is also invigorated by the possibility of seeing the effects of the Fall pushed back. Sin will not be silenced until the Lord returns, but it can be occasionally quieted and its incessant chatter cut short. Those moments of reconciliation, though few compared to the moments of division, are resplendent and provoke a passionate shout of exaltation and healing tears of joy.

CONSEQUENCES OF DENYING HOPE OF RECONCILIATION

Consider the byproducts of attempting to deny the hope for reconciliation with anyone, including those who have perpetrated terrible harm. Hope for heaven (that is, for beauty restored) is deeply imbedded in all human relationships. It takes a lot—a whole lot—to keep it down or trivialize it. The only force strong enough to deaden hope is hatred.

Does that mean we are not to hate the harm perpetrated against us and the one bearing the evil tidings? Nothing could be further from the truth. The hatred I am talking about, a hatred of the desire for reconciliation, is as different from a hatred of evil as night is different from day. A hatred of evil produces a passion to live righteously in accord with what enhances relationship. A hatred of evil deepens our passion for repentance that increases "earnestness, what eagerness to clear yourselves, what indignation, what alarm, what longing, what concern, what readiness to see justice done" (2 Corinthians 7:11).

Hardness
A hatred of the hope for restoration, however, is a hatred of beauty. Such hatred leads to a hardness that might appear

passionate, but in fact saps passion through contempt, bitterness, and cynicism. The person who hates the thought of reconciliation would never allow himself to visualize his abuser radically changed, deeply committed to love, and powerfully involved in making the gospel known. Imagine your betrayer humbly acknowledging the harm that was perpetrated against you, in tears, broken by the damage that was done and sorrowing over the sin against God. In turn, imagine his or her life being a wonderful, redemptive tool in the hand of God to allow other abusers and betrayers to face the damage they have perpetrated against beauty and God's glory. The only way these images will remain unable to touch or move us is if they are surrounded by hardness.

Hardness is the concrete casing that attempts to imprison hope. Even though hardness will never be entirely effective, it may block or redefine hope to a point that a desire for heaven's beauty may be almost entirely lost. When that occurs, the soul loses something of its dignity and its humanness. The most obvious result is the denial of emotions. Emotions are the interplay of our soul with what is and what was meant to be. A loss of craving for what was meant to be leads to a shutting down of our sorrow and anger, and in turn, distorts our ability to prize and richly experience moments of joy and exaltation. Our culture's loss of an ability to feel deeply is directly related to its loss of heaven as a central anchor of desire and hope.

Myopic Self-Interest
Another consequence of a hardened heart is the intensification of myopic self-interest and commitment. When the hope of heaven and the passion for small tastes of reconciliation is denied or relegated to trivial importance, then nothing is more important than my pleasure in the present. In simple terms, once the beauty of restoration is denied, then nothing is more precious than myself.

Our culture is frighteningly myopic. If you ask someone why they see a counselor, why they go to a recovery group, or even why they read a self-help book, the answer usually is either to relieve a symptom or to gain greater control or happiness. It is rare to hear someone say, "I want to deal with my depression so that I can better understand what God has for me to learn about loving others and Him as a result of these struggles."

My words must sound like naive, almost vacuous, idealism. Then what must the Lord's words sound like to our culture: "Whoever finds his life will lose it, and whoever loses his life for my sake will find it" (Matthew 10:39)? His words seem violently opposed to the grandiosity and self-centeredness of our age. But even more, His words strike at the very motive most of us have for pursuing change. The desire for change in another that is essentially for my pleasure, convenience, or vindication will lead away from restoration and will not deepen my love for beauty or hunger for heaven.

If the hunger for reconciliation with my abuser is discarded, I will lose part of the freedom and joy of my own salvation and my eager anticipation of heaven. How can that ever be replaced? If I am living for heaven, then little matters, but much can be enjoyed—in its limited and fleeting moment. But if I am not drawn out of the moment by a hope greater than a passing fancy, then I will always be frenetic and absorbed in hunting for what only heaven can fill. It is a fruitless and futile search—as silly as a dog intent on biting its own tail. Self-absorption, either in the form of always finding fault with myself or in the style of requiring others to serve me, is self-destructive. It leads to the eventual loss of the self because one lives primarily to find oneself.

Matthew is a sad example of this principle. Matthew's Christian parents were dutiful and distant. He cannot report a tragic story of abuse, but he lived with a chronic sense of emptiness and boredom. He currently struggles with compulsive overeating, pornography, and fear in relationships. He was told by countless friends and well-meaning Christians to shape up and get control over his eating and immorality, and to stop being so controlled by others. The advice fell on a divided heart. As much as he desired to change, a deeper desire controlled his life.

Matthew lived to be free, but the more he lived, the more

he felt enslaved by his symptoms. His addictions provoked shame, but they also gave him his deepest sense of passion and purpose in life. He eventually joined some recovery groups that specialize in working with addictive behaviors. He began to face his loneliness and insecurity and saw that he was trying to fill the empty parts of his soul by food, sex, and people pleasing.

He tried to become more assertive and more independent from the desires of others, especially his parents. He faced some anger in his relationship with his parents, but overall, Matthew remained numb to feeling and dead to desiring anything other than to be free of hassles. After some time, he gained a degree of control over food and sex, but he felt a gnawing self-absorption that followed him like his shadow. The self-care he practiced seemed more often than not to strengthen his sophisticated justification for doing whatever he wanted with little regard for others, and the self-assertion he learned often degenerated into cruelty. He was not a happy man. His only passion for life was in being free of the struggles with sex, food, and dependency.

When I counseled with him, he displayed a noticeable disinterest in anything spiritual. His only desire was to be symptom-free. The level of interest he had in the Bible was solely in those texts that seemed to affirm the self and gave him hope that he could be free of shame. Matthew knew something was desperately wrong, and he knew it went far beyond the problem with the symptoms of food, sex, and people. Yet his friends and the leader of his recovery group viewed his personal struggles as nothing more than the outcome of growing up in a dysfunctional family. Matthew sensed that his problems might be tied to bigger issues than merely his past. His culture, however, encouraged him to do little more than grieve past relational disappointments and learn to take better care of himself. Matthew, at first, found this desirable, but over time saw that it ignored far deeper issues in his heart.

Our work terrified him. He began to see that his deadness of soul was significantly related to his hatred of a God who required him to love in spite of his perceived inability and lack of good modeling. As he faced his contempt toward God, he also began to face, in far greater horror, how badly he was failed by his folks. Facing their failure exposed not only his hunger for a better relationship with them, but also illuminated how he avoided any movement toward them that might be rebuffed by their passionless patronization. Their failure opened the door for Matthew to see his failure and his longing. His hunger for a restored relationship with them increased his desperate need for a perfect home that is full of love, passion, and joy. In turn, that desire compelled him to pursue the God with whom he was confused and angry.

In Matthew's case, a renewed desire for something more than a change in his symptoms and happiness brought forth a sense of connection to the great march of heaven. Joining a far more important crusade than symptom resolution brought about an ennobling passion that made the passion for pornography, food, and codependent relationships look pale in contrast. No one will leave an addiction or compulsion unless a competing passion is offered that gives a taste of what the soul was meant to enjoy. Only heaven with the beauty of restoration is a big enough passion to draw us away from the petty distractions and cheap addictions of this sorry world.

PITFALLS THAT HINDER RECONCILIATION

So what part can we play in cooperating with God to deepen our desire for reconciliation? In essence, we must avoid the pitfall that will keep us from moving toward change and be sure to move toward an end that will bring forth good fruit. There are three things to avoid and three things to pursue.

Don't Run from Hope. Do Allow for the Ambivalence that Comes with Honest Desire.

We can attempt to flee from hope, but it will rise in our heart unless we work hard at weighting it down. A client I saw for many months not only was not changing, but she was getting worse. I lost hope. Better said, I gave up hope. I simply did not want to feel the disappointment of seeing her languish in her despair. I did not pray for her as often as I prayed for others, and I felt a knot in my stomach when she came to a session. I ran from hope.

It was crucial for me to see that I was feeling strong ambivalence. I wanted to work with her, yet on the other hand, I wanted to quit. That is true even in my family. As I see my teenage daughter grow up, I know I will feel loss and sorrow, no matter what she chooses to do with her life. If she turns her back on the Lord, I will be full of sorrow; if she pursues God, she will still move into her own life and calling. I will feel joy, but I know I will also experience the loss that comes in seeing her orbit of life chart a course away from our family. *Loss is inevitable, therefore hope feels dangerous.*

In fact, if I am honest, all relationships seem suffused in danger and ambivalence. A student came up to talk with me after a class and told me, "I feel personally attacked by what you said in class today. Do you have an hour to talk this through?" Unfortunately, I did not have an hour to give her for several weeks. When I told her I was unavailable, she turned away in disgust. I was furious. I knew her well enough to realize that her assumption behind even asking for my time was that an hour's discussion could alleviate a deep and ongoing battle in her soul that went far beyond our recent skirmish. I also felt her fury and suspicion toward me. Her disgust barely disguised her belief that my heart was bad and destructive. She did not really want a relationship with me that honored God by bringing to the surface the things in each of us that kept us from loving well.

For several days when I saw her, I ruminated about every unattractive quality in her life and I grew stronger in my dislike of her. The last thing I wanted was reconciliation. I wanted distance, and occasionally, I wanted her to know she was vicious. I handled her by hardening my heart to her sin, pain, desire, and history. She was now a nonperson. After a few days, my hardness began to weigh on my other efforts to love and to receive love. I knew a block existed that was keeping me from being the man I desire to be. I knew I was grieving God. At times that bothered me, and at other times I did not care. The battle raged quietly at times and then erupted in a hailstorm of conviction, only to melt in my lukewarm indifference.

If one wants to learn to forgive, these ups and downs of ambivalence must be entered as he bumps along a path that will lead to change. Over the months since our unpleasant exchange, I have ridden the crest of love as it has occasionally swelled above my sinful apathy, and I have discovered a capacity to move toward this woman with a heart and deeds of kindness. If I embrace my ambivalence with love and forgiveness as an inevitability of living in a fallen world, I will neither quit hoping nor frantically labor to fix my double-mindedness. I will long to be single-minded in hope, but I know that it will always be a battle. My confidence is knowing the war is won; heaven will dawn and ambivalence will fade as an unpleasant dream in the light of the new day.

Don't Be Naive About the Prospects of Change. Do Be a Visionary Who Can See What Change Would Look Like.

Hope is often hopelessly naive. Merely hoping change will occur, obviously, does not bring about the end result. God does not succumb to the arrogance of "name it and claim it." It is imperative to understand the difference between good and naive hope, although few things are as difficult to clarify.

Naive hope is trust that the awful will change to what is desired. Period. Naive hope seldom goes beyond to the deeper domain of desire—to the soul and to eternity. For example, when my father was diagnosed with cancer, I was told by a friend that we needed to pray for his healing and God would grant our desire. I asked him what gave him such confidence. He said, "I know God will keep you from unnecessary suffering at this busy time in your life." I wanted his confidence, but his hope seemed naive. I can hope for a cure, but more soundly, I can with confidence know that God will use my father's illness to soften or harden his heart, and mine as well.

Good hope is trust that greater good will prevail no matter how awful the awful remains. For example, during a friend's divorce, I asked her, a young believer, how she was handling the terrible loss. She replied, "I have hope my husband will be changed by Jesus and he will return to our family." I too prayed for his return, but my hope included more than his return. I wanted him to change, but my hope also went beyond the present battle to what might occur in her life if he did not change.

Good hope is secure, because tragedy will either soften or harden the heart. In either case, God will work to see His Kingdom come to pass. Good hope, regarding any tragedy, is not only in the present, but in the power of the moment to press us beyond the struggle to the day of beauty and justice.

Good hope is full of visualized specifics. One ought to be able to envision the desired reconciliation. It is not wrong for my friend who is on the brink of divorce to imagine what it would be like to see her husband return, repentant and committed to her. A picture of what restoration to a deeply changed person might be like is an utterly legitimate ground for desire. It would be naive hope, however, if this were her only picture. The images of desire must go beyond the immediate concepts of reconciliation to imagine what will occur in the day when the lion lies down with the lamb—when all that is secret is made known, and all bend their knee to the victorious King.

In the same way, it is utterly right to pray, anticipate, and visualize my father's physical healing, but if I stop there, I have narrowed the scope of my desire. I want to see *all* cancer destroyed. And why stop there? I can visualize a day when all disease, sickness, loneliness, and sin is sucked into the lake of fire and vanquished in the destruction of the Evil One.

We must strive to see each moment from the larger perspective of heaven. Then hope for the day of victory has the potential to infiltrate and energize the moment in which we live. It adds color to our understanding of what real change will one day look like, and it clarifies what our heart really desires in contrast to what would merely make the situation more tolerable.

For example, the student I supposedly attacked in class, who grimaced in contempt when I chose not to make time to see her, was boxed into the category of nonperson. Over time, I saw my hardness and sin, and I began to look at her as a tough, angry woman who occasionally had a nice smile. I began to wonder why she was so angry. I also pondered what caused her to feel attacked in my class. As I thought, I began to pray, and as I put my heart into wondering about what it meant to love her, I found that I wanted her to grow, to soften, and to deal with the crustiness in her relationships with men. At one point, I thought about how wonderful it would be to be able to weep and rejoice together over what God had done in our lives, and I found that my heart was not as hard. I felt tender and excited, albeit unsure, at the thought of being involved in her life.

A picture of hope, fleshed out in cinematic detail and color, gives us some broad direction for how to love and forgive. In the case of my near-divorced friend, deepening her hope for the moment and then increasing her hope for what lies beyond the moment helped her clarify what she really desired for her marriage and for her life, even if the marriage was not restored. A rich vision of hope intensifies our desire to live courageously today.

Don't Be Pressured
to Make Change Occur in Another Person's Life.
Do Accept the Part You Play in Seeing Change Occur.

Clarity about what we really desire in a relationship with another person always intensifies the desire to a point that no human action alone will be able to bring about the hoped-for conclusion. Frederick Buechner put it succinctly in his book *The Magnificent Defeat*, when he wrote, "The birth of righteousness and love in this stern world is always a virgin birth. It is never men nor the nations of men nor all the power and wisdom of men that bring it forth but always God."[1]

If our hope is limited to the mundane or the merely endurable, then in many cases we may be able, by our own strength, to pull it off. If my friend was willing to let her husband see his girlfriend and still live at home while he made up his mind, it is likely he would return. But if she desired the kind of change that leads to a restored relationship with God and others (which she should), then both their hearts must be transfórmed. Such change will occur only through repentance and the touch of God's grace.

Repentance involves facing the homelessness of my heart, which says, "I am lost and helpless and hungry, and I will not find rest in my own power." The first step of repentance is accepting the powerlessness of my condition. But that step can quickly lead to a subtle form of arrogance, which claims, "I am hungry and God will feed me, if I trust Him." Often the unstated assumption is not only that He will but that He ought to feed me: "I am hungry, and it is God's job to feed me."

Repentance is more—much more—than merely seeing that I am hungry and alone. It is embracing the reality of how deeply I deserve something far more terrible. Repentance is facing the reality of my condition in the light of the holiness of God and then crying out to Him for mercy, which He longs to give. When we are deeply humbled, broken, and then thrilled in the light of God's perfection and compassion, we are transformed.

No one can produce repentance in another person's heart. Perhaps under duress or demand, a change of behavior may be made, but never a real change in the deepest convictions of the heart. If I desire what only God can bring about, I am less likely to feel pressure to lift a burden that is clearly outside the range of my strength. I can sweep out the garage, but I cannot make my wife love me. I can speak kindly to my neighbor, but I cannot orchestrate his salvation. The major work of change in what matters is entirely God's problem, not mine. It is too big a task for my soul.

On the other hand, I am a part of His supernatural work. In many cases I am used as His ambassador to announce the good news or as His emissary to pronounce the bad news. Jesus said, "If your brother sins, rebuke him, and if he repents, forgive him. If he sins against you seven times in a day, and seven times comes back to you and says, 'I repent,' forgive him" (Luke 17:3-4).

Because forgiveness is conditional on repentance, we need to learn more about how to recognize genuine change. In later chapters repentance will be explored in greater detail. At this point we will consider our part in the process. First, we are to rebuke. This goes beyond merely telling a person what is on our heart and mind, and sharing our feelings, though it certainly may involve doing so. *Rebuke is bringing truth to bear in a person's life in the hope he will repent so the relationship can be restored.*

Truth may come in the form of a letter, a phone call, a court subpoena, an intervention by the family, a book, or even a ticket to see *Phantom of the Opera*. Rebuke is the wise and shrewd story telling of Nathan and the serene, faithful witness of Stephen's martyrdom. It is any form of communication that parlays truth before the eyes of the abuser.

A second key to biblical restoration is withholding forgiveness from an unrepentant person while pursuing reconciliation. Many will no doubt say, "Forgiveness is absolutely unconditional; it does not depend on the response of the offender; it is gift from the offended." I agree. Forgiveness cancels the debt of the undeserving. But forgiveness is also passionately expectant. *We cancel the debt in order to invite the offender to return from the pigpen and join us at the banquet table.* A forgiving heart does not settle for a stain on beauty; it aches for the return of the offender to the house of God and the heart of the offended.

But entry is conditional. I may invite you to my home for dinner, but I will not let you in if you are wearing filthy shoes. The door is open and I desire for you to enter, but entry is not a given if you have not chosen to repent and take off your shoes. My part is to offer and hold firm to the principles of beauty in order to truly invite you to the freeing taste of repentance. When your head is lowered and your heart is broken over sin, I am privileged to welcome you to join me for a staggering feast.

I have my part to play, and I want to do it as well as I possibly can, but I can offer to others only what I have experienced. If I am no more thrilled about being forgiven by God for my sins than the French queen who said, "It is God's job to forgive," then I will offer others little more than demands and ingratitude. If, on the other hand, I am still surprised by His response of favor, I can (to some degree) say as Paul did in 2 Corinthians 5:18-20:

> All this is from God, who reconciled us to himself through Christ and gave us the ministry of reconciliation: that God was reconciling the world to himself in Christ, not counting men's sins against them. And he has committed to us the message of reconciliation. We are therefore Christ's ambassadors, as though God were making his appeal through us. We implore you on Christ's behalf: Be reconciled to God.

If we are ever to be Christ's ambassadors in this broken world, we need to look closely at something that keeps our hearts from desiring restoration—the even stronger desire for revenge.

NOTE
1. Frederick Buechner, *The Magnificent Defeat* (New York: Harper and Row Publishers, 1966), page 65.

CHAPTER EIGHT

REVOKING REVENGE:
A Merciful Invitation to Brokenness

One night, in a quaint Italian villa hidden in a ramshackle little mountain town, I spent an enjoyable evening hobnobbing with a few Christian leaders. My nearest seatmate made the unfortunate decision to ask about my current area of interest, so I began talking about love. I find the topic fascinating. My dinner companion, however, seemed bored. At one point, I compared love to war, and his ears perked up. Later, I suggested love's intention was, in part, to destroy the arrogance and ugliness in the beloved's soul in order to enhance their God-given beauty. His eyes widened and his shrimp scampi did a back flip off his fork onto his plate. I could not have had a more rapt, curious, and dubious table companion.

It seemed inconceivable to him that love could be so purposeful and cunning, so strong and potentially destructive. Perhaps I am naive, but I was astounded by his astonishment. Why is it so inconceivable that love, in this fallen world, is a weapon to destroy evil? Why is it so hard to embrace the force and resourcefulness of love?

It seems we have perceived love as something saccharine

and frilly, best described as "unconditional acceptance." The assumption seems to be that if I ignore how bad you are and continue to be kind, maybe somehow something will occur to make you a nicer person. Love is magic, and if the fairy dust is sprinkled long enough, change will occur. In that case, love is looking the other way when someone steals from your home; it is pretending the vicious comment was not vicious; it is trying to cloak the stench of sin in a more attractive scent.

I am walking a very thin line. Love, in many cases, is a covering over of the offense with long-suffering patience. But even when love covers over the dead remains of a vicious comment, it does not pretend or naively hope things will be fine once we get through the current unpleasantness and return to a more comfortable status quo. Love may pardon an offense, but it does not ignore the ugliness and arrogance that blights beauty. In a later chapter, we'll explore what it means to cover over sin. For now, I hope it is clear that covering it over is not another word for pretending it doesn't exist.

Pretense is the work of distorting truth. It is the art of deceit. It is the friendly spiel of the used car salesmen describing the best car ever built, which has hardly ever been driven, and is available to you for only fifty dollars down, a small monthly payment for a few decades, and the life of your firstborn. It is the pleasant smile that hides eyes of hurt or anger. It is the conviction that love is nice. Therefore, any interaction that is not pleasant is by definition unloving.

Let me clarify what I am not saying. I am certainly not arguing for wanton honesty. I am not an advocate of saying everything I feel, even when my opinion may be quite helpful. There are many who share their feelings or ask, "May I be honest with you?" and proceed to unleash a stream of invective that comes from the bowels of hell and not from the sanctuary of beauty. I am advocating a view of love that is consistent with doing ultimate good for the other. There are times when a hard, painful rebuke is good. There are other times when it would crush a broken reed. There are moments when the gentle wind of encouragement deepens a resolve to live for God. There are, of course, other times when encouragement will be misheard as support for a direction that is deadly. Therefore, confrontation may be the kindest word possible. Love is the offer of a good gift that fits the circumstance, needs, and personal variables of the one being loved.

Love embraces another for the great work of redemption. It captures someone by a goodness that is anything but "unconditional." It is remarkably conditional in that love cannot flourish and bring forth fruit in arrogant and unrighteous soil. Therefore, love must be an intrusion of a good gift of word or deed that makes the greatest demand of life: Follow Christ and serve Him with your whole heart, soul, strength, and mind. *Bold love is the tenacious, irrepressible energy to do good in order to surprise and conquer evil.* We will explore this further in the next chapter.

The dilemma for my dinner companion was that love now sounds a lot like revenge. Love may demand change; love may bring consequences for a failure to change; love may withhold involvement until beauty is pursued; love may hurt the other for the sake of a greater good. But many might say this sounds very similar to hatred and vengeance! I wish the matter were not so complicated. What often appears to be loving may be infused with wretched self-interest and hidden hatred. What may appear to be unloving—in fact, cruel—may be a passionate wounding that is designed to heal (Proverbs 20:30). No wonder we yearn for the simplicity of quick formulas or pat answers, they appear to relieve the agony of the Fall. But we must press on to understand the difference between loving with a boldness that provokes change and executing with a vengeance that destroys hope for restoration.

IS REVENGE EVER RIGHT?

Revenge has a bad reputation. It is an emotion from the other side of the tracks that no good Christian should embrace. Revenge is a bully, a thug that must be controlled by more noble and godly sentiments. Ask most Christians, "Is it desirable to want revenge? Or is it ever godly to seek revenge?" I am confident that most would heartily say, "Absolutely not."

I beg to differ. Revenge is a wondrous and lovely passion that ought to be embraced as a trusted friend who offers the strength of his arm in order to take the journey. I would go so far as to say that without the desire for revenge, we will lack the necessary energy to end well our long journey of life.

WHAT IS REVENGE?

I am amazed how many Christians view revenge as intrinsically evil. I asked one man if vengeance was ever good. He answered, "It is the most vile of human desires. It goes back to the tribal demand of an eye for an eye. As Christians, we've gone beyond tribal vengeance to an ethic of love that offers the cheek, rather than requiring the repayment of an eye." Again, there is a measure (small as it may be) of truth in his words. We do operate on an ethic of love, but his assumption is that love and vengeance are in opposition.

The same disturbing assumption sees an inherent contradiction between mercy and justice. I asked the same man why he believed he was more righteous and pure than God. He was stunned. He argued vociferously that he loved God and did not presume he was better than God. At one point during his protestations, I quietly said, "Vengeance is mine, says the Lord." His expression softened, and he remarked, "I see your point." If vengeance is inherently perverse, then God is wrong for claiming it as His domain.

Our vengeance, of course, may be wrong and involve utterly impure motives, but it is base only when it is taken in the wrong form and at the wrong time. Illegitimate revenge can come in many different forms. It can be as overt and clear as a public vendetta. The proverbial Hatfield and McCoy feud was fueled by the endless spiral of revenge. Almost every office knows the politics of revenge. I recently heard an employee of a Christian organization remark that her boss was conniving to oust another executive who had failed to vote for her boss's pet project. Most office politics are likely energized by the dual desire to acquire more power and to destroy those who currently hold it. At other times, revenge is as subtle as a casually placed comment that so and so is not quite up to par in his work and needs our prayer and concern. In an instant, a person's reputation and work may be imperceptibly tarnished. A word spoken or a smile withheld can bear the sting of revenge.

The key to illicit revenge is making someone pay — now! — for a real or perceived crime without any desire for reconciliation. Illegitimate revenge is assessing and executing final judgment today without working to see beauty restored in the one who perpetrated the harm.

Vengeance, at times, can be illegitimate, but it is not inherently wrong. Vengeance is part of the character of God and is not in contradiction with His love and mercy. Revenge involves a desire for justice. It is the intense wish to see ugliness destroyed, wrongs righted, and beauty restored. It is as inherent to the human soul as a desire for loveliness.

Paying for Wrongs

Revenge is, in part, a desire to see someone pay for the wrongs that have been done to us. The desire for restitution is the basis of our justice system. If I take something from you, I should not only give it back, but repay you for your loss. Revenge invites restitution. Repayment of the harm done is always a symbol of what is ultimately required of us all — our life as payment for sin.

When a thief is sentenced to ten years in jail, it is a symbolic repayment for violating the fabric of God's order. Instead of requiring him to pay at this point with his life, he is given the opportunity to face the consequences of sin in a smaller and less final degree in the hope that he'll turn away from his destructive course and devote his life to good. Restitution, then, is a form of discipline — a small, symbolic taste of judgment forced on the evildoer to warn him of the direction his sin will eventually take him.

The energy behind godly discipline, which is a form of revenge, is not "getting even" but "getting restored." Without repentance, the evildoer will ultimately be required at the Judgment to account for his life, and if he is unable to plead for mercy on the basis of the blood of Christ, he will be required to pay for his sin with his life.

But what does it mean for an abuser who is a Christian to face justice when he is already forgiven? Many struggle with the frustration that vengeance will not be forthcoming because the person who harmed them is a Christian and is already forgiven. Several thoughts need to be considered with regard to this frustration. First, many who appear to be believers are not. The Lord said clearly, "Not everyone who says to me, 'Lord, Lord,' will enter the kingdom of heaven, but only he who does the will of my Father who is in heaven. Many will say to me on that day, 'Lord, Lord, did we not prophesy in your name, and in your name drive out demons and perform many miracles?' Then I will tell them plainly, 'I never knew you. Away from me, you evildoers!'" (Matthew 7:21-23). A person who has made a confession of faith but shows no heart for repentance or love does not bear the marks of a believer. It seems that many who served the Lord fruitfully with public ministries and good reputations may be sent away.

One woman I worked with struggled with her anger toward her father, a successful pastor, who sexually abused her from ages nine to fourteen. She confronted him after her memories of the abuse returned, and he denied her allegations. Even more, he attempted to institutionalize her and have her declared mentally incompetent. He went so far as to ruin her reputation in other areas. Though several family members admitted strong suspicions of abuse in her life and were witness to her father's highly inappropriate sexual comments and gestures, he was exonerated on the basis of his successful ministry. One relative asked me, "How could God use him to lead countless people to Christ, if he really sexually abused his daughter?"

Thankfully, I am not his judge, but the evidence of vicious denial, slander, coercion, and punitive destruction of his daughter does not add up to the marks of a Christian. The facts indicate that his heart is so deceived and so ruled by arrogance that he is to be counted among those who will be turned away from Christ and left in the darkness of eternal

judgment. Many apparent Christians, who consistently perpetrate soul-shattering harm without repentant sorrow and a
passionate desire to be humbled, ought to (but usually won't)
quake in their souls at the thought of being rudely and harshly
turned away by the Lord. This man's daughter wanted to see
him pay for his sin, and her desire was wholly consistent with
God's own just character.

But what if the evidence indicates that, without question,
the person who did harm *is* a believer, mercifully spared final
condemnation because of Christ's shed blood? The desire for
restitution or justice is still legitimate. The desire for justice is
derived from our hunger for order, righteousness, and beauty.
It is the yearning to see true beauty and life restored to the
person who is entrapped by the ugly weeds of his arrogance
and harm. Anyone who strays outside the parameters of love
and acts to destroy God's order is a weed that might diminish
the beauty or destroy the fruitfulness of His garden. Consequently, vengeance is merely the pulling of the weed to keep
the garden lovely and fruitful.

A Complete Restoration of Beauty

A commitment to beauty — that is, to doing everything we can
to birth good and destroy evil — is the heartbeat of biblical
revenge. The person who does harm must pay for his sin,
now and perhaps later. Without payment, arrogance — like a
weed — will grow, and a disregard of God — like a thicket — will
become thicker and more impenetrable. Punishment, in the
form of legal consequences, church discipline, biblical rebuke,
or supernatural discipline, is both a warning and an opportunity for repentance, as much for the believer as for the
unbeliever.

Bearing the stripes of discipline will either increase arrogance ("I will not be broken") or deepen humility ("I will not
pursue death"). If repayment leads to repentance, the relationship can be restored and beauty is enhanced. If it leads to
arrogance, greater crimes will undoubtedly be committed and
more repayment will be required. Ultimately, over a lengthy
period of repeated crimes or given the ultimate crime (taking

life), an evildoer may be required to make repayment with life imprisonment or life itself.

Given the state of a person's hardness (measured in part by the crime), the payment may need to be very severe to give the best opportunity for hardness to be dissolved. The goal, nevertheless, remains restoration and a return to beauty. This will continue until the day when repentance and brokenness are no longer options. In that day, vengeance will no longer be for a warning or as a path to pursue change, but as a clearing away of the weeds, thorns, and thistles to be burned and destroyed.

The final day of revenge will be a day of complete restoration because evil will be bound together and incinerated in a bonfire of holiness. Beauty will be supreme and ugliness and disorder will be destroyed. Isaiah speaks about the interaction between beauty and justice in a profoundly moving passage:

> You have been a refuge for the poor,
>   a refuge for the needy in his distress,
> a shelter from the storm
>   and a shade from the heat.
> For the breath of the ruthless
>   is like a storm driving against a wall
>   and like the heat of the desert.
> You silence the uproar of foreigners;
>   as heat is reduced by the shadow of a cloud,
>   so the song of the ruthless is stilled.
>
> On this mountain the LORD Almighty will prepare
>   a feast of rich food for all peoples,
> a banquet of aged wine —
>   the best of meats and the finest of wines.
> On this mountain he will destroy
>   the shroud that enfolds all peoples,
> the sheet that covers all nations;
>   he will swallow up death forever.
> The Sovereign LORD will wipe away the tears
>   from all faces;

he will remove the disgrace of his people
    from all the earth.

                        The LORD has spoken.

In that day they will say,

"Surely this is our God;
    we trusted in him, and he saved us.
This is the LORD, we trusted in him;
    let us rejoice and be glad in his salvation."

The hand of the LORD will rest on this mountain;
    but Moab will be trampled under him
    as straw is trampled down in the manure.
They will spread out their hands in it,
    as a swimmer spreads out his hands to swim.
God will bring down their pride
    despite the cleverness of their hands.
He will bring down your high fortified walls
    and lay them low;
he will bring them down to the ground,
    to the very dust. (Isaiah 25:4-12)

The final day will dawn when God's glory will dispel the darkness, and all the uproar and songs of the wicked will be silenced (vengeance). When the wicked have been silenced, all the tears of God's people will be wiped away and their cries quieted (beauty restored). God will fill His people with gourmet food and delicious wines (beauty restored). His enemies will lie face down in dung and be filled with the byproduct of decay (vengeance). The contrast could not be more profound: The arrogant will die, and the weak and needy will be exalted. Vengeance, in its final form, is a clearing away of evil so that beauty may flourish unencumbered by the weeds of sin.

Since the unrepentant will be destroyed in God's final sweep of wrath, we who have been forgiven much should feel compelled to prod evildoers—Christians or not—toward brokenness and restoration. How much better to taste the bite of restorative revenge today than to be face forward in dung, drowning in judgment later. Many might agree that revenge is a form of mercy — a legitimate desire on the part of the offended and a painful gift to the offender that is meant to awaken his heart to a path that is leading to death. But we are clearly told in the Bible to not repay evil for evil because vengeance is God's prerogative and not ours. Although that fact cannot be disputed or ignored, it seems to lead many to assume that we are not part of God's ultimate plan for vengeance nor free to anticipate its arrival.

WITHHOLDING REVENGE

Leaving Room for God's Wrath

Is vengeance something we will be part of in the great day? Is it something we are called to look forward to today? And, are we actually to practice a form of revenge that anticipates the final day?

Paul says without equivocation, "Do not take revenge, my friends, but leave room for God's wrath, for it is written: 'It is mine to avenge: I will repay,' says the Lord" (Romans 12:19). In a final sense, revenge of judgment pronounced and executed is beyond us. Why? Paul uses a fascinating phrase to explain why we are not to seek it today. He tells us to "leave room for God's wrath."

There seem to be several ways to understand his words. First, it implies that I am to step out of God's way, because I am not as good at executing final revenge as He is. There are times I will let my children work at a task until it is clear that a stronger hand is necessary to finish the job. At that point, I will ask my children to make room for my presence: "Step back, kids; your father is about to take over." I will intercede because I know how to lift the box without breaking the contents, and I have the physical strength to accomplish what is required.

We are told to leave room and not crowd out the One who knows how to do it right. Do we know how to make someone pay? Do we know what is the perfect, just penalty for the offense? I am constantly confronted with determining what is an appropriate discipline for one of my children's crimes. I am either too severe or too lenient. I never seem to find, at the moment, the perfect consequence for the offense. Think how much more difficult it is when determining the exact nature of the penalty for a lifetime of arrogance, hatred, and abuse. Our minds simply are unable to fathom the internal, hidden crimes against God that have been committed. We would be overwhelmed beyond words if we could see the extent of any one person's offense against God and others. How do we assess the consequences for what a person deserves?

It is my opinion that our final vengeance, no matter how well it has been thought through or planned, would never be enough to cover every offense. I asked one enraged victim of a spousal affair what she would do to her husband if she could make him pay. She said, "I would scream at him for hours, then I would shoot him." I told her that she was far more lenient and generous than God would be. She had never read Isaiah 25:4-12, so I asked her if she would be willing to let him lie face down in his dung, slowly drown, and be trampled underfoot by teams of horses. She was disgusted with my suggestion and said outright that I was a strange and violent man. When I argued that I was merely reflecting the essence of what God would eventually do to all those whose citizenship is with Moab, she was startled and miffed.

She wanted her husband to pay, but she really did not want him to pay too severely. Her "mercy," though, was less merciful than it was squeamish. If God hates sin so deeply that He is willing to severely punish it, then perhaps He does not take too kindly her own manifestations of arrogance. We naturally tend to limit the extent of our desire for vengeance on the basis of an innate knowledge that we deserve the same. Consequently, final vengeance taken today is anemic and puny. It tries to squeeze God into a form of punishment that is substantially less than what is deserved.

Paul is encouraging Christians to wait because the fireworks will be far more spectacular when they all go off at one time. Lighting one cherry bomb today and then a Roman candle next week tends to water down the boom. Do we really want to be part of a spectacular show? If we do, we are to wait until the Lord arrives before we take our best shot at revenge. He does promise that we will have our opportunity to participate.

Crushing Satan

Paul told the Roman Christians that God would "soon crush Satan" under their feet (Romans 16:20). Paul promised they would have the opportunity to make the Evil One pay. The promise was first given in Genesis 3:15 when the serpent was told that it would strike the heel of humankind, but its head would be crushed by the offspring of the woman. We will be given the opportunity to put our foot on the head of Satan and crush him. I don't know what that will actually look like or how it will occur, but I am promised an opportunity to destroy the Evil One and all who are aligned under his flag.

And I will be utterly shocked to see both the number and nature of those aligned with the Evil One. There will be many who were not obviously evil or damaging, yet spent their lives in wanton disregard of the gospel. All who served evil by not serving good will pay. In that day, we will also watch every believer kneel before the great white throne of God and hear every word that was spoken in secret and every deed that was done in darkness. Judgment will be tasted even by Christians, as rewards and honor are dispensed before His justice. Not only does that encourage us to wait, but it further deepens the importance of an honest look at how we are living our lives. The day will come when revenge is fully possible, and our heart is to yearn for that moment.

I imagine a long line of believers, who have faced the torment and attacks of the Evil One, waiting single file for the opportunity to kick Satan in the face before God delivers the final blow. Those who have let God be God will be at the front of the line; those who have chosen to deliver revenge today will be at the rear. By the time the Evil One has faced the righteous indignation of centuries of Christians, I don't think there will be much response to the kicks of those near the end of the line.

I want to be near (very near) the front. I want him to pay for the forty years of physical agony my grandmother endured under the crippling force of rheumatoid arthritis. I want him to pay for my father's cancer, the divorce he caused my good friend to endure, and the heartache of every child who has experienced the violent shame of sexual abuse. I want him to pay, and I want to be part of his destruction. Consequently, I am able, at times, to resist taking a puny form of revenge today, knowing that I don't want to lose my place in line. Make room for God's wrath and He will give you opportunity to unleash every ounce of righteous rage on the right day.

Hindering Redemption

A second reason why we are to "leave room" is our inability to see who will and who will not trust in the death and resurrection of Christ. If we pronounce judgment through taking revenge now, we are a hindrance to the work of redemption. Let me share a typical example, where revenge was taken out of season and the fruit of repentance was blocked from becoming ripe. A husband caught his wife in a lie. It was not a major deception, like an affair, but it was a clear effort to deceive. He went nuts. He ranted and raved and assailed her character. He presented the ramifications of the loss of trust and soon made a serious offense into a capital crime. He used fear and intimidation to attempt to forestall another deception or lie. In fact, what he did was tragically to multiply sin by sin against his wife so that her transgression was lost in the maze of his own destructive revenge.

Vengeance sought today shifts the offense from the one who committed the sin to the one who is handling the sin with even greater sin. The work of exposure, reflection, dialogue, and prayer is hindered and change made more difficult. How many believers are blinded to their own sin because of another's inopportune pursuit of revenge? How many unbelievers have been given greater grounds to dismiss the gospel on the basis of petty, almost absurdly small, grudges held by one believer against another? When the gospel is hindered by illicit revenge, Satan smiles. It is a small but significant victory for the devouring lion. Our choice to seek or not withhold vengeance brings sorrow to our Father and, in turn, tears our hearts away from the joy of our reconciliation with Him.

I recently experienced the sickening emptiness of not withholding revenge. I saw an acquaintance who felt slighted and harmed by my unwillingness to write a good letter of recommendation for a job he desired. When I saw his face, I recalled the parking lot where he coldly and viciously told me that I had failed him and brought terrible hurt to his life. As he approached me, I felt my throat constrict and my eyes narrow. His face was warm and inviting. He greeted me with kindness, and I responded as best as I could. I neither trusted him nor did I want to believe he had changed. I still felt the sting of his words, and I did not want to open myself up for more, nor did I want to give up the sting and lose the justification for my distance. Even if he had changed, I still wanted him to work to regain my favor. As self-righteous and ugly as I felt, I did not want to release my claim to vengeance.

We spoke for only a few moments, but I was impressed by his unswerving kindness and boldness in sharing with me what God had done in his life since our last interaction. I felt a tug to rejoice, but I held back excitement like a father who is ashamed of his young son's reckless spontaneity. I was cordial, but with an undertone of coolness. After he left, I felt like I had turned down a wonderful gift to attend opening day of baseball season because I had to polish my shoes. How ridiculous! Even worse, I just gave comfort and pleasure to the Evil One. By withholding grace and offering subtle, cool revenge, I gave Satan reason to smile. I not only lost my place in line and gave the Evil One a thrill, but I lost the opportunity to see eye to eye a glimpse of the beauty of redemption. I lost; he lost; and most importantly, God was deprived of a moment of joy.

It is too great a cost to seek final revenge today. It is far better to wait and leave room for God's wrath. I can be assured He will give me my moment if I only wait for Him. But that does not mean I am to sit impotently, passively hopeful that good will somehow prevail someday. There is an active part for me to play in God's drama of mercy and justice.

HOW DO WE SEEK GODLY VENGEANCE TODAY?

Though I must wait for the Day of the Lord for the final expression of revenge, I am given opportunity to put a dent in evil today. Paul says, "On the contrary: 'If your enemy is hungry, feed him; if he is thirsty, give him something to drink. In doing this, you will heap burning coals on his head.' Do not be overcome by evil, but overcome evil with good" (Romans 12:20-21).

There is something about "doing good" that has the potential to surprise and supplant evil. It is an odd, precarious, and at first, absurd approach to evil, but it is our Father's wise strategy. Our goal must be to conquer—that is, to entirely annihilate—evil, but we are to do so by feeding those who have done us harm. In the next chapter we'll think through how this occurs and how we are to go about doing it.

For now, we'll look at the framework for seeking godly revenge today. As in living out a hunger for restoration, we need to avoid the pitfall that will keep us from moving toward change while being sure to move toward an end that will bring forth good fruit. There are three things to avoid and three things to pursue.

Don't Pretend You Don't Desire Revenge.
Do Anticipate Revenge by Groaning for It.

It is effete and self-righteous to pretend that you are above the desire for revenge. Many Christians feel guilt at the discovery of such a desire in their hearts, and they assume the desire is dangerous. I have heard it argued that a desire for vengeance unleashes hatred like a swollen river that sweeps both the guilty and the innocent to their deaths. Vengeance, it is presumed, needs to be cornered and caged in the human heart in order to keep vigilantes and do-gooders from hanging every stranger who looks like a criminal.

The truth is, however, that the desire for revenge is far from being merely a fallen human emotion; it is a reflection of the purest longing for justice. Hatred is a torrent of passion, but it need not be recklessly released. A hunger for legitimate revenge may, in fact, increase self-control and long-sufferance, knowing that the taunts of the Evil One will one day be vanquished. Indeed, it may be the energy that enables the tired and wounded heart to stay in the battle.

Others argue that revenge is beneath the true motive of love. A man of God as brilliant as C. S. Lewis presumed that many psalms are not to be used in worship or as a basis of prayer because they are full of hate and contradictory to the Christian ethic of love. At first glance, it is not hard to understand why many feel opposed to the imprecatory psalms. Listen to one psalmist's attitude toward those who hurt him:

> May the table set before them become a snare;
>   may it become retribution and a trap.
> May their eyes be darkened so they cannot see,
>   and their backs be bent forever.
> Pour out your wrath on them;
>   let your fierce anger overtake them.
> May their place be deserted;
>   let there be no one to dwell in their tents.
> For they persecute those you wound
>   and talk about the pain of those you hurt.
> Charge them with crime upon crime;
>   do not let them share in your salvation.
> May they be blotted out of the book of life
>   and not be listed with the righteous.
>   (Psalm 69:22-28)

The psalmist is angry and wants revenge so badly he can taste it. Is this hymn ever to be sung by a Christian? The answer is yes, based on the assumption that God's Word infallibly reflects God's desire for our hearts. Yet how are we to pray this prayer against a husband who has just spoken cruel words, a father who refuses to care deeply for his child, or a ministry partner who has undermined us before our boss?

First, it is appropriate to pray for the Lord to destroy all evil — to pray fervently and daily that He will come quickly and stick Moab's face in the dung. The Lord also waits for that day in the agony of childbirth. God says, "For a long time I have kept silent, I have been quiet and held myself back. But now, like a woman in childbirth, I cry out, I gasp and pant. I will lay waste the mountains and hills and dry up all their vegetation; I will turn rivers into islands and dry up the pools" (Isaiah 42:14-15).

God is in travail, waiting for the opportunity to lay waste to evil. Not only is He in childbirth, but so are creation (Romans 8:22), all believers (Romans 8:23; 2 Corinthians 5:2,4), and the Spirit (Romans 8:26). We are to wait for the day when beauty will be victorious and the Evil One destroyed, groaning with a longing similar to the passion of a woman who wants to give birth.

Who do we want to destroy—the private in the army of evil or the mastermind of the entire war? The deep desire to destroy evil will never be satiated by taking vengeance against a private in the army of evil. Imagine offering an aspirin to someone who is groaning in the agony of a kidney stone. It simply would not satisfy the ache. In the same way, why attempt to satisfy the groaning for revenge by being mean to a spouse, parent, or boss who is nothing more than a peon or pawn in the army of the prince of darkness? I personally would prefer kicking the general in the face than pinching a private on the arm. I want to damage the general, first and foremost, but I also want the opportunity to kick those who serve under him, in one form or another.

Paul, in one of his final letters, told Timothy about his anger and hope for vengeance against a specific man. Paul said, "Alexander the metalworker did me a great deal of harm. The Lord will repay him for what he has done. You too should be on your guard against him, because he strongly opposed our message" (2 Timothy 4:14-16). Paul wants him to pay, but he wisely puts aside the opportunity to seek vengeance now. The psalmist, then, can teach us what it means to pray against the one we desire to see trapped, bent over, and blotted out from life forever.

Second, it is appropriate to pray for a specific person to be broken, humbled, and brought low in order to see their evil destroyed. In one sense, we are praying for the death of their arrogance and self-sufficiency. The psalmist prayed for the ultimate obliteration of evil. So can we, but we can also pray for the temporary trapping, bending over, and blotting out of sin. Change in the human personality comes only through repentance. Repentance will catch the sinner in his foolishness, break the back of arrogance, and blot out the path of death. It is what the psalmist prayed for in wishing harm on his enemy. I can do that for my spouse, parent, friend, and authority. It is a cry of battle that asks God to intervene to destroy that which mars beauty.

Don't Seek to Destroy Evil in Others
Until You First Seek to Destroy Evil in Yourself.
A hatred of evil in another will either harden our heart to goodness or soften our sensitivity to evil. A woman I know is bitter and consumed by hatred. Her husband has decided to selfishly live the last years of his life doing precisely what he wants to do. His wife is enraged at his selfishness. She should be, but her hatred of his sin has not opened her eyes to her own selfishness. Consequently, she is even more convinced of her righteousness and regularly speaks against him to friends and family. Her heart has hardened, and she views anyone who differs with her as an enemy.

How different the scenario would be if her husband's sin, which is hate-worthy, provoked her to look at her own selfishness to see how she may have added to her husband's commitment to seek life apart from a relationship with her! Evil in another ought to serve as a mirror to better reflect evil in our own eye. Jesus told us,

> "Do not judge, or you too will be judged. For in the same way you judge others, you will be judged, and with the measure you use, it will be measured to you. Why do you look at the speck of sawdust in your brother's eye and pay no attention to the plank in your own eye? How can you say to your brother, 'Let me take the speck out of your eye,' when all the time there is a plank

in your own eye? You hypocrite, first take the plank out of your own eye, and then you will see clearly to remove the speck from your brother's eye." (Matthew 7:1-5)

Our first warning is not to judge unless we are willing to be measured by the same criterion. If you are hurt because someone slighted you, then you are implying that you equally hate the same tendency in yourself. If you are angry that someone used deception to gain advantage over you, then you are saying that deceit is equally despised in your own heart. If that is not the case, then hardness of heart will deepen and sin will flourish in layer after layer of weeds.

A second warning is to take the log out of our eye before we take the speck out of our brother's eye. Jesus is not implying that we are to be so "judgment-free" that we are not to notice our brother's inability to see. We are to reflect, assess, and develop a strategy on how to remove the speck in our brother's eye. The implication is that we have judged his sight to be blocked, assessed the nature of the block, and figured out how to get it out. There is nothing wrong with being burdened and furious about a spouse's sin, but only if the huge log is being plucked from our own eye. The priority is always to look first in yourself. You will not stand before God required to deal with any life but your own. Therefore, let judgment begin first with the house of God.

This takes a unique heart to accomplish without falling into several traps. One error is to always assume that you are at fault, no matter what occurs. The log in this case is viewed as a virgin forest of sequoias. People who refuse to see anything but their own sin when they see sin in another are really attempting to flee from ever dealing with the speck in their friend's eye.

A friend of mine is a self-serving lumberjack. She is constantly working to improve herself and is almost always the first to confess her sin, her hard-heartedness, and her failure to love others. She is a pain in the neck. The reason is that her log pulling is not designed to enter more powerfully into the lives of others. It seems to be motivated by a desire to ingratiate on one hand and, on the other, to beat others to the punch of seeing her sin.

A second trap is to assume we cannot love another until our log is gone. This person says, "I really can't deal with your speck because my log is so big." Indeed, if this were the case, no one would ever be rightly involved with another's sin. We are called to restore one another and to pluck the sinner from the fire through tenderness and strength (Galatians 6:1, Jude 22-23). We must live with the ongoing work of removing our log, first and foremost, without neglecting the work of removing the specks in the eyes of those whom we are privileged to love.

Don't Withhold Good from Those Who Do You Harm.
Do Good in Order to Unnerve Evil.

My counseling practice is primarily with victims of sexual abuse. One question seems to arise more than any other: "Why should I be good to someone who did me such harm?" The answer is never simple. In one sense, this whole book is an effort to answer that question. But part of the answer is, do good to destroy evil. Withholding goodness or offering a cold shoulder, biting words, indifference, or overt or covert hatred adds more ugliness to an already ugly world and deepens the commitment of the Evil One to do more harm. Only goodness has the power to destroy evil before the final judgment. The issue for many is, do we really want those who did us harm to receive the severe mercy of God in order for their lives to be changed?

A good friend of mine was sexually abused by her stepfather. He would regularly attempt to catch her in various settings where she was undressing or showering. Her mother excused his "dirty-old-man behavior" because it seemed so mild and playful. At one point her mother said, "He never touched you, so what's the big deal? You are making a mountain out of a molehill." She was significantly harmed by many others in her life, but the depth of her rage and refusal to forgive was directed against her stepfather. The same desire for immediate vengeance was not as intensely felt toward her mother, her father, or the others who had perpetrated significant harm in her life.

This is a classically common phenomenon. Often we will find one person to hate, which is safer than feeling anger and hurt toward those we still hope will love us. Her hatred of her stepfather and the intensity of her desire for revenge dulled her senses to her mother's unconscionable betrayal. In one sense, her mother's choice to ignore the abuse and turn her daughter's pain against her was at least as great a betrayal as the actual abuse. But hidden under the rage was a naive hope, a little girl's wishful desire that her mother would one day come through for her and offer a warm lap in which to rest. The desire for a mother was barely acknowledged and was mostly hidden under the fury she felt toward her stepfather.

Once I talked with her about vengeance that desires the destruction of sin in order for beauty to be restored, and she retorted, "Hank can just go to hell for all I care. I want him dead. I don't want reconciliation. I certainly don't want to do anything that he might interpret as kind." I asked her what would happen if she were to forgive Hank. Her response was visceral and intense: "Then Mom would never see how badly she treated me." The real issue was not with the one she hated and wanted to destroy, but with the one she was afraid to hate with godly vengeance.

Her heart was afraid to feel the depths of betrayal perpetrated by her mother. Her battle was not really with Hank; it was with her mother. So often the one who draws our greatest desire for vengeance is merely a pawn that is concealing the person who has perpetrated even greater harm. In an odd way, our struggle to do good to those who harm us is really an unwillingness to feel the full weight of hatred against sin, especially the sin of those we still deeply hope may come through for us.

The ability to grieve for her stepfather and hunger for his restoration to God and to her could not occur until she faced his usefulness as a stand-in for the even deeper hatred she harbored for her mother. Once her heart faced the evil complicity of her mother, she was compelled to struggle with her heart's deep reluctance to be deeply wounded and angered by her mother. With her mother on center stage, she was finally free to deal with what was blocking her desire to offer redemptive goodness to Hank.

Only redemptive goodness has the ability to destroy evil and express the wonder of the work God has done in our life. This is indeed an odd thought. We experience the opposite from the playground to the board room. A heart of mercy seems to invite abuse; intimidation invites (cold) respect. The offering of goodness to those who have done us harm seems absurd. Indeed, it is utterly out of kilter with what makes sense.

It would be logical to avoid someone who has harmed you or, at least, to do all that is necessary to limit his ability to do harm again. It would make even more sense, if it were safe, to destroy someone who did you harm, so that harm could not be perpetrated again. Instead, the Bible tells us to love our enemies, turn the other cheek, and do them good. Why? What is the point behind such odd commands?

Evil knows the ways of evil. Evil has its own perverse logic and rationale, even if it appears to be illogical and unreasonable. What evil cannot comprehend is goodness. Goodness offers life; evil seeks death. Goodness walks in light; evil slinks in darkness. Evil may be contemptuous of the good, but it is equally baffled by its power and beauty.

Good draws forth rage from evil because evil desires to get the good to operate from the same principles of warfare. Good does not (ultimately) succumb to the principles of evil. Instead, it conquers by the force of redemptive beauty. Goodness is not weak or sentimental. It is a force of power that is designed to surprise, supplant, and shame evil.

One should never choose to be "good" for goodness' sake. The choice to pursue and embrace goodness toward others must be motivated by a passion to overcome evil and destroy it from its roots. We will now turn to what it means to "do good."

CHAPTER NINE

GIVING GOOD GIFTS:
A Cunning Intrusion of Truth

❖

I sat with a friend late into the night, wrestling with the question, "What does it mean to love, forgive, and do good to someone who has hurt you?" The situation he faced may not be common, but the issues involved in his struggle are universal.

He told me about a scene that typified his relationship with his mother. His grandmother, who was very dear to him, died and left her estate to be divided by her three children. Each head of the household had the opportunity to pick certain household items that were of value to that wing of the family. My friend's mother asked him to make a list of what he would like to have from his grandmother's estate. He listed five things that reminded him of his grandmother's kind heart. He presented the list to his mother, who would represent him at the dividing of the estate, and waited.

Several months passed, and his mother announced that she would be visiting and when she came would give him his "present." He awaited with keen anticipation. The weeks prior to her visit were filled with rich memories of his grandmother as he thought about the five objects on his list. Although none of his choices were of much monetary value, each represented some of the happiest moments of his childhood.

The day arrived, and he sat with his wife, family, and mother in the living room and unwrapped the package. The gift was a very expensive pearl-handled silverware set. He was stunned. The gift was known in the family as the prize possession. His mother, beaming, informed him of the great cost she suffered to assure him the finest of all the possessions. He was speechless; nothing on his list was included with this gift. He was hurt and confused. He had asked for objects worth little more than fifty dollars and, instead, received a gift worth thousands of dollars. He felt like he ought to be grateful, but he was overwhelmed with sorrow and confusion. He thanked his mother, but he did not feel grateful.

His war began and lasted for several months. He would alternate between hurt, confusion, and the beginnings of anger, then he would slide to guilt and self-hatred, which would end only when he abandoned the whole mess by frenzied activity at work and church.

It dawned on him that the same thing occurred often at Christmas and birthdays. He was invited to ask for what he wanted and he never got it. What he did receive was far more than he desired. He never felt like he could complain, nor was there much point in asking for what he wanted. At the point I talked with him, he was no longer (severely) questioning whether or not the wound was legitimate. He knew his lack of joy in receiving the expensive gift was not a deficit in his character and the angry feelings were not the result of an overly sensitive nature. He began to ponder what it meant to love his mother at the moment the gift was opened, later at the dinner table, and even then, months after the event. It is a question that returns us to the issue of what it means to forgive.

Forgiving someone who hurts us requires humility, imagination, and courage. We need the kind of humility that rises out of a deep understanding of our sin and a redemptive imagination that honestly faces where a person is and longs for where he might be. When our hearts deeply admit that our own sin is, at core, no less heinous in its direction than our enemy's and when we taste the restorative grace of God, we grow in courage to wisely plan ways of destroying anything that mars beauty in the souls of others. A formula of sorts can be constructed that gives direction for loving boldly:

Hungering for restoration + revoking revenge + pursuing goodness = forgiveness that invites repentance and the opportunity for reconciliation.

If we trust in the superlative wisdom of the One who has masterminded the battle between good and evil and will one day end the war with glorious victory, we must seek His perspective on what it means to overcome evil with good.

WHAT DOES IT MEAN TO LOVE AN ENEMY?

As we are more captured by a gospel that is perfectly balanced in justice and mercy, light begins to shine on the path toward forgiving others who are guilty, but who might be restored by the same capturing process. Bold love is not a reasonable idea that some self-help guru is likely to promote or use to attract a large audience. It is the intrusion of the naked, scandalous gospel into human relationships. Love is a violation of the natural order of meeting power with power and an affront to the visceral response of shielding our soul when an attacker swings in our direction. Consequently, the concept of loving one's enemy is usually mocked as pathetic, ignored as irrelevant, or admired as noble, but certainly not seen as practical.

If we're honest, we'll find each perspective, in its own way of dismissing the radical call of love, attractive. We want to find some way to ease the sting and salve the wound of the command to love. It seems utterly mad to either want or attempt to practice the redemptive love of God, especially when we can't even come close to approximating it. We are, nevertheless, relentlessly drawn by the Spirit of God to do good to those who have done harm to us. The siren song of grace cannot be ignored or snuffed out in the heart of the person who has tasted forgiveness unless she opts for a growing hardness of heart.

Feeding Our Enemies What They Need

Grace is the gift of nourishment to one who will die unless he eats the bread of life. Bold love involves feeding those who have done us harm. Unfortunately, many define goodness in terms that may not be good enough. It would not be wise to put rich, spicy Indian curry before someone who was hungry but struggling with a stomach disorder. It would be utterly insensitive to put pork before a hungry man or woman of Jewish faith. It would be cruel to offer a man who is dying of thirst a large basket of thick, pasty bread, without first satisfying his parched throat. The art of love is not merely in feeding your enemy, but in feeding your enemy what he desperately needs.

What a person needs may be utterly foreign to what he wants. My young son recently required antibiotics to deal with bronchitis. Four times a day we wrestled him to the ground like a steer. I held his mouth open, and with a towel wrapped around his chest and arms, my wife poured a seemingly innocuous-tasting liquid down his throat. By the time we finished, we all looked like the canvas of a wildly modern painting. We fed him "grace," but he experienced it as a terrible assault. So will many we love.

What is best for the angry father who dictatorially makes every decision in the home, even for his adult children, is a gracious, tender strength that judiciously chooses a different direction than he desires. Loving a frightened and passive friend who always leaves every decision in your lap may mean making no choice, leaving a decision entirely up to her. *In many cases, bold love will unnerve, offend, hurt, disturb, and compel the one who is loved to deal with the internal disease that is robbing him and others of joy.*

At first, and perhaps for a long time, the food we serve may not be appreciated. Paul gives us an admonition: "Do not let any unwholesome talk come out of your mouths, but only what is helpful for building others up according to their needs, that it may benefit those who listen" (Ephesians 4:29). Our task is to continually learn and relearn what it means to offer what the other person really needs.

The image of feeding and giving drink implies an awareness

of hunger and thirst, and a knowledge of how to get the needed "food" to the person who is without. This is no small task. What does the perpetrator of harm need from you? In the broadest terms, what does every human being desire? The answer can be put very simply — love and honor. These realities have been wandered around, in various ways, throughout this book. We all long for union and connection, a taste of being drawn to another and intertwined in his soul, so that we are known and fully received in spite of the deformities of sin. We also long to enter the other and the world with the kind of presence and power that sees beauty and goodness grow as a result of our existence.

The rub is that true connection and impact require a heart that knows the ground of true love and the basis of true meaning in life, which is a right relationship with God. God made us to worship Him. At all times we are beings who will worship something. That is how we have been created. Our hearts were meant to worship God in His splendor, glory, and beauty. The desire for beauty, the hunger for union, the passion to be part of someone or something greater than self, all arise out of our bent to worship.

Our hearts are poisoned, however, toward worshiping God, because our bent is toward serving other gods, and He will not share His glory. He is intolerant of a divided heart; therefore, He works, mysteriously and often ruthlessly, to destroy all that violates true worship and love. Most people intuitively know that God requires the deepest part of their heart, if they desire to worship Him. Though we are made to worship, we want to find another way to live out what we are made for without offering what we do not want to lose — sovereign control over our life.

The false routes chosen to satisfy the hunger for connection and impact are legion. They are seen in every addiction, manipulation, and denial. They are as obvious as the person who dulls the ache and rage through alcohol, or as subtle as the person who uses humble servanthood to ingratiate and obligate others to serve them through awe ("How could anyone love so well?!") and gratitude ("I would do anything for that man!"). We want to eat our cake without paying the price of caloric intake. We want God's blessing and favor without repentance or faithfulness.

What is the greatest gift—the most tasty and life-giving food—you can give to the one who did harm? The answer is, *anything that increases a desire for true love and honor, and anything that decreases the penchant to pursue false paths to satisfaction.* For example, over the months of my father's illness, I talked to him daily on the phone. Every phone call began with the same litany from him: "Why did you call? Do you have any idea how expensive it is to call every day?" For months I bowed to his words and truncated the call, sticking to questions of health and current circumstances. My father had always found it very difficult to express his feelings, but he had demonstrated love in countless physical ways. A typical phone call always ended with the uncomfortable hesitancy of whether to say "I love you, Dad."

Our phone calls did little to increase his (or my) passion or decrease his (or my) self-protection. Finally, the truncated phone calls and passionless chats seemed as violating and destructive as the disease that devoured his health. The next time he questioned why I called, I told him, "Because I love you and I have no idea how long you will live. I want to know more about you than I do now. I want more of your heart before you are gone." He was stunned. He fumbled and backpedaled, but I didn't let him off the hook. I said, "I know without a question you love me and you know I love you, but I am unwilling to let your awkwardness with personal conversations keep us at a distance. Now let's be clear. I'll call when I want to, for as long as I want to, and I will ask anything I want about how you are feeling, what you think of as you face death, what your relationship is with the Lord, and anything else I want to know. You can do as you choose. Hang up on me. Refuse to answer. Refuse to feel. Do what you want, but I will too."

Our relationship changed. He began, in his own way, to share realities that I never heard him talk about before, because in part, I finally offered him the kind of food that I had been too proud, too frightened, too busy to serve before.

Our love ought to draw others to a taste of life that satisfies like no other, and our strength ought to warn others that
pursuit of a false god leads to an abyss that will eventually
violate and destroy their soul. Feeding our enemies means
giving them a taste of life that both draws them to hunger
for what they've been created for and repels them from what
would destroy their life. In essence, bold love is a unique blend
of invitation and warning—a pull toward life and push away
from death.

HOW IS GOOD FOOD DELIVERED?

How can we respect and deepen someone's hunger for love
and honor? It is no easy task because the portrait of our love
is always signed (unfortunately) by our signature of sin. We
can grow and we can offer better food, but only if our failures
serve to deepen our awareness of how good God's food of
forgiveness tastes in the midst of our sin.

In many cases, "doing good" is simply being thoughtful
and kind. It boils down to nothing more glamorous than pour-
ing a cup of coffee for someone or warmly greeting them at
church and asking about their weekend. Kindness is the gift of
thoughtfulness ("Let me look for ways I can serve you") and
compassion ("Let me know how I can enter your heart").

Unfortunately, our food is rarely delivered piping hot and
with the full complement of love that is desired. Sin always
tears at the fabric of thoughtfulness and compassion. Sometimes thoughtfulness is not even in our mind, and compassion
is not felt. Other times, a thoughtful person may make too
many assumptions as to what another may want or offer only
what seems safe to give. And a compassionate person may feel
another's pain so deeply that issues of respect and responsibility are set aside.

A friend called me at an inopportune time and poured out
a long story of real pain. She had no idea of my other commitments at that time or the concerns she had taken me from as a
result of her call. I talked with her for a while, but I was aware
that I could speak only briefly. I was afraid of offending her

or hurting her more, so I ignored my other commitments and talked with her far longer than I desired. I failed her. I may have appeared to be loving, but I did not respect her ability to accept the realities of living in a fallen world, where even a good friend may not be for her as she would desire. If I love someone, then I will not serve her in a way that violates her beauty or diminishes her responsibility to pursue life.

Tenderness

The two central passions of the heart are a desire for connection that does not consume or destroy the other (is not dependent and weak) and a hunger for impact that leads to greater beauty and justice. Connection, or love, is experienced in countless ways, but we can synthesize the multifaceted elements of love with the word *tenderness*.

Love feels the pain of the offender's sin and ugliness. At a church gathering, I watch an acquaintance — who has gossiped behind my back and brought deep pain to my family — talk in hushed whispers. I can turn my eyes and ignore her, stare at her in amused disgust, wondering whom she is talking about now, or see her as a sinful, lonely woman who has chosen to offer little other than her Pony Express mouth. Her sin still rankles me. I am apt to write her off. But when I allow myself to imagine how her heart has damaged so many and what she could become if her heart did not require the power of gossip, I am caught with the simple thought, *My sin is no less damaging than hers*. If I desire connection and love, then why do I suppose her heart desires it any less? Tenderness is a response of mercy that can see through the sin to the parts of the human heart that were designed for more.

Strength

We will not stir a person's hunger for connection unless we are tender, and we will not increase their desire for impact if we are not strong. Doing good in a fallen world requires an ability to wrap our hands around a thorny weed, feel the pain of needles piercing through our gloves, and yet pull with the kind of might that does not stop at the first signs of resistance.

Strength involves a willingness to bleed in the midst of unpleasant, undesired conflict.

Strength is most needed in exposing violations of relationship. For example, a friend who gossips regularly behind your back will eventually be exposed. At least part of the allure of gossip is the excitement of seeing how far one can go without being caught and how powerful one's resources are to withstand loss once discovered. True biblical strength will not hunt and track down every violation of relationship, but it will have the wisdom to wait until the offense is ripe and undisputed in order to face the offense directly with the force of tender and angry eyes. A gossip must be caught in the act, and the deeper pattern of betrayal that underlies her sinful episodes must be exposed.

Strength laced with tenderness is required if the roots of the betrayal are to be radically pulled from the ground. The sorrow of tenderness and courage of strength guides the journey of love that may lead to deeper and more profound restoration.

What occurs if one element of love is missing? In isolation from the other, both tenderness and strength are hideous. Tenderness without strength is saccharine and sentimental. It will invite only weakness and dependence. Strength without tenderness is harsh and dictatorial. It will command fear and distance. In either case, it does not emulate the holiness, justice, love, and mercy of God.

Love is never weak, nor is true strength ever lacking in tenderness. When someone gives love, it should be with a strength that does not fear the loss of the relationship. When someone is strong, it should be with a tenderness that does not use fear to intimidate. If we want to feed our enemy, then we must freely and wisely offer her tenderness and strength. The proportion of strength to tenderness, or vice versa, may be different for every person or situation we encounter, but in any case, there will never be a total eclipse of one over the other.

We are to feed our enemy because we love beauty and hate arrogance. We want to see beauty enhanced through the healing work of repentance, which leads to a sorrow unto life

(2 Corinthians 7:8-16). How exactly can "doing good" to an enemy work to move him toward brokenness?

Burning Coals

Paul tells us that when we offer food and drink to our enemy, "you will heap burning coals on his head. Do not be overcome by evil, but overcome evil by good" (Romans 12:20-21). If the core of change is repentance, then what do "burning coals" have to do with deep-hearted change? At issue is the meaning of the metaphor—burning coals. The idea of heaping burning coals on someone's head has been understood as a symbol of God's smoldering, hot justice (Psalm 140:9-10). Others have argued it is a Bedouin sign of favor to give hot coals to someone who is without fire. Others see it as a metaphor of shame. Coals on one's head turn the face red, and obviously, the color of shame is the same. Commentators seem to agree on one manner for interpreting the odd metaphor—begin with what is clear and then work back to what seems unclear.

The reason for doing good is clear: it conquers evil. There is something about feeding your enemy with tenderness and strength that puts "burning coals on his head." Perhaps a clearer understanding of the metaphor will come as we consider how goodness overcomes evil.

HOW DOES GOODNESS OVERCOME EVIL?

Goodness Surprises the Enemy

Anyone can be an enemy. There are times when I am my wife's enemy, and other times when she is my foe. An enemy is anyone who intentionally or unwittingly harms you for their gain. Intentional harm involves a conscious commitment to make the other person pay and usually is clothed in the language of justice or love. The other person "deserves" the harm and one's actions are for the other's "good." If one traces the motivation back to the heart, one will often see the stain of deceit, manipulation, and personal advantage wrapped up in the harm. For example, a husband who shouts at his wife for her insensitivity at a party and, without tenderness or concern,

accuses her of betraying him is more than likely intentionally punishing his wife.

Unwitting harm, on the other hand, involves patterns of
relating that are so deeply ingrained that one does not think
or plan to harm; it merely happens as a matter of fact. For
example, another spouse may handle a perceived insensitivity
at a party by ignoring his anger and avoiding his wife. His
silence may not be a conscious means of punishing his wife,
but the damaging effects are the same.

In a world where harm comes our way as a matter of
course, we will eventually have to deal with an enemy. Everyone is someone's enemy, at least some of the time. If we are
to love boldly, we must surprise our enemy and invite him to
deal with his offense.

Surprise disrupts the expectations of your enemy. When
I speak to my wife in angry, intimidating words, consciously
or unwittingly, I want a response. I want her to do as I desire.
When we have related to the same person for some time, we
anticipate how they will respond in different situations. When
I yell, I anticipate my wife will close down and let me have
my way. When I speak in words that are guilt-producing, I
expect her to take on responsibility for something I do not
want to bear. When I speak in words that are frail and helpless,
I expect her to be strong and bear both our shares of the burden. At times, I am sinful enough to fully know the effect of my
words, and I fully intend on making her pay. There are other
times when I am blind as a bat and I am only intent on sharing
with her my feelings, but the effect, and often the unconscious
intention, is still to make her pay. Words and behavior are
always expended with some expectation of what we want others to do.

Love is not naive. It faces what may be intended in the
enemy's words or behavior and does not ignore harm, nor
redefine it, to make it more palatable. Love anticipates what
may be intended and is willing to ponder, pray, and explore
the depths of the enemy's heart for the purpose of determining
what kind of meal to prepare the enemy (Proverbs 20:5).

What does the enemy usually expect? The enemy usually

has an idea, even if it's vague and unconscious, about what one will do in response to his words or deeds. He operates according to a paradigm, as complicated as a chess match, which anticipates what action will be taken to his opening move. Therefore, any word or behavior that is unanticipated throws the match into higher gear. The more radical the response, the more likely the paradigm of defense will crumble under surprise and uncertainty. If the one violated does not react predictably to the violation, but instead offers to feed the enemy with kindness (without compliance) and strength (without harshness), the enemy's setup is foiled and his plan violated.

The goal is to disrupt the enemy's expectations and thus take away his power and strategy, to unnerve him. A classic example of this is Ghandi's philosophy of nonviolent confrontation of the enemy. A scene of immense power in the story of Ghandi is his followers' attempt to take over a salt factory. His forces walked into the face of barbarous assault—bloodied by the cruelty of men with bludgeons. The assaults provoked a worldwide cry against the violence and control of the British.

Goodness surprises evil because it does not fight according to the principles of brute force, power, intimidation, and shame. It is creative and unpredictable, and can be powerfully overwhelming to an enemy whose victory depends on using his skill to play the same game over and over again.

Goodness Supplants the Enemy
To supplant is defined as tripping someone up or unnerving them by force or plotting. Goodness trips up the enemy by foiling his battle plans. The enemy anticipates compliance or defensive coldness, harshness, or withdrawal. The last thing he expects is sustained kindness and steadfast strength. Therefore, when evil is met with goodness, it is apt to respond with either exasperated fury or stunned incredulity. Goodness breaks the spell the enemy tries to cast and renders him powerless.

A friend told me about an encounter with her mother, who is a malicious enemy. In almost every phone call, her mother finds some way to assail her daughter's wisdom and integrity. For years my friend attempted to defend her actions, but would eventually succumb to her mother's criticism. After extensive reflection, she realized she hated her mother and wished her terrible harm. She lived out her hatred by developing an impermeable fortress around her soul that kept her both numb and quietly enraged at her mother's cruel comments. It was as if she talked to her mother through layers of gauze, hearing only the mere echo of the venom being spewed toward her.

As she matured over a long period of time, her own hatred became an even greater offense to her than her mother's sin. Her passion to love grew, and at one point, she began asking her mother questions. Never before had she asked her mother anything of importance because she thought it would invite an even longer harangue of her stupid choices. But when she began to ask her mother how she made difficult choices, how she handled regret, and what she did with loneliness, she saw her mother backpedal, offer silly, almost pathetic advice, and then work quickly to get off the phone. It seemed that the more curious she became about her mother, the more her mother could not wait to curtail the conversation.

One day when her mother offered Ann Landers' advice from that morning's paper, claiming the words as her own, my friend wept. She felt so sad and grieved for her tragically cruel, soullessly empty mother that she could barely remain on the phone. Her heart changed toward her mother. She was no longer as afraid of her, although she knew that any interaction of depth would lead to greater personal loneliness and sorrow. She had a high price to pay if she was to remain in a relationship with her mother, but at least it would no longer cost her the integrity of her lively soul. The price of hatred she had been paying to avoid sorrow was too costly when the reward of love, which is a deepening of desire for heaven, was too wondrous to refuse.

Change in her soul and in their relationship came when she challenged the power of hatred with the supplanting goodness of love. Goodness strips away the deceit of denial and the power of harm, and forces it to come out in the open as an emperor with no clothes. The cold father is exposed as angry and afraid. The workaholic husband is seen as impotent and driven by the demons of failure. Once the Wizard of Oz, who held such terrible power over us, is exposed as a mere human, we are free to offer our mind, heart, and courage to one who has lacked those resources all along. And once the setup is exposed and evil has lost its power to intimidate or enrage, it will either scurry back into darkness or be forced to fight out in the open. Goodness exposes the nakedness and hunger of the enemy, and offers clothing and food. Goodness, in other words, shames the enemy and then offers the opportunity for restoration.

Goodness Shames the Enemy

Darkness has never been too fond of light. If you were to watch light enter a dark room at super slow motion, you would see light progressively force darkness to flee in its presence. Darkness cannot bear to inhabit the same environment as light. In the same way, evil cannot tolerate the intrusion of goodness. Evil has its own snarl, dress code, favorite beer, and sports team, and when someone comes into its lair sporting a smile, out-of-fashion wide lapels, and a root beer, it can hardly bear to coexist with this alien and stranger. It depends on its ability to mock and shame the intruder into retreat.

What unnerves evil more than any one thing is someone who is not controlled by shame and yet is not (like evil) shameless. The one who does harm uses shame to force the eyes of the victim to look at some inner deficiency as the explanation for the pain. The abuser abuses, but it is the victim's fault—she was too fat, too thin, too smart, too dumb. The greatest shock to the abuser comes not only when the victim is no longer controlled by shame, but also has the power to expose the little man behind the curtain who uses big words, spouts angry commands, and sends innocents on long, dangerous journeys. In other words, goodness has the power to expose and shame the one who did harm.

Shame is the experience of being naked and seen, of

having the curtain lifted and being recognized as the wizard of a sham kingdom. Shame can be the gift of exposure to an enemy when it offers him an opportunity to look deep inside to see what rules his heart. For that reason, I understand the metaphor of "heaping burning coals on the head" to mean offering goodness that surprises, supplants, and shames the sin of the one who does harm, lest it remain and destroy his heart. Shame can be a severe mercy, a gift of sight that either hardens or softens the heart.

Essentially, goodness is designed to expose darkness in the other and call him into the light. There are countless examples of this in the Bible. For instance, the Lord Jesus interacted with two betrayers at His final meal, offering both the opportunity to dine with Him and speaking with the most unrestrained and fervent passion about His calling (Matthew 26:17-35). He made no effort to keep the pain of their impending betrayal at a minimum. He told Peter He prayed for him and would receive him back when he fell (tenderness), and when Peter remonstrated that he would never fall, Jesus spoke directly and forcefully about Peter's sin (strength). Over time, Peter softened and repented in the face of Jesus' goodness (John 21:15-19). Judas, on the other hand, hardened his heart and pursued his black path of betrayal and death (Matthew 27:3-5).

Shame always elicits change. The result will either be an intensification of the evil or a melting of the heart to face the damage done. The repentant heart will come out of the woods to declare defeat and ask for honorable terms for surrender. The hardened heart will come out of the woods and brandish its sword, declaring a call to arms. In either case, goodness will recognize what it is up against and will no longer be fighting against an unnamed and crafty foe.

The rest of this chapter will outline in general terms how to offer a restorative coal of shame to the enemies we deal with every day. The remainder of the book will explore in more detail how to boldly love different kinds of people who are hooked in to greater or lesser degrees with the Evil One's drama of destruction.

HOW CAN WE DO GOOD TO OUR ENEMIES?

Jesus put words to the radical call of bold love: "Love your enemies, do good to those who hate you, bless those who curse you, pray for those who mistreat you. If someone strikes you on one cheek, turn to him the other also. If someone takes your cloak, do not stop him from taking your tunic. Give to everyone who asks you, and if anyone takes what belongs to you, do not demand it back" (Luke 6:27-31).

Doing good is accomplished by words and deeds—by praying and blessing, and by turning and giving. These verbs do not describe all that is involved in the process of doing good, but they are way markers that point us toward what it means to love boldly.

Good Words

To bless is to give words of life that nourish the soul and deepen its desire for truth. Words offer grace to our enemy and ask God the Father for grace that benefits our enemy. What might that look like in a relationship with a demanding friend who calls and says, "I cannot find anyone else to babysit, and I just have to get to the store before the sale ends. It won't be a problem if I drop my kids off for the afternoon, will it?" Before considering a range of possible loving responses to her question, first think through what needs to be quickly processed before a good response can be made: "Am I able to do what she has requested? She has not considered my schedule, my situation, or my desires in making what is likely an insensitive request. Making it to a sale is not a life-threatening situation, but it is a legitimate desire. What is best for her and for our relationship? Is there any way to respond to the situation and the issues of her character with tenderness and strength?"

Many will immediately say, "No way! I can't think that fast." Of course, in most cases it is impossible to process all that needs to be thought about before a response is required. We usually can't say to a friend, "Let me call you back in a moment." The only way we can hope to think quickly on our feet is by preparing our hearts through prayer.

Praying for wisdom. Before entering a war, we need to enter the heavenly realm, asking for help. We are to pray to the Father to act on behalf of our enemies; we are to pray for God to work in our enemies' lives, to restrain evil, to deepen consciousness of harm, to destroy their arrogance so that life and grace might flourish. We are equally to pray for wisdom and all that blocks the development of wisdom in our life.

Wisdom must be developed to learn how to apply truth to the different situations and people we encounter. A fascinating study is to walk through the book of Proverbs with an eye to questions like, "How am I to use my tongue?" "What should my attitude be toward my neighbors?" "How am I to deal with fools?" What we see are very practical, pithy statements about when to hold our tongue and when to speak, how to avoid certain unnecessary conflicts, and how to confront when necessary. No one proverb spells out what to do in any one situation, but studying the elements of wisdom helps us develop a grid for thinking about how to live shrewdly in a fallen world with love and integrity. Wisdom is a skill that is mastered only after the expenditure of heart, soul, strength, and mind to grow in ability and sophistication of performance.

Most would consider it appropriate to ask God for wisdom but stop there. Why not go further and take a long walk to talk with God about your friend who is, at times, insensitive and demanding? On the walk, you might rehearse typical scenes; ponder out loud with God what might be going on in her heart; review what you know about her relationship with her spouse, children, and friends; and consider how she deals with others when she is angry, hurt, alone, frustrated, scared, ashamed.

Many may find it inconceivable to put that kind of time into praying about someone they relate to on a daily basis, although they'll often spend a half hour reading a newspaper to learn about events and people who, in fact, matter little to them. But prayer is the best way to invite God to use us and to teach us what it means to love boldly. If prayer is a part of our relationships with others, especially those close enough to be enemies, then in most cases we will seldom be caught off guard by sin. We will often, then, have a sense as to what may be involved in loving a friend who calls to ask for on-the-spot babysitting service.

What might it mean to speak "good" words to such an enemy/friend? One possible response may simply be, "I'd be delighted to give you the chance to go shopping." Period. Many times the most simple response is the best. A perfectly "good" response may be, "I'd be delighted to do so, but I am committed to finishing this project for my husband, so I won't be able to do so." Again, a simple, straightforward answer may be all that is appropriate to say. However, more may be required. There are very few cases where a direct, frontal rebuke is helpful or wise.

On the other hand, wisdom (defined as skillful kindness and strength, tempered with shrewdness, armed with courage, clear about calling, and hungry to see arrogance destroyed and beauty enhanced) may lead to saying a few more words. For example, in addition to saying yes, one might also say, "I'll take care of your kids, on two conditions: (1) you take care of my kids tomorrow while I take a walk, and (2) you take five minutes to show me what you bought. You've got such good taste in clothes." The friend is held accountable to do more than take, yet she is given the opportunity to shine in an area of ability. Who knows where the five-minute conversation may go, but goodness can always build on greater kindness. Stiff, angry interactions, on the other hand, take away the opportunity for developing greater connection.

A True Blessing

It would be a mistake, however, to see the idea of blessing as merely being nice. An Old Testament blessing was a bestowal of truth that would guide and shape the person's life. In a number of cases, the blessing of the father to the son was not pleasant news, but words of warning and consequence (Genesis 49:2-27). The blessing is always tailored to the person and his circumstances. A blessing to a person who has defrauded your business is likely not, "Hey, it's all right. No problem. If you want more money, here is my checkbook."

Why? The reason is that your words would invite the thief to take advantage of another, which defrauds him of honorable labor (impact) and righteous concern for others (love). In other words, it invites him to mar his own beauty. Words of blessing will never contradict true tenderness or strength, nor violate the beauty of relationships or the holiness of order. A blessing may be warm and tender, and it also may be emphatic and strong. What it will not lack is either tenderness or strength. The model for offering words of blessing is, of course, the Lord Jesus Christ.

Peter says about the Lord, "When they hurled their insults at him, he did not retaliate; when he suffered, he made no threats" (1 Peter 2:23). The Lord did not use contempt or intimidation to shame and frighten His accusers. On the other hand, He didn't hesitate to tell them He could call down a host of angels for His protection. He also was not exactly a cooperative witness at His mock trial. He refused to answer and made no defense — to the absolute astonishment of His accusers. His silence was a quiet, mime-like indictment of their charade. His words were not harsh, but He thoroughly exposed the sham of their accusations.

Our words of blessing are meant to arouse legitimate longing, expose emptiness, and deflate the enemy's attempts to shame or intimidate. Blessing should be designed to open the heart of an enemy to astonishment and curiosity.

Good Deeds
No matter how powerful, clever, and penetrating words are, they are never enough. Words may be the quarterback that masterminds the success of the team, but deeds are the sturdy, in-your-face linemen who win the terrain by hand-to-hand combat. Words that are not backed by behavior are as sound as a bankrupt businessman. Our behavior may be faltering and clumsy, but it must contain a consistency of direction and a clear, deep desire to be even more faithful in order to back the currency of our words. The Lord said we are to bless and pray, but He also defined bold love as turning the cheek and offering our coat.

Few commands are more difficult to understand. Does He mean that we are not to protect ourselves against physical harm or safeguard our financial well-being against theft? I believe we are to protect ourselves from unnecessary, random harm. For example, if we are falsely accused, it is appropriate to defend our reputation. Our reputation is the calling card we use to get in the door of the heart in order to live out the gospel. Paul defended his reputation as an apostle in order to retain the opportunity to minister the gospel. I also believe we are to guard against the insatiable appetites of others who might eat us alive. I am often asked to help fund a ministry endeavor. The moment someone asks for my shirt, am I to give them my coat as well? I would answer no, because doing good rarely involves giving to every solicitation without thought or planning.

Shrewd sacrifice. So what are we to do with our Lord's radical words? The key to both turning our cheek and offering our cloak is the principle of *shrewd sacrifice.* It is giving that is designed for an enemy, not a friend. A friend—one whose agenda does not include harm—can be responded to directly and honestly. If a friend asks for a coat, then it is up to the giver as to what seems consistent with the principle of love. But with an enemy, any sacrifice we offer should attempt to expose the heart of the one doing harm. If he demands I carry his bag one mile, then let me carry it two miles. Remember, what the enemy expects is that intimidation and shame will get him what he wants. When he hits someone in the face, he expects the normal reaction—fight or flight. Kindness and generosity are good gifts that can cause him to stumble, because they bear a redemptive bite.

Voluntarily turning the other cheek removes the pleasure of the first blow, even if the second blow is taken. The enemy's real pleasure in striking out is the power he enjoys to intimidate and shame. He enjoys inflicting the harm, to some degree, because it gives him a sense of control and the fantasy of being like God. Turning one's cheek to the assault of the enemy demonstrates, without question, that the first blow was impotent and shameful. What was meant to enslave is foiled. Like a boomerang, the harm swoops around and smacks the back of the head of the one who meant harm. A sorehead may, with the working of the Spirit of God, ask, "Why did I strike that man?" and eventually ask of the one he hit, "Why didn't you retaliate?" Again, a measure of astonishment and curiosity is stirred, and the path toward repentance becomes slightly less dim.

Shrewd sacrifice is a gift of grace that exposes hatred and rage, and invites the enemy to wrestle with his sin. Every situation is unique, and there are no rules for giving good words and deeds, but perhaps an illustration will reveal the redemptive heart of one who desires to love boldly.

A woman who had strong suspicion that her husband was having an affair flew to the city where he was conducting a business meeting. He had the pattern over several years of staying several days longer than needed in the same hotel, getting work done that he could as easily do at home. She got a separate room near his suite and waited and watched until he arrived late one night with a young woman in tow. They entered the room and remained there all night.

When they went to breakfast the next morning, she waited until they were seated and then walked to their table. She first spoke warmly to her husband and then introduced herself to her other enemy. She said, "We have a great deal to talk about, but I am not sure this is an appropriate time or place. If you would prefer, we could all talk in private or schedule another time to do so. Please talk about that between the two of you, and I'll wait in my room for a response. Have a good breakfast."

She had not been hostile or subtly vindictive. She was in terrible pain, but her desire was to offer both of them grace so God would have room to work in their hearts. The offer of the other cheek had nothing to do with ignoring the harm or, as grotesque as it sounds, encouraging the affair.

Her husband came alone. She again greeted him with warmth and kindness, and then made it clear that the marriage was over unless radical, very radical, movement was made to deal with his sexual and relational violations of their covenant. In word and in deed, she was shrewd and innocent, tender and strong. She offered him a taste of life and the consequences of death. It was his choice and she neither threatened nor reviled, nor did she withdraw or attack. Instead, she offered the vulnerable honesty and strength of her soul and the opportunity for repentance.

He was stunned—almost to a point of inarticulate madness. She had never flown by herself or stayed in a hotel alone in her life. She was a dependent and frightened woman in most situations, yet she won over fear and loneliness and the shame and rage of facing her husband's lover. And of all things, she not only gave her husband the freedom to divorce her, but insisted he do so if he was unwilling to change. No greater gift of grace could have been offered and no greater slap endured than the manner in which she shamed her husband and received him back, if he chose to repent.

Good words and deeds are the elixir of life and the antidote against death. Their radical force draws the response of shame and invites the enemy (eventually) to repent so the relationship can be restored. The words and deeds we offer will depend on the scope and particulars of our battle plan, which will be determined according to the kind of enemy we are facing. Doing good to a truly evil person will look different from doing good to a normal sinner who occasionally behaves in evil ways, but whose heart is open to truth.

Most of us are called to deal with three kinds of enemies in our lives—evil people, fools, and simpletons. We need to have a unique plan of attack for each.

PART THREE

Combat for the Soul

CHAPTER TEN

LOVING AN EVIL PERSON:
Siege Warfare

❖

T he world is made up of many different kinds of people. This is an obvious and intuitive observation that is often obscured by the complexity of human behavior. There are massive differences between people, but there are often enough commonalities to allow for categorization. The next three chapters will deal with the question of what it means to boldly love those who are evil, foolish, and "normally" sinful. The premise is that different kinds of "good gifts" are required to impact different kinds of people with truth and life. There are dangers involved in any labeling of persons, but there is some legitimacy for dividing humanity into these three categories.

People can be categorized according to almost any organizing theme. For example, a person can be put in a group by demographics — nationality, race, socioeconomic status, educational level, profession — or by psychological structures — temperaments, personality disorders, psychiatric classifications (depression, anxiety), addictions (eating disorder, alcoholism, sex addiction). There are probably as many schemes for organizing people in groups as there are groups.

The schemes are often highly illuminating and profitable in helping us group, assess, and predict human behavior. If I know that you are an engineer, who is a conservative Republican who attends a very conservative church, then I can usually predict certain things about you that will be different than if I learn you are an artist, who lives up in the mountains, away from people, and are part of a non-traditional Christian community that meets in the upstairs of a rock-and-roll bar.

Demographics are usually highly interesting, but in most cases, they do not lead to a deep understanding about what makes a person tick. Psychological categories, at first glance, do a better job of guiding our understanding of human motivation, because psychological information tunes us into more substantial concerns. The facts involve patterns of response to our inner world and the world of people, which is definitely more illuminating than knowing if a person is an engineer or an artist.

But psychological information usually misses another dimension that is crucial in the process of categorization, and that is what a person does with God — with truth, beauty, and justice. The categories used in Proverbs — mocker (evil), fool, and simpleton (normal sinner; Proverbs 1:22) — deal with horizontal information (such as psychological categories), but also address the vertical dimension of our existence (what a person does with God). For that reason, we will focus on the categories of people found in the wisdom literature that addresses how a person is motivated to relate to self, other people, and God.

THE DANGERS OF LABELS

Imprecision
We need to be aware, however, of the dangers in the use of any label when attempting to account for the unique, mysterious human soul. First, all categories are imprecise and fuzzy. In order to put the diversity of humanity into any comprehensive group (given the fact that no one is precisely the same as the others in the group), a degree of precision and specificity will be sacrificed for the benefit of categorization. For example, not

all evil people do the same thing. It is nearly impossible to define evil on the basis of behavior. I've worked with people who have murdered their children and found those people not to be evil. On the other hand, I have worked with parents who have spent a lifetime grooming, displaying, and using their children and whose evil sent horrible shudders through my heart. Categories are dangerous when we require them to do more than they can bear. A label simply cannot tell us what someone will do, although it may help us assess something about their heart.

Even among the categories found in Proverbs, there is a great deal of imprecision and overlap in description. The mocker is a fool. The fool is simple. The simpleton makes foolish choices. The fool despises wisdom. At first glance, there seems to be little point in attempting to subdivide the three terms into specific categories. However, the mocker (evil) is more vicious and destructive than the fool; the fool is more resistant to change and more committed to pleasure than the simpleton; and the simpleton is more precariously disposed toward sin than the wise person. There are gradations and differences, even if there are points of considerable overlap. Labels may be fuzzy, but they are useful, especially to those who hate to be bothered by all the diversity and mystery of human existence. If we label all Republicans as white conservatives who are committed to decentralized government, states' rights, private enterprise, fewer welfare programs, and trickle-down economics, then we can simplify life and political decisions. For most people, labels are stereotypes that strip life of its complexity in order to make it more tolerable. When labels are used to generalize in this manner, they are destructive.

Labels can be useful without being destructive when they push us to consider (given the differences) the common themes that tie the different people in a subgroup together. They help us to reflect on the central, core passions that drive divergent human behavior. What is common (given that it will not be mere behavior) about those who are evil, or foolish, or normally sinful? The answer will be imprecise. But if reasonably accurate, it will enable us to consider what it means to spur a person to love and good deeds (Hebrews 10:24). We need to be more concerned with increasing perspective than in formulating a fine-tuned, detailed plan of attack. With perspective, we can form adaptable and unique strategies that fit the person and situation, rather than attempting to formulate a plan that fits everyone at all times and circumstances.

Clear, Rigid Definitions

A significant danger in any scheme of categorization is creating a definition that is too clear. A well-defined definition asserts too much clarity over the enormous complexity of life. Any time a category is too clever or clear, it allows for the illusion of control. For example, to assume that every person who is labeled "codependent" is always afraid to speak his mind or never shows anger to others creates parameters that are too rigid. Or to assume that everyone who reads her Bible an hour a day, conducts a Bible study, and is very pleasant and kind is godly assumes too much clarity in defining godliness. We should struggle (to a degree) to define who is and who is not in a category.

A second danger involves rigid definitions. A rigid definition implies that I am what I am and will always be that in the future. But the heart and soul of a person are not eternally enslaved to a particular direction or to certain symptoms. Change can occur to a point where it can be said of the thief, the gossip, or the adulterer, "That is what some of you were" (1 Corinthians 6:11). Sufficient change can occur that invalidates the label. For that reason, I am never to judge you. I may assess your current condition and offer a tentative hypothesis, "You appear to be a fool," but I am never to say, "You are and will always be a fool." That statement is the dictum of a judge who has passed a final, unchangeable verdict. It is imperative never to feel certain or resolute about our opinion. We must remain open to seeing the facts from a new perspective and equally open to the possibility that our perception is distorted by the log in our own eye.

The central reason for resisting rigid, final judgment is the warning that we will be judged according to the sure categories we use to judge others (Matthew 7:1-2). Further, the way we forgive others will be the way God will forgive us (Matthew 6:12). Our internal paradigm of judgment and forgiveness is of eternal importance. We must resist two extremes: a penchant to judge too freely, labeling others with condescending confidence and snarlish anger, or a refusal to assess data given the potential for error. The risks are great, but the task is crucial if we are to love with boldness and wisdom.

THE MOCKER: DEALING WITH EVIL

There are people in this world who seem to live and breathe evil. In every generation, masters of evil (Hitler, Stalin, Amin, Pol Pot) seem to serve as caricatures of the demonic. There are others, less known, who are involved in ritualistic abuse — the sadistic physical, emotional, and sexual abuse of children. Few would dispute, even without definition, the accuracy of calling these people evil. Indeed, they are evil. There are many people, however, who do not perpetrate societal or individual barbarity to this demonic extent but who are more than simply arrogant, hard, and hurtful. All of us are capable of doing evil things, but evil people are driven by a self-interest that is so heartless, conscious, and cruel that it delights in stealing from others the lifeblood of their soul.

Often the one who delights in evil is an ordinary, unassuming person who hides behind a facade of normalcy. Few people who are evil ever appear evil, even after the evidence of their deceit, destructiveness, and hardness is exposed. The little old man who feeds birds and smiles warmly as you walk by his home might be a person who has abused a hundred children over the last fifty years. If he is caught, most will doubt the charge, or at least the extent of the harm. This is true, even more so, when the behavior is not societally condemned, but may nevertheless emanate from an evil heart. The father who craftily and pervasively undermines his children at every point of decision, criticizing their reasoning or their motives, superintending every one of their relationships with solicitousness and overprotection, may appear to outsiders to be a committed and sacrificial parent, but in fact may be a jealous, obsessive accuser who devours their hearts.

One problem in defining evil, and even seeing evil in others, is that it is so common. We all behave in evil ways at times. Jesus says, "You, then, though you are evil, know how to give good gifts to your children" (Matthew 7:11). He implies we are all capable of evil and commit evil in our most intimate of relationships, yet we are still able to do good. If my heart and hands are looked at from the perspective of any one event, it may be very possible to say that I have done evil. But I would argue that my life, looked at over time and in various situations, would produce evidence that would warrant a different classification for my heart. I am capable of being an evildoer, as anyone is, and actually at times do evil things, but I am not an evil person. A person's heart can be diagnosed as evil only after he is observed in repeated interactions where the patterns of harm are committed without sorrow or openness to feedback.

WHAT IS EVIL?

Evil is present when there is a profound absence of empathy, shame, and goodness. Empathy involves a connectedness to the heart of another and a respect for their personal boundaries. An evil person is unmoved by the inner world of the other and has no respect for boundaries. Shame involves an ability to be exposed and disturbed about actual or perceived violations of relationships. An evil person is unaffected by exposure, so is consequently shameless. Finally, goodness involves a desire to see someone or something grow in strength, freedom, and beauty. An evil person seems to delight in stripping away purpose, individuality, and vitality.

Evil Is Cold

Evil is (for the most part) unfeeling. It lacks sorrow when someone suffers and joy when there is happiness. But an evil person is more than emotionally detached; he simply will not allow himself to enter the heart of his victim as a person. The victim is an object — an entity to be controlled or destroyed — and not a living, breathing being who feels hurt, fear, sorrow, and shame. In that regard, evil sees the other as nothing more than a service to itself. Most of us will use a paper cup and, when finished, discard it without feeling or concern. As long as the cup is useful, it is used, but when its use is finished, there is no reason to keep it or honor it as valuable. Similarly, an evil person feels nothing toward those who are used to satisfy his craving for unlimited power and control.

A husband of one of my clients spent the vast majority of every waking moment exposing the errors of her ungodly thinking. If she expressed an opinion about a friend or if she ordered a meal without his approval, he began a long discourse on the flaws of her logic. His lecture might literally last for hours, and if she differed with his facts, he intensified his onslaught of criticism. He was more than intolerant of other viewpoints; he was methodical and relentless in stalking every thought that differed from his until it was tracked down, shot, and left to die. She felt like she was a prisoner of his words. If she tried to get out, she was forced to endure even more relentless torture. If she sat quietly and endured his tirade, she would be spared the full extent of his violation.

Evil may exhibit normal emotion at appropriate points. In many cases, evil is able to offer sorrow at a funeral or joy at a wedding, but the feelings are not connected to those who are suffering or rejoicing. They are a facade that hides a coldness of heart. I once met the father of one of my clients who was sexually abused by him over a ten-year period of time. He introduced himself and gratefully thanked me for my work with his daughter. He spoke glowingly about the changes he saw in her and then remarked, "I'm sure you are aware she has suffered a great many delusions about her past. What I have been most pleased by is that you seem to be concentrating on her sin, unlike her other therapists, who get caught up in her exaggerated stories." I answered, "I am honored to work with a woman of such integrity and willingness to grow in spite of her wounds," then I stood and looked into his face. When I did not respond enthusiastically to his compliment, he smiled wanly and his eyes turned dark. We parted, and I felt a chill run through me.

Part of my work with her was to free her from his grasp. I concentrated on her refusal to face the real state of his heart and her tendency to assume responsibility for the abuse in order to hide his stalking evil. She was terrified to face the extent of his heartlessness. At one time when she was six, he put a noose around her neck and forced her to stand all day long on a chair underneath a tree limb. If she fell or swooned, the noose would hang her like a condemned criminal. After standing for hours, she felt weak and began to faint. Her knees crumpled and the noose pulled tight. She fought to regain her balance, but the chair toppled below her and the rope snapped around her throat and then gave way. He had tied the rope so that it would cinch tight and then release when the pressure was strong enough. She blamed herself for being so naive. She thought she should have known as a six-year-old that her father would not really kill her. He was only teaching her a lesson to obey him the next time he asked for something.

In one emotional fight with him twenty years after the event, she recounted the feelings of torture she experienced that day and in many other equally evil assaults. His demeanor was the same as it was with me — pleasant and condescending. He did not deny the event; he merely reinterpreted it as an acceptable means of making a dramatic statement to a little girl who would not listen to or obey her father. He was utterly estranged from the feelings a six-year-old girl might experience at the prospect of hanging to death. He felt no empathy or concern for her pain, then or now. From his perspective, he was trying to be a good parent, and she misinterpreted his concern as cruelty.

An evil person, regularly and masterfully, portrays his motives and behavior as innocent. Others just do not understand. He is deceitfully gifted in making the victim of his abuse feel like the perpetrator of the harm. When the victim protests and exposes the abuse, he will accuse the victim of being too sensitive, emotional, troubled, or unreasonable. He portrays himself as the real victim, cruelly misunderstood and falsely accused.

The coldness of evil is a passionless hatred toward any who resist or fail to succumb to the evil person's desires. The hatred is passionless in that even passionate hatred involves an entanglement with those who are hated. Evil seems to transcend passion and feeling. It finds its nourishment in the ability to soullessly eschew relational and emotional entanglements. It is as if the Devil offers the person freedom from human emotion, including the ability to harm others without guilt or fear, if he merely gives his soul to evil. When the innocent veneer is stripped away and his methods are exposed, the eyes of an evil person may look straight into yours with an unflinching strength born of an absence of shame. A second attribute of evil is shamelessness.

Evil Is Hard
Evil is devoid of conscience. It lacks moral boundaries; right is whatever it desires. A seared conscience does not respond with mercy to a cry for help, nor is it stopped by the threat of shame. Evil has an energy that continues to move without restraint or rest. In one sense, it seems boundless, consuming, and all powerful. Its power lies in its coldness and hardness — the fact that it is neither caught up in human suffering nor bound by a dread of shame. Therefore, it does not succumb to the normal give and take of loneliness and fear of rejection.

Most of us don't want to be isolated; loneliness draws us into the will of the group. Evil, on the other hand, allows no feelings of true loneliness, so it is free to violate the values of the group. Similarly, the fear of rejection may repel us from offending the powerful in a group so we won't become the object of contempt. Evil rarely feels shame, so it is free to do as it pleases. It is no wonder evil is a powerful option in a fallen world; it gives a person almost absolute freedom from pain and almost total control over others.

Shame. Shamelessness thrives on the ability to avoid exposure. The experience of shame always involves an exposure of one's inner world by another and is usually a potent deterrent to proceeding in a shameless direction. Shame involves the gut-wrenching threat of being seen and cast away from relationships. But a person can avoid the experience of shame if he can put out the eyes that see inside him. When his accuser is blind, he can escape the gaze that penetrates his soul. For that reason, evil almost always works to shame the other. Shame works to blind the eyes that expose.

Evil uses arrogance and mockery to escape being shamed. The ability to cover loneliness and fear of rejection without reliance on the mercy of God is predicated on a hardening of the soul through arrogance and a blinding of the eyes through mockery (Proverbs 21:24). Mockery may take obvious forms, such as biting sarcasm and vicious cynicism, or it can be much more subtle.

One client's mother is a pleasant and hospitable woman who is known as a "good" Christian. She bakes meals for shut-ins, serves on church committees, and is involved in many civic organizations. A negative trait, overlooked by most, is a significant temper that never explodes, but oozes molten contempt. Behind closed doors, however, her volcanic fury melts everyone who dares stand in her path. One time, her daughter refused to participate in an activity because she believed it was morally compromising, so the mother slapped her, pulled out a shank of hair, and explosively recounted every wrong her daughter had ever committed. Her daughter finally caved in and agreed to participate. The mother remarked, "I'm glad you've come to your senses."

One awful, abusive event does not make a person evil, but when it represents a repetitive pattern of excessive disregard for others (mockery) and a wanton, vicious refusal to look at the damage done (arrogance), then one can ascertain a significant inclination to evil.

Arrogance. An arrogant heart assumes the prerogatives of God. It claims one's own status, gifts, power, health, and/or finances emanate from oneself—and from nowhere else. It is more than self-sufficiency; it is the boastful claim that one's life is a byproduct of a personal fiat to be powerful and successful. An arrogant person, at core, hates God (Psalm 74:10). He sees God as an affront to his claim of dominion. Does this mean that an evil person will be an atheist or obvious God-hater? No, evil can parade as an angel of light committed to observing certain religious tendencies, but despising the law of love with a cold, unbridled contempt.

Arrogance swaggers to its own inner rhythm. It sings its own boastful songs of conquering potency. The bravado of arrogance is, at times, enormously attractive. It walks into potentially dangerous and shameful situations, and calmly and powerfully exerts control. There is a sense of confidence, a *savoir faire*, a leader's energy that allows others to abdicate choice and relax in the swagger of their boldness. Arrogance creates a mood of "follow me or get lost." And who wants to be lost in a world such as ours?

Consequently, arrogant men and women rule the world and offer the illusion of rest (from choice) for the weary, and hope (for protection) for the frightened. An arrogant heart is hardened to its own sin and blinds the hearts of those it controls. The more evil a person is, the greater the degree of arrogant hardness ruling his heart. In turn, the greater the hardness, the more likely the control of others will be achieved through vicious contempt.

Mockery. Contemptuous mockery is the language of accusation. It is the bony finger that uses shame to cut through our defense to the fragile, lonely parts of our heart. Few experiences are as difficult to endure as being the object of someone's cackling contempt. For that reason, we will often do anything in the world to avoid the fiery eyes of mockery, including a denial, or at least a hiding of our deepest convictions and beliefs. Mockery is the weapon that evil uses powerfully to strip its victim of a sense of self and life. The withering look of mockery shames the heart and seems to compel it to flee to higher ground in order to avoid the impending flood.

For example, I recently spoke to a prominent physician who is respected as a leader in his community and in his field. He told me of an interaction at a professional conference where he presented a paper. A fellow physician, in a tone of incredulity and contempt, asked him, "Are your findings based on enough research, or do they come from the same kind of hope you have in an unprovable God?" He told me that he wilted.

He felt a wave of heat surge around his face, and he melted into a pool of confusion and despair. In a single, withering surge, he felt like his career, his walk with God, and his integrity vanished in the turbulent foam of mockery.

Mockery can come in the form of an outburst of invective that accuses the other of failure or, in the slightest turn of the mouth, takes the form of a sly, knowing smile that accuses the other of stupidity. *Mockery is any heartless accusation that lacks tenderness and a desire for reconciliation.* Evil uses its ability to wound and destroy to terrify those under its control.

A third attribute of evil is its destructiveness.

Evil Is Destructive

Evil is bad. That is, it is persistently destructive. But it is also deceitfully subtle. Consequently, evil rarely shows itself as bad. In fact, it often portrays itself as helpful, open, kind, generous, long-suffering. An inclination to evil taints all activity, even the gifts of kindness that appear genuine. Such kindness or generosity seems to entangle the victim deeper in the evil person's web. If one is in a relationship with an evil person for long, the signs of death will begin to show — anemia (a loss of self, vitality, and strength), despair (a loss of desire and hope), and disorientation (a loss of direction and purpose). Many of these symptoms are also the byproduct of a relationship with an arrogant, hard, and destructive person who may not be inclined to deeper shades of evil. How does one make a distinction between an evil person and a less destructive person (a fool)?

A fool might withhold involvement unless you conform to his will and might intimidate or manipulate to gain advantage. His goal is to get you to conform, and once that end is achieved, he is at peace. An evil person, on the other hand, wants conformity and much more. He wants unearned devotion that borders on worship — a form of sacrifice that requires the loss of one's will, mind, and soul. He displays a craving to suck the other's soul dry until every drop of life has been drawn for his own benefit.

Evil steals faith, hope, and love. Faith involves trusting in what is unseen and unknown, and is required in almost every moment of our existence. For example, I put my faith in faceless, unknown drivers who are coming toward me on the road. I trust they are not drunk. Faith in a person is trust in her character—a confidence that if I am hurt by her, the damage will eventually be resolved because her heart, ultimately, wants to do good. An evil person uses the access of trust to obliterate any desire to trust others, and even to trust in oneself. Consequently, the effect of evil is to remove from its victim any discernment or sense of caution in relating to evil and, at the same time, to create a hypervigilant fear of anyone good. Evil betrays trust and makes faith look ridiculously foolish. Evil misuses power and then claims innocence. If that is questioned, then evil uses shame or mockery to bludgeon the victim into accepting the blame.

In most cases, it seems easier to be at fault than to bear an evil person's scorn. I have worked with sexual abuse victims who at age forty still believe that they provoked their abuser to violate them because they were told they were precociously seductive. Evil disseminates disinformation, pinning the blame on the victim and eventually robbing her of the adventure found in faith.

Stripping Hope
Evil also strips people of their hope. Evil not only betrays, but also attempts to entrap the innocent in bondage. Bondage is a form of slavery that dulls the senses and steals from the soul a vision of what could be. Almost all dictatorships, be they political or ecclesiastical, attempt to limit access to freedom. Restricted freedom of speech, thought, or soul evokes a disappointment in what is and a hunger for what is not. Hope unsettles the soul in the present and urges it to imagine what might be. Evil kills hope by deadening the soul through bondage and terror.

Evil works to supplant hope through destroying perspective. Hope is visionary and motivating, even when the anticipation is no more profound than the reward of a break once a task is finished. Hope, or anticipation, draws us out of the moment to see what is ahead, while paradoxically energizing the moment in order to press on to what lies beyond. A loss of hope, in the moment or in what lies beyond, is a death knell for productive, vital choice. Evil wants control and absolute power over choice; therefore, it must numb hope.

A person's hope is deadened when nothing she does is good enough, or when all her choices, no matter what they are, are used to punish her. We all fear (to some degree) being cast out of another garden — be it a tightly knit family or an authoritarian church — yet to defy evil results in sure banishment. An evil person addresses any difference of opinion with fury, cruelty, and hatred, using terror to drive home the idiocy of ever wanting or working for change. Terror snuffs out the longing for a better day, or more specifically, makes the hope of heaven seem too painful to desire. Terror propels flight to the safety of conformity and compels one to leave behind the heavy baggage of hope. Once hope is under bondage, one is left shackled to a passionless present where energy to live and grow is lost to the more primitive goal of survival. It seems easier to live a lifeless, futureless, choiceless present in conformity to evil than to risk the ruthless scrutiny of evil by stepping outside its will.

Once evil violates trust through horrendous betrayal, intimacy with others seems too dangerous to enjoy. All connection, pleasure, and joy is lost in an unbridgeable chasm. Evil hates love, even more than it does faith and hope. Evil delights in fanning the flames of hatred, as long as the passion of hatred does not also cling to what is good. When a victim is full of a frenzied and vulgar desire for vengeance, an evil person can easily continue his deadly dance. But a hatred that despises evil and clings to truth and beauty infuriates evil and draws forth its most compelling assaults of shame (Romans 12:9). Evil wants love to be a pointless, insane spitting against the wind.

Love seems so puny and inconsequential in the face of the enormity of evil. Most mornings after reading the paper, where the forces of evil publicize yesterday's victories, I want to quit. It seems so foolish to stumble into a world inflamed by hatred to offer a pitiful cup of love, so flawed and incomplete. Evil shames the desire to love by making love seem so small and powerless. Once love is squashed by the enormity of evil, the heart loses purpose and passion. Even more, love, a shining guide to the character of God, is darkened and our desire to be like God is shamed.

Though evil is cold, hard, and destructive, no person is so evil, or so beyond the grace of God, that His light is unable to penetrate. Our task is to know what lurks inside the heart of the evil person so we can excavate a pathway toward the part of his heart that is made in the image of God and, consequently, still hungers for love and meaning. In every person, no matter how reprobate, there is some remnant of desire for beauty and justice. If we know what to expect from evil, then we will be better disposed to fight it with the weapons of God in order to claim the evil heart for the God who can redeem even the most despicable of souls.

THE GIFT OF DEFEAT

An enormously good gift to give someone evil is to foil their effort to win. Evil is used to winning. It uses conscienceless seduction and shameless mockery to win ground and frighten others away from taking it back. If evil consistently wins, it will see more evil as the only strategy for keeping its victory spoils and gaining new rewards. One of the greatest gifts one can give a person inclined to evil is the strength to frustrate their attempts to dominate.

Such strength must be full of cunning and precision. Evil can never be overthrown through rational, reasonable argumentation. It may dialogue and debate, but its direction is already determined. Evil will never stop long enough to consider its destructiveness unless it is held accountable, under strong, clear, and unwavering consequences of righteousness. What is required for righteous consequences to be established?

A Willingness to Endure Loss

Evil instinctively knows what you are unwilling to lose and will tempt you with the possibility of loss and heartbreak. When one man spoke to his apparently evil father about their relationship, his father said, "Son, I don't think I can bear this conversation and still believe you love me. I am in the midst of changing my will, and I want to know you really do support me." The message was clear: "If you disturb me, then you can't love me. And if you don't love me, then you can count on getting nothing from my estate."

Evil has a keen smell for false gods. It will sense what our heart truly loves and worships, and threaten the weakest, most ungodly chinks in our armor in order to keep love mute. Evil will not be conquered as long as our hearts live to obtain immediate relief or escape profound loss. *Only when we have little or nothing to lose will we be willing to love.*

A Willingness to Face Shame and Hatred

Evil also instinctively knows where you can be shamed. Whatever will provoke shame will be used to stifle your voice and compel you to back down from serving good gifts. A friend of mine perceives herself to be slow of thought and speech. She is certainly no brain or speed demon, but she is bright and articulate. Whenever she attempts to talk to her overwhelmingly shaming, hateful mother, she blanks out and eventually consents to do whatever her mother desires. She is easily shamed; therefore, she opts for dissociative deadness rather than facing her mother's efforts to destroy her.

I don't believe that in this life we can be entirely free from the effects of shame. To be shameless is, most likely, to be arrogant, narcissistic, and inclined to evil (Philippians 3:18-19). But it is possible to be face to face with the most shaming accusations of the Evil One and find the Lord's mercy sufficient to withstand the brutal assault of contempt. His mercy will not only enable us to survive the attack, but also to declare and offer freedom from condemnation to any who choose to trust in the blood of Christ (Romans 8:1).

But when shame continues to hold a vise-like grip on our heart's movement toward freedom and love, we cannot face evil. We will be too afraid to be hated and alone. Evil recognizes a heart that fears hatred. Hatred intensifies our dread of being an alien and a stranger, cast out from a home that may be evil, but at least is ours. Most people would rather accept evil as the daily menu than be pronounced an orphan and barred from reentering the parental garden. Evil will push us to see if we will bear loss, shame, and hatred. If we are not prepared for the attack, we will wilt under the seduction and mockery of evil.

The preparation we must undergo is training in righteousness, where our senses are aligned with truth and our hearts have been strengthened by discipline (Hebrews 12:1-12). God promises in due season we will yield a harvest of righteous fruit if we enter and pursue His purposes in the midst of pain. If our heart desires to know Him in the midst of suffering, growth will be our reward (1 Peter 4:1-2).

A Willingness to Set and Enforce Clear Parameters

Evil must be caught in the act. Discussing evil with an evil person is rarely useful. It's like giving a gun to an imbalanced and impulsive husband after he has had a vicious fight with his wife; it just gives him more opportunity to turn his hatred against you.

In order to stop evil in its tracks, parameters must be set in the moment of transgression. A parameter (or boundary) is any line in human relations that honors separateness and respects individual dignity. For example, in our home a closed bedroom door should not be opened without knocking and asking for an invitation to enter. In the same way, the inner thoughts of a person should not be infringed upon without invitation. Honoring parameters is a reflection of righteousness, or right living in relationships.

We learn to honor parameters when we experience the consequences of violating them. A consequence is a warning and/or a small dose of pain that alerts others to a violation of love. The consequence, like discipline, is therefore a merciful gift of discomfort, pain, or loss that invites the offender to deal with his harm. A consequence might be no more severe than telling someone, "I am troubled by your remark. Please explain what you mean," or so severe it might involve legal prosecution when the violation of boundaries involves a criminal offense.

One woman, whose husband often verbally attacked her with vicious and cruel contempt, told him, "If you choose to continue this tirade, I will tape it and give a copy to your elder board to allow them to see what kind of man you are outside of the pulpit." The parameter was clear: Don't verbally abuse me. The consequence was equally clear: If you do, then it will be brought to the attention of our church.

Some may protest, "But the church will not listen!" or "I don't have a church that will take action," or "My husband won't be affected by the consequence of being brought before church discipline." I agree that effective consequences are not easy, at times, to determine, but they always exist. And they will eventually be received as the wounds of a friend by one who desires to do good, or attacked ruthlessly as a betrayal of a relationship by those whose hearts refuse to be humbled and broken.

Evil is fairly predictable in its efforts to intimidate through manipulation and shame. Therefore, involvement with an evil person ought to involve surprise and unpredictability. There should be incredible strength on one hand, and warmth and kindness on the other. Whenever a violation of the clear parameters occurs, consequences must follow—but without resorting to cold, detached hatred. Consequences should be offered with a benevolent matter-of-fact demeanor that further offers the opportunity to deal with the evil, if that be the offender's desire.

We need to catch evil in the act and smile, calmly and confidently stating what we are willing and unwilling to endure—then watch hell rise out of the fury and explode. When we are prepared for the assault, we can calmly and confidently (even if we're shaking inside) restate the parameters of acceptable human response, and then warn the evil person what the consequences will be if there is a further violation of those parameters. Inform the evil person that you will walk out of her office, or hang up the phone, or call the police, then do so with deliberation, without apology, and with an absence of rancor or vindictiveness.

Our biggest problem is seldom in finding reasonable and biblical consequences, but in the risk of setting parameters.

Our refusal to accept potential abandonment blocks most of us from setting limits and establishing consequences. But when we find the courage to do so, we will find love to be a powerful weapon against the forces of darkness. We will then be prepared to offer the next good gift, which is an opportunity to repent.

THE GIFT OF AN OPPORTUNITY TO REPENT

After parameters have been set and consequences enforced with strength and kindness, unflinching in the face of loss, shame, and hatred, then it is not uncommon for there to be slight change in the evil person. He can be expected to be moderately contrite, or at least nicer the next time you interact with him. But don't be fooled. It can be easy to be lulled into thinking, "Great! This stuff works!" But his change is probably only a regrouping, not repentance. Evil uses false contrition to lull its victim to sleep so that it can regroup and try a different tactic. It is best to use this lull in the battle to further enrage evil so it will know the battle is not over until righteousness reigns.

The offer of an opportunity to consider the harm that is done, if delivered with passion and wisdom, unnerves and intensifies coldness, hardness, and destructiveness. An intensification of evil draws it to the surface, to the clearing, rather than allowing it to fight under the camouflage of the forest. Once evil exerts its threats about loss, intensifies its shame, and bears down with hatred, then goodness can shine with searing light and penetrate the heart if there is any desire in it at all for life.

Evil is enraged when it is treated with strength and mercy. A good example is an interaction between a daughter, Jane, and her evil father after a terrible fight ensued over her decision not to come home for vacation. For years, she had been put in the position of being a pawn who was attacked by both her mother and father when they were angry at each other. Each parent viewed her as the other's favorite. Therefore, she was assailed for any perceived loyalty toward the other. She was

in the constant bind of being a target for both, no matter what
she did. Here is one boldly loving conversation.

> DAD: Hi, honey, I'm calling to see when you will be
> arriving.
> JANE (chuckling out loud): Well, Dad, I can at least say
> it won't be in this calendar year.
> DAD: What?! You know your mom is counting on you
> helping with the big Fourth of July party. She won't be
> able to do it without your help!
> JANE: Oh, that's too bad, Dad. You know, a lot of cater-
> ing firms do holiday spreads, and I bet there are some
> in your area.
> DAD: Don't get cute with me. You know your mother
> wants you here, not a catering firm. Now let's get seri-
> ous. You will be coming home.
> JANE: Dad, do you recall the conversation a few nights
> ago when you yelled and called me some terrible
> names? Well, I told you then I would no longer allow
> you to sin against me or yourself by enduring your
> use of rage and shame. Before you get too much more
> intense, let me make it clear again: I will not stay on
> the phone if that is your manner of relating to me.
> Dad, are you willing to think with me about the way
> you deal with me and, frankly, almost everyone else
> in our family?
> DAD: Well, fine! I'll tell your mother about your deci-
> sion. And let me tell you I have no interest in being
> lectured by a kid who has no more sense than . . .
> JANE: Dad, I will look forward to the day you do
> desire to interact, so I'll be talking with you soon.
> Bye, Dad.

The phone call was a major first for Jane. She had never
before been able to stand firm with grace and dignity. After
the call, she shook like a leaf for hours. She told me, "I felt
like I was giving birth to evil incarnate one minute and to a
totally new and wonderful life the next. I don't know if I ever

felt so crazy." Her response is not surprising. The breaking of any bondage thrusts the freed prisoner into a frightening new world that, at first, seems alien and awful. Jane struggled with bouts of terrible guilt and fear, but in time, she continued to offer both her parents the opportunity to address realities about their lives that had never been exposed before.

Once parameters are established and consequences are clear, then it is a bittersweet joy to pray, meditate, and ponder on how to use words and deeds to offer the enemy forgiveness. I am amazed how many evil persons, far from consciousness, desire what no one has had the courage to offer them — a taste of strength surrounded with mercy.

The Issues of Repentance
An offer to repent eventually will address, over time, the issues of (1) the violation of relationship and details regarding the damage done, (2) a perspective on forgiveness and hope, (3) a statement of the parameters of love and consequences of violation, (4) a picture of what would need to occur in behavior and heart before the relationship can be reconciled, and (5) a negotiated agreement about what will occur now to begin the process of change. Let me illustrate from the story of Jane.

Her father was emotionally abusive — calling her names and attacking almost every aspect of her character. Her mother was equally abusive, as she withdrew involvement to a point where she'd pretend her daughter did not exist. If Jane asked for the salt during a meal, her mother would act as if she did not hear. Jane once shook her mother in fury, and her mother looked straight through her and then walked away.

At separate times, she talked with her father and mother about the chronic violations of their relationship. She provided each parent with specific situations where the details of their response were beyond comprehension (issue 1). Several times in each encounter, vociferous accusations were made against her, and explanations were offered to justify their behavior. She neither succumbed to the virulent attack nor to the cold silence. She used the data of their attacks as new evidence to illustrate their commitment to intimidate and destroy.

She told them what it was like to be humiliated and abandoned. She explained how she had mishandled them, others, and God in the midst of her sin. This opened the door for sharing with her parents the good news of the gospel. She spoke about her own sin with a stunning passion and pointed to Christ's work on the cross as one's only hope in face of the terrifying judgment that lies ahead. She told me later that for a brief, fleeting moment, she understood how the harsh words of Stephen, "You stiff-necked people, with uncircumcised hearts and ears! You are just like your fathers" (Acts 7:51), no longer seemed inconsistent with his final words, "Lord, do not hold this sin against them" (verse 60). The rebuke was not a punishment, but a door of hope to enter into repentant, forgiven life (issue 2).

She shared with them what it meant for her to love them. She reiterated that her commitment to them would no longer allow her to be a go-between or a punching bag. She was detailed and specific about loving parameters and the consequences that would occur if the violations continued. She restated again her desire to see their relationship reconciled on the basis of forgiveness and respect (issue 3).

She made it clear that deep, abiding change could not occur if the problems were superficially swept under the carpet. Their hearts had to be open to dealing with their sin, or the same destructive litany would repeat itself again and again. Jane had the wisdom to ask both her parents why each seemed so committed to doing terrible damage to her. She asked about their past histories of abuse and abandonment. What she discovered was a long history of intergenerational abuse, alcoholism, depression, and evil. Her parents' abusive past saddened her, but she did not use it to excuse their inclinations to do evil.

Unfortunately, her parents' disclosure of past harm hardened their hearts to facing the abuse of their daughter. At countless points in the conversation, she had to warn each parent of the consequences of continued harm. She went on to paint a picture of what could happen in their relationship if they wanted to be reconciled (issue 4).

She told me later that no moment in her life was more difficult than looking each parent in the face and directly asking, "Do you want to be my father (or mother) and own your part in the rupture of our relationship?" Neither parent desired to do so. Her strength kept the abuse at bay, but there seemed to be no spark of life that drew them to deal with their perpetration of evil. If there had been a movement to change, then Jane could have talked about the slow, arduous process of rebuilding trust (issue 5).

Almost two years later, Jane has not given up. Her parents are no closer to repentance, but her love, witnessed in new parameters and consequences, and even more in her moments of genuine sorrow for them, has curtailed the extent of their damage. She continues to shock and surprise them with her kindness, strength, and vitality. The change has even surprised her. She feels, at times, deeply alone and occasionally walks (somewhat) knowingly back into abusive situations, but overall, she has experienced renewed passion and a wonder in the gospel.

No one encounter will likely address all the issues I've outlined. But over time, each point must be passed in order for reconciliation to occur. If each is not passed with heartfelt joint agreement, then ongoing surprise, rebuke, kindness, and consequences must continue. *If forgiveness, fulfilled in reconciliation, is to occur, evil must repent with clarity and conviction.* Does this mean that if repentance does not occur, then forgiveness cannot be offered? If forgiveness is defined as a continuing process of hungering for restoration, revoking revenge, and offering good gifts, then we are to forgive until there is reconciliation. But reconciliation should not occur until there is repentance.

Repentance on the part of the evil person will include a renunciation of rage and mockery. He will need to demonstrate a willingness to be humbled and broken by the weight of guilt for his use of shame and contempt. He will further desire to see wrongs righted and other relationships restored through a process of humbly asking forgiveness for the effects of his sin and through the process of carefully rebuilding trust.

If such a deep change in direction does not occur, then there is a final good gift to give to an evil person—the grace of excommunication. No one can tell another with certainty when this gift should be offered. Jane does not yet feel free to stop the process of active battle with her parents' evil hearts. The time may come, however, when cutting off all relationship may be the most strategic step toward their restoration.

THE GIFT OF EXCOMMUNICATION

The gift of excommunication is the withholding of the relationship. It is a kind gift because it removes the immediate opportunity for sin and opens the door to loneliness and shame. Paul talks about the purpose behind the process as destroying sinful inclinations (1 Corinthians 5:5) and intensifying shame (2 Thessalonians 3:14-15). It serves the same purpose as disciplining a child. A child is given a small taste of pain in order to warn him about an even greater sorrow that may lie ahead if the destructive direction continues. Being cut off from a relationship is a taste of hell.

Cutting off relationships, however, is not done merely to minimize our own pain, nor to decree the offender beyond hope. Paul tells us, "Do not regard him as an enemy, but to warn him as a brother" (2 Thessalonians 3:15). Cutting someone off from communion should be done only after significant time and prayer has been expended to set parameters, apply consequences, and offer the opportunity to repent. Further, the step should not be taken without consultation and prayer with older and wiser believers. No one has the right to tell another what is the right thing to do or the right time to act, but consultation and prayer is useful to help us consider the issues in our life that might be blocking our ability to love. In other words, excommunication should not occur rashly in a moment of anger, nor quickly after only a few interactions with the evil person. Nevertheless, at some point, it is not loving to continue an evil relationship with a person who consistently and perniciously sins against you without some sign of repentance and change.

Cutting off the relationship will spark new kinds of battles in the soul. Jesus tells us it is unwise to go to war without first counting the cost (Luke 14:31-32). A major battle will likely occur with doubt and guilt. The choice to separate yourself from another should never be done with arrogant certainty that a right choice has been made. There is seldom that much clarity. And without question, the evil person and his family and friends will set off tremors of doubt in the one who boldly loves through the intensification of shame and rage.

What is to be done with doubt and guilt? Again, the answer in part is to anticipate it, to prepare for it. When it arrives, smile and cry. The smile acknowledges its arrival and the utter predictability of evil. The tears embrace the inner reality of the terror of loneliness that likely underlies doubt and guilt. The fact that we are children of God, and truly never orphans, seems to matter very little at the prospect of losing a parent or other significant person. Tears acknowledge the sorrow of living in a fallen world. They mingle with the tears of God over the necessity of applying such radical surgery to the advanced cancer of sin.

New external issues must also be considered when relationship is severed. Family or friends who continue to relate to the evil person may not agree the person is inclined to evil, or if they do, they may continue to encourage an approach to forgiveness which prefers that your head and the head of the family, church, or organization be kept in the sand. What is to be done? Wisdom, again, never tells us exactly what to do, but I would suggest, in most cases, to continue relationships with those who are still in contact with the evil person.

Without doubt, the evil person has spread vicious, uncontested lies about you to those who know you. You will be called judgmental, holier-than-thou, arrogant, unbiblical, cruel, heartless. Others will often be watching to see if the evil person is correct. It is not your responsibility to counter every lie, but a life that is full of joy and sorrow, tenderness and strength, and brokenness and boldness will discount at least some of the virulent untruths and half-truths told about you. In many cases, the more the gossip, the better the opportunity to shine with humbly passionate light. The contrast between good and evil will, over time and certainly in God's time, intensify a hatred of life's fragrance or soften hatred to a point where the smell of death repulses and the fragrance of life draws.

The task of loving an evil person requires (as it does in all cases) supernatural intervention. The battle is not yours; it is the Lord's. That, however, will not take away the cold gaze of hatred and the sting of shame. The only motivation strong enough to propel you in battle is an unquenchable desire to know the mighty God who changed your heart and can change the evil person's as well.

CHAPTER ELEVEN

LOVING A FOOL:
Guerilla Warfare

A friend told me about his recent visit to a city he called a "fool's paradise." I asked him why he labeled the city and several million of its inhabitants "fools." "People seem to live for little more than the moment," he answered. "They furiously grab for whatever satisfies their bellies." His perspective on an entire city may not be accurate, but with few words he portrayed the key characteristics of what the book of Proverbs calls a fool—angry, arrogant, and self-centered.

A man I counseled was a hard-driving, self-confident, opinionated businessman. His self-assurance dominated every stage onto which he stepped (Proverbs 12:15, 28:26, 30:32). When I first met John and walked with him down the hallway to my office, he commented on our choice of computers. He informed me that we had made a poor choice and that a brand he used would serve our purposes much better (Proverbs 18:2). When we began the session, he told me that his marriage problems were really the result of his wife's lack of submissiveness and his only problem was not exerting more control in his family. He was sick of his wife trying to analyze him and tell him what to do (Proverbs 1:7, 15:5). He knew he had a bad temper, but his problem with anger was her fault (Proverbs 14:16, 29:11; Ecclesiastes 7:9). Later, he admitted a long history of drinking problems and pornography, which he viewed as wrong, but normal and not that big a deal (Proverbs 13:19). He was intimidating, reflexively self-centered, and manipulative. He could be called a fool.

Foolishness can be present in a person who does not look as obviously angry and arrogant. John's wife, Mary, is a good example. Mary got angry whenever she made a mistake. She was vicious and vindictive toward herself when she failed. Her arrogance surfaced in her frenetic effort to make every relationship perfect. Mary was afraid of failure and relational tension, but the quiet arrogance in her life grew out of a disdain for intimacy and kindness. When I addressed this in counseling, she warmly but condescendingly informed me that she did not need better relationships, but more energy to be obedient. She viewed the struggles with her husband as her fault. When I began to point out his failures and how hard he would be to love, she quietly and subtly turned her barrage against me for misunderstanding his motives, then against herself for her failure to trust his attempts to change.

In many respects, she was the mirror opposite of her husband. To the degree he blamed others, she blamed herself. His opinionated assault on those around him was countered by her confident assurance that she was at fault, but could not change because she lacked faith and conviction. Her failures, in a perverse sense, were the central focus of most of her day. But her efforts to change seemed more important than the wonder of being forgiven. Both John and Mary were utterly self-centered. It is tragic to say their marriage was a parody of fools.

CHARACTERISTICS OF A FOOL

A fool's hot anger (directed at self or others), self-centeredness, and hatred of discipline and wisdom are not essentially different from the qualities that line the heart of an evil person, but there is a difference in degree. Sin is essentially the same in the saint as it is in the reprobate. The most godly men and women I know still struggle with petty anger, jealousy, selfishness, and an ambivalence toward wisdom. Nevertheless, they are lovers of wisdom and imbued with a fragrant scent of heaven. At first blush, one can say we all struggle with sin; therefore, the one inclined to evil and the one who hungers after wisdom with regard to the capacity to do harm are much more alike than different. On the other hand, with regard to living out truth and love, they are different enough to warrant notice.

In many respects, an evil person is simply a more severe fool who has progressed to a level of foolishness that is deeply severed from human emotion (empathy and shame) and human involvement (devouring destruction). An evil person is a more crafty and deceitful fool who is more artful at escaping exposure. Further, an evil person delights in the destructive thrill of controlling and then consuming his victim. The points of similarity and difference may help further clarify each category.

ANGER: A FLIGHT FROM EMPATHY

Empathy is the human reflection of the incarnation, or God with us. God not only feels what we feel, but in fact, enters our condition and our flesh in order to fully bear our reality. Human empathy does not take away sin, but it mirrors the incarnation in that we possess the ability to (remotely) enter the pain and joy of others.

Although an evil person does not feel the pain of another, he is highly perceptive and often a master of predicting other people's shame, fear, and loneliness. Evil does not truly feel for the sake of coming alongside, but only for better enslaving and devouring. An evil person's anger is cold-blooded and merely a prelude to stunning his victims in order to draw close enough to swallow them up.

A fool, on the other hand, is not usually cold and unfeeling. In fact, he may be very warm and sympathetic, but not for long. His feelings are usually like a travelogue instead of a real trip. They are a brief emotional excursion that hits the highlights, but never ventures into the smells and sounds that make up a real city. Once real depth of feeling and relationship is required, the fool is usually bored or distracted to other matters that are more personally rewarding. The fool, unlike the one inclined to evil, feels connected to the inner world of others, but only to the degree that it requires little of him. Once something is required, the fool will deaden his own inner world and cut off the connection with the other through anger.

A fool's anger is often intimidating and intense. Overt behavior can be misleading, however, because evil can be explosive and foolishness can appear calm. It takes a wise heart to discern the motivational energy behind appearances. The evil person is like a black widow who frightens, stuns, and traps her victim with the intention of moving in closer to do more harm. The fool is more like a grizzly bear whose primary goal is to intimidate and frighten in order to establish his preeminence and independence, and gain compliance and control. Evil wants to enslave and destroy; foolishness desires to be adored and obeyed. A fool's anger is disproportionate to the situation, impulsive, and repetitive.

Disproportionate Anger

A fool's anger at others or himself almost always seems to be far more severe than appropriate. I watched a father scream at his son for dropping an almost-finished ice cream cone on the ground. He did not drop it on his pants or on the back seat of the car. I'm not saying the father's anger would have been appropriate if the child wasted the treat or made a mess of himself or the car. The fact that nothing of the sort occurred only heightened the absurdity of the father's intense storm. It almost appeared that his anger was simply waiting for a gate to open so that the penned-up bull could come crashing out of the stall and inflict wounds on the first who dared stand in its way.

Disproportionate anger is a fight waiting to happen. In that sense, it is not anger that stimulates constructive action toward a reasonable goal; it is merely the desire to find relief for some inner turbulence that is not quieted without a sacrifice of one's own or another person's blood.

Disproportionate anger is almost always a hot anger. It comes quickly and fades as rapidly. It seems to burn itself out after expression and then returns to a normal, pleasant interaction within a few minutes. The fool seems legitimately surprised that anyone would be hurt or upset by the furious display. Whatever was said or done was necessary to resolve the problem. Those who turn furious anger on themselves are equally convinced that stability and hope for change would be entirely lost if failure were not handled with viciousness. In that case, the rage is not interpreted as extreme, but as minor compared to what is deserved. Disproportionate anger is intense, but it is also impulsive.

Impulsive Anger

The fool lacks self-control and is reckless (Proverbs 12:23, 14:16, 20:3, 29:20). Not only is the fool a thunderous storm, but the storm is also one that can develop suddenly out of a clear, sunny day. Most people find such storm fronts utterly intimidating, to a point that they are too frightened to wander out in the open terrain, not knowing when and if lightning will strike.

An acquaintance of ours is easily hurt. She is pleasant and obsequious, but without notice or, at times, even without context, she will withdraw into an angry, blue funk. She is not an obviously angry woman, but her funk is experienced by others as dangerous and radioactive. There is an ongoing uncertainty whether she is going to implode and collapse, or explode and destroy. Repeated efforts to draw her out only seem to intensify her loneliness and hurt. The depth of her pain is matched only by her destructive self-hatred. Both alternate in intensity until she seems to spiral into a chasm of despair. It is easy to expend immense energy trying to keep her from misinterpreting an interaction and tumbling into a fit.

Impulsivity is a means of acting without bearing responsibility for an act. We seem to live with the presumption that if we did not do something with calculating intentionality, then we cannot be held as responsible. Impulsivity is a decoy, a cover-up of the deeper commitment to find satisfaction, irrespective of the consequences to self or others. Impulsivity is seldom a one-shot experience. Oddly, the activity of erratic, unpredictable, rash behavior is a pattern that can be predicted over time like clockwork. The fool regularly repeats his folly.

Repetitive Anger

The classic proverb establishes a key element in the personality of the fool: "As a dog returns to its vomit, so a fool repeats his folly" (Proverbs 26:11). It is a disgusting simile. A fool falls on his knees to lap up the vile substance of his foolishness and does so again and again. A fool compulsively returns to what has worked to keep shame and loneliness at a distance.

Anger is effective in keeping people at bay and the inner ache subdued. Anger is used to intimidate ("Stay away, I don't want you close enough to see me and provoke shame"). It is also used to demand ("Don't go too far away, I don't want you to leave me and provoke loneliness"). Anger, like a thick wall, keeps alien, unwanted inner realities outside awareness. The fool uses anger to demand that nothing inhibits him from being on the center stage of life. His rage is utterly self-centered.

SELF-CENTEREDNESS: A FLIGHT FROM BROKENNESS

Both evil and foolishness want to avoid the experience of shame, but an evil heart is harder and more impenetrable. Unlike the evil person who deflects exposure so that it is nearly impossible to develop conviction about sin, the fool is not entirely hardened to exposure.

The fool normally uses arrogant pride as a shield against the shame provoked by exposure. Arrogant pride can swell to a ridiculous grandiosity and spill over to distorted paranoia, but at core, it is an intense self-centeredness. The more the fool attempts to steal fire from the gods, the more freedom he seems to enjoy from the ill effects of shame. Consequently, the fool uses self-centered arrogance to hide his enormous fragility.

Pride can be defined as self-sufficiency. It is the assumption of completeness that allows no other to add to or take away from the obviously empty heart. The heart of the fool is empty, but it feels full because it finds satisfaction in the transitory and material world. When the fool says, "There is no God" (Psalms 14:1, 53:1), he is not saying that God does not exist, but that God does not matter. What does matter is what he can lay his hands on to fill his soul.

In arrogance, the fool says to himself, "You have plenty of good things laid up for many years. Take life easy; eat, drink and be merry" (Luke 12:19). Arrogance believes that life is manageable and under our ultimate control. The Lord says, "You fool! This very night your life will be demanded from you. Then who will get what you have prepared for yourself?" (verse 20). The passage indicates that a fool's self-sufficiency is easily satisfied and morally and pragmatically stupid.

Easily Satisfied
A fool is insatiable but easily pleased. The sentence may appear to be contradictory, but there is an odd logic to the point. A fool lives to fill his belly, but the only true fullness comes from humble dependence on the mercy of God. The fool sees God as an interloper who meddles in the rightful business of life. Consequently, the fool either ignores God or compartmentalizes God and then sanitizes Him to be as he desires. Dealing with God in this way leaves an untouched emptiness in the fool's heart that can never be filled as long as he lives in rebellion. The fool will always be insatiable, always looking for more to fill the emptiness, and even more, to numb the awareness of his hatred of God.

Yet the choice to ignore God makes temporary satisfaction much more fulfilling. I have always been amazed that fools seem to be happier than those who are wise. One reason is that the fool has options available for happiness that those who seek wisdom know will only deepen shame and sorrow, and will harm those they love. At times, I am less than thrilled with the options of holiness. I'd prefer a denial-based, hedonistic holiday like Mardi Gras to the pew-sitting solemnity of a Christmas Eve children's pageant. The fool can sate his appetite on folly without bearing much of an inner battle of shame. I am sad to say that at times I envy him, until I see his demise (Psalm 73).

What seems to thrill the soul of the fool more than drugs, sex, food, or any other quick-filling addiction is the sound of his own voice. I have met recovering alcoholics, sexaholics, bulimics, Christians of all stripes, pastors, counselors, Indian chiefs, and CEOs who were transported by the sound of their own intoxicating babble. They were no longer as enslaved by their primary addiction, but they were still addicted to the presumption that they had the steps to life and the knowhow to lead everyone to the new Promised Land. Nothing is more difficult to bear than a bore or a person who "delights in airing his own opinions" (Proverbs 18:2). The fool thinks he's right in everything he does (Proverbs 12:15), whether it's interpreting a Bible passage or operating a sewing machine. The fool is easily filled, especially with his own grandiosity, but he is blind to the consequences of his direction in life.

Morally and Pragmatically Stupid

The fool may be brilliant in his chosen field or in academic pursuits, but he is a jackass in life. In fact, it is a slur to donkeys to be compared to a fool. The fool may be a follower of the gurus of positive self-talk or a devotee of the most recent cure for the ills of the soul, but he always believes something can be gained in this life that will make the sorrow of sin and the tragedy of the Fall pale in significance.

The fool believes there is an answer to the emptiness that only heaven can fill. Consequently, he will give his heart to whatever activity or substance seems to provide relief from the dull internal ache. He will not question the wisdom or power of positive thinking ("Things will work out and life will be happy because I have all that I need to survive loss and disappointment"). The fool seems to be an expert at calculating gain, but is unable to look deeply at the inevitability of loss.

The fool is so self-centered and self-reliant that he is deaf, dumb, and blind to the consequences of his choices.

He will follow a path that seems to be right, even when the blacktop gives way to gravel and gravel to dirt and dirt to rocks and debris. Almost nothing will stop the fool from plunging ahead into peril. I spoke to one woman who was ruining her marriage by demanding that her quiet and meek husband pursue counseling. Her evaluation of the marriage problems was precise and accurate, and her desire for a deep and intimate relationship with him was legitimate. Her heart toward him, however, was full of foolish anger. She regularly chided him and then erupted in seismic tears and vicious self-reproach. Later she apologized, but her pattern of rage, self-reproach, and apology occurred again and again.

Few of her friends would ever call her a fool. She was not boastful or obviously opinionated, but she was resistant to change and unswervingly believed the emptiness in her marriage was essentially the result of her husband's refusal to go for counseling. Her complaints about him may have been valid, but she did not wisely and tenaciously interact with him in a way that could have provoked change.

As more evidence of her foolishness was exposed, she simply became more committed to finding a cure through self-help books, seminars, advice from friends, counseling, and recovery groups. None of these resources is essentially foolish, but she pursued each with the energy of a fool, bent on satisfaction of her desire regardless of the cost or the damage done to herself or others in the process. Eventually, she found friends who agreed she should divorce her weak husband, and she found new and revitalized freedom to do her own will. Fools hate the pain of discipline and the inherent fear involved in growing in wisdom and knowledge.

HATRED OF DISCIPLINE AND WISDOM: A FLIGHT FROM BEAUTY

A fool despises the cost of growth. A fool demands quick relief, and if it is not forthcoming, he will rant and rave until someone offers a counterfeit solution. Growth invariably involves fear and trembling (Philippians 2:12) and suffering and death

(Hebrews 2:10, 5:8-9; 1 Peter 4:1-3). The fool seeks pleasure instead of redemptive pain, and proud indulgence rather than the trembling terror of knowledge.

A person who is evil despises truth and all humanness because God infuses every cell of humanity with His goodness. Evil hates God and delights in destroying God through violating His image in personkind. The fool, on the other hand, does not hate beauty and truth at the same level. He will often enjoy beauty and seek truth, up to the point that it exposes his hubris. While the evil person hates anything that is human and reflects the beauty and glory of God, the fool hates anything that exposes the ugliness of his heart. Consequently, the fool is repelled by the process of honestly facing his life and embracing the pain that produces lasting beauty.

Hatred of Discipline
Discipline is painful, so the fool hates it (Proverbs 15:5). Whether we are talking about the discipline of a good father (Hebrews 12:5-11) or the discipline required to master the violin, a tennis stroke, or surgical procedures, there is a cost that is difficult. I am reminded of that as I put down a second Hershey's chocolate kiss. I just ate one and I want another, but I also want to lose weight and I am at war over a delicious little morsel of fat. Discipline involves loss and emptiness, whereas the fool is committed to pleasure and fullness.

Discipline is personal engagement with thorns and thistles that moves to subdue the unruly chaos of the Fall. Self-control or discipline embraces the reality that the first time I put my lips to the flute I will not hear the melodic and lithe melody of Bach. Discipline is a battle against the effects of the Fall, where beautiful notes are not easily coaxed out of an instrument, nor where thorns and thistles eagerly give themselves over to being pulled out of the ground. Discipline is a form of warfare that wrestles with a world that is not Eden, without succumbing to the pointlessness of pulling weeds today that will be back tomorrow. It is right for me to work to push back the Fall, even though I will see little fruit in the years I may be allotted.

A fool wants to find a way around the Fall and the discipline required to slog through the waist-deep mire of sin. The sorrow of reality is too much to bear; the rage against evil is too great a passion to feel. The fool would rather turn his eyes away from reality and indulge them in pleasure. Every time I come home from work, walk into the pantry, grab a few bags of processed junk food, and engage in a fifteen-minute culinary orgy, I live out a foolish hatred of discipline. Many days I eat sensibly—until I get home and feel consumed by the desire for a break. In truth, I want more than a temporary respite; I want to abandon discipline and make an assault on heaven to give me a secular Sabbath, a rest that will last, rather than a rest that only prepares me for even more difficult labor.

Most of us retain foolish ways but are not actually fools. The fool is deeply committed to a life of disengagement that refuses to tangle with the ugly, overwhelming confusion of the world. The primary crucible the fool avoids is integrity in relationships.

Relationships require enormous struggle and passion to cultivate a crop worthy to be called tasty. We will not have healthy relationships unless we have a commitment to personal holiness. My foolish indulgence in the pantry (or any other giving of self over to rebellious satisfaction) weakens my character. It calls into question my desire and ability to grapple with the far more significant weeds in my garden. If I cannot handle my appetite, how am I going to deal with the more imposing chaos that exists in my heart and outside my door?

The fool refuses to struggle with issues of character. Rather, he gives himself over to something that provides relief without enticing him toward heaven. The fool lives for pleasure in order to hide from the decay of the world and his body. As death and loss impinge more and more, the fool must deepen his pursuit of pleasure in order to eat, drink, and laugh death away. But death will catch him mid-sentence, and without warning, his soul will be required to stand naked before an unflinching and Holy God.

All discipline invokes an intuitive sense of the entropy that waits like a vulture if we merely slow our pace down to a crawl. No wonder the fool hates discipline; it exposes his inability to ever gain unlimited and complete mastery of the world. The fool wants to believe he can win the superficial spoils of battle, and thus win the war.

Hatred of Knowledge

Knowledge is always personal and relational. Every fact we learn, imperceptibly, sometimes dramatically, affects our inner world and the universe of relationships. My six-year-old daughter, Amanda, plopped in my lap the other night and said, "Watch this. You are going to be amazed." She took out a book and began to read. She came to a sizable word and stopped. I began to help her sound it out, but she put her finger to her lips and signalled, hush. She worked her mouth around the letters, and before my eyes, she mastered another word in the English language. She had no idea what it meant, but it didn't matter. Her joy was full. She bounced into the kitchen to read the word again and again to any who would listen. She will never be the same (precisely) again.

Ultimately, all knowledge is connected to a covenantal relationship with God. I cannot truly know any fact about the created world without being drawn into a deeper relationship with the Creator whose being is interwoven in every multiplication table, zoological classification, or psychological observation, let alone in my wife. I know my wife. She is a beautiful, near forty-year-old, five-foot-six-inch, 112-pound, quiet, wild, sweet, thoroughly inexplicable lover of our Lord. I have told you a great deal about her, but I've virtually told you nothing. She is so much more rich and complex than my description. The facts I've told you do not reveal what triggers her tears or her wry wit, or how she makes me laugh when she dances. Whatever detail I describe to you adds little to your appreciation of her, but every detail I write makes me yearn to put aside this paragraph and run home to tell her how much I love her.

To ponder any fact is to be eventually drawn beyond the immediate entity to the very meaning of the universe. Any knowing will compel us to look to the unknown, unless truth is forcefully held down in unrighteousness and the beyond is allowed to be only as far as we can see. Knowledge always provokes a personal response toward what is known and demands a change in whatever would keep deeper knowledge from taking root in the soul. I cannot learn or recall knowledge about my wife and remain detached from the essence of her soul that I love and long to embrace. The same is true with knowledge of God. I cannot know about God without being changed by the One who draws me, confuses me, frightens me, intrigues me, and is utterly and completely unlike me, yet is closer to me than the sound of my beating heart. Knowledge points to God and compels change—either deepening hardness or prompting brokenness.

A possible reason for the fool's hatred of knowledge is an unwillingness to experience fear. Wisdom is gained primarily through personal disruption and pain that urges one to seek understanding of life and, ultimately, of God. Life lived honestly and humbly can be frightening because we must face that there are so many elements of it that are beyond our control. Fear is an awareness of danger, an experience of being eye to eye with something uncontrollable that is also unknown. I've talked to many cancer patients who said their most difficult time was not hearing the bad news, but the period between taking the diagnostic tests and the disclosure of the results. Fear in the midst of the uncontrollable and the unknown is closer to the experience of dread—a deep, internal foreboding that is unable to find relief in any distraction. Dread is wide-eyed, stunned anticipation.

Fear describes the experience of waiting for God, unsure of what will descend, but sufficiently quieted by helplessness to know it is pointless to run or scream. The fear of God also involves something deeper than dread, and that is awe. The fear of God is wide-eyed, stunned anticipation conjoined with a Spirit-guided awareness that the One who is unknown and uncontrollable is also good. Perhaps not good in the way we might naturally envision, but good in a way that is almost more terrifying than facing annihilation.

Fear of God strips away certainty, exposes our nakedness

and puny self-centeredness, and then invites us to know Him as He has chosen to reveal Himself — as both holy and merciful. The fool despises wisdom because he must abandon his anger and bravado, and experience the shame of his helplessness. The fool must bend his knees and extend his hands to ask for mercy, knowing he deserves nothing but condemnation. "The fear of the LORD is the beginning of knowledge" (Proverbs 1:7), but the fool wants none of it because it leads to humble, broken dependence on mercy.

How are we to love an angry, arrogant, pain-denying, pleasure-seeking hater of discipline and wisdom? What kinds of good gifts might we offer to bring a fool to his knees and back into relationship that reflects the glory of God?

HOW TO LOVE A FOOL

A fool is probably more difficult to love than a person who is evil. An evil person may be difficult to recognize because he is crafty, but once understood, he can be followed like a snake in the grass. A fool is easier to see, but is more difficult to interact with because he is not sufficiently evil to excommunicate, nor sufficiently broken to hope for change. The fool seems to be both perilously close to hardness and frustratingly close to repentance. The fool may live in this twilight zone for years, and the tension of dealing with him can be overwhelming.

Let me illustrate the difficulty of loving a foolish person who has some desire to repent, before tackling the topic of dealing with one who has a foolish heart. A friend told me about an eruption between her and her husband when he got lost in a large city during their family's vacation. She made the almost incomprehensible, wicked error of suggesting that her husband ask for directions. He began screaming at her, "I can't do everything! Why don't you go do something helpful instead of giving me stupid advice?!" His verbal assault did not stop there. His face puffed up like a blowfish, and his fists shook at the wheel. Rather than back down and cower under his scandalous diatribe, she told him, "I will get out and ask where we are. But I am taking the kids with me because you are being irresponsible and wicked. I hope you deal with whatever is provoking your viciousness."

After she and the kids got out of the car, her husband sat at the wheel and fumed. After many minutes, his fury turned to shame and then to sadness. He told me later, "I was overwhelmed with sorrow. I knew I ruined a perfectly good time and there was no way to cover it over and pretend it didn't occur or that I could make it up to them. I knew I was responsible for the whole family's hurt and confusion. I went to find them and apologized. We sat on a small curb outside a large office building, and I told each person what I did wrong and why I wanted them to forgive me. My wife and I spent a long night praying and talking about what my anger has done to her in the past. It was awful and wonderful."

This man behaved foolishly, but he is not a fool. He certainly qualified as a fool during the explosion, but his heart was truly grieved and full of sorrow over his harm. He humbled himself in the moment and hours after the failure and took responsibility to deal with the consequences.

A person with a foolish heart would have handled this painful event quite differently. A fool will not bow to feedback; it will only intensify his rage. He will find some way to avoid being humbled and shamed by putting the blame back on the victim. He may cap off such an event by demanding sex that night, secretly going out to buy a pornographic magazine, bingeing on food, drinking too much alcohol, or furiously reading his Bible. As he tries to push down the shame of violating a relationship, he will need more rage or another shot of pleasure to quell the inner hemorrhage. Once the event is passed, he'll expect everyone else to forgive and forget and let bygones be bygones.

For many married to a fool, the kind of event described happens several times a day, year in and year out. The fool turns almost every event into an occasion for more damage. He seems like a rampaging torrent of water that never stops its destructive descent. If a person's heart has not hardened to such an extent, the damage he causes during foolish episodes can be used to deepen his heart's wonder over grace and expose even deeper patterns of sin that will be dealt with over time. The fool, on the other hand, does not seem to change over time. Therefore, loving him cannot consist of "forgiving" his angry episodes because "that's just the way he is." Loving a fool is difficult.

Loving a fool can be difficult beyond words, but it can yield the fruit of righteousness. What is involved? A fool's folly must be exposed, consequences experienced, and the failure of love discussed and worked through toward repentance.

Exposing Folly

Proverbs tells us, "Do not answer a fool according to his folly, lest you be like him. Answer a fool as his folly deserves, lest he be wise in his own eyes" (Proverbs 26:5, NASB). In other words, don't be naive. We are called to use the highest degree of wisdom in knowing whether to rebuke or to remain silent. In either case, we are to mirror back to the fool a response that allows him to see the reality of his foolishness, without standing in the way of his wrath (folly). Strong and loving interactions with a fool will not be lightly or warmly received; therefore, we must prepare for his assault by getting out of his way.

What does it mean to get out of the way of a fool's folly? *The essence of love is not foolhardy sacrifice, but judicious, well-planned disruption.* The fool must be caught so far out in the open, so obviously violating the relationship, that he is forced to take a momentary break in his strategy in order to pull up his pants after the exposure. Exposure involves forethought, planning, and acceptance of the likely loss of relationship that might be temporary or, sadly, long-term.

One woman I know used to endure her husband's rude and abusive humor at social gatherings. After much reflection and thought, she decided to wage a war of love against him. One night at a party, he was on a roll with degrading remarks about women. She finally spoke to the group of men standing around him. She looked in the eyes of one man who had two daughters and said, "John, if your daughters were here, would you put up with his rude and unkind remarks?" The whole group grew somber and tense. Her husband was furious, but for a moment quiet. She looked in his eyes and said, "I think you at least owe an apology to the men who have daughters, who ought to be offended, and if they are not, are as boorish as you." She had not been harsh, although she spoke with great strength and conviction. He was mortified, and the men who had quietly acquiesced to his foolish machinations were equally silent.

She had known for some time that his foolishness and hateful critiques of women surfaced most often in social settings, so she had been prepared to launch her attack of bold love at the party. She had also made prior arrangements for another way home if she should need it and had a plan to deal with his rage if he chose to come home that night. She was aware her "betrayal" would be the beginning of the end. It would either lead to increased rage and shaming abuse or to a reformulation of their relationship where he was invited to deal with his extreme harm. The fool cannot be required to offer love, nor to repent, but he can be made to feel the piercing exposure of shame when his heart-crushing arrogance bears down on those in his way. Getting out of the way of foolish wrath involves insightful preparation, clear boundaries, and courageous consequences.

Let me give another example. One foolish husband used to go on binges of shaming behavior in which he would verbally abuse his wife and children for hours. He would then retreat into a severe depression that usually lifted only after his exhausted wife coaxed him back into the family circle. For several hours, he would excoriate himself for being such a terrible man. If anyone in the family slightly agreed with him, he would retreat to a blue funk or return to self-pitying attacks of his wife. His family learned over time to endure his protestations of guilt as the last major phase before things returned to a shaky calm. The calm would last for a few days and then some unseen shift would occur that started the shaming cycle over again. His family acted like well-orchestrated backup vocalists for his front-stage shenanigans.

Finally, after many such episodes, his wife sought

counseling and began to see how misled she was in her understanding of biblical submission. Submission is not a straitjacket of mindless obedience; it is the freedom to serve the deepest needs of the other with all that we are. She really wanted to love her husband, so she was willing to enter the significant battle to own her responsibility in keeping the maddening cycle of shame alive. She began to change.

Her husband met her changes with constant threats that he would divorce her. In order to love him, she had to be prepared to support her children financially. She set boundaries and continued to limit his ability to do terrible harm. But she put off major confrontations until she could renew her teaching certificate. During that time, a portion of her inheritance came to her, and she consulted with a lawyer in order to keep the money separate from their joint income. Everything she did was intended to foil his efforts to win the sick battle by keeping her under his control. She was neither detached from the pain in her family nor vulnerable to his shaming abuse. Like a good matador, she put out a red flag, but turned her heels whenever he kicked up dirt and ran to gore her.

An excellent biblical example of getting out of a fool's way is the prophet Nathan, who used great wisdom to expose David's foolish course. The Lord Jesus Himself, however, was the master tactician of exposure. Two situations in particular reveal the way in which the Lord handled foolishness with redemptive wisdom and strength—one with the rich young ruler (Luke 18:18-25) and the other with the Samaritan woman at the well (John 4:1-30). In neither case did the Lord get pulled into the quicksand of arrogant presumption or shame-based defensiveness.

The rich young ruler came to the Lord for a few finishing points on how to be righteous. He was sincere and good-intentioned, but diseased with the fatal flaws of arrogance and greed. He asked the Lord, "Good teacher, what must I do to inherit eternal life?" (Luke 18:18). A normal, kind response to his question would have affirmed his sincerity, but missed his disease. Instead, the Lord challenged his understanding of the word *good* in order to expose what he really desired—

affirmation or radical change. In one brief interaction, Jesus dismantled the rich man's presumption that he knew what pleased God.

At Jacob's well, the Lord met a Samaritan outcast who was likely unwelcome at the well during the normal hours when the other women of the city came to draw water. The implication is that she was a whore, hated by the women and used by the men. The Lord engaged her in conversation. The cultural weight of this fact alone is overwhelming. First, she was a woman. Men in that day did not speak directly to strange women. She was also a Samaritan. Jews did not converse with this mongrel, religiously heterodox people. And she was a whore. She certainly did not possess the kind of attractive résumé that might encourage the normal religious leader to engage her in conversation. But Jesus not only talked with her, He pulled her into a lengthy, convoluted debate.

She attempted to ward Him off by pointing out His inappropriate behavior in talking to her (John 4:9), His inability to draw water (verse 11), and His apparent arrogance (verse 12). In each case, He did not get embroiled in her defensive maneuver, but continued to deepen her curiosity and hunger for what she knew she did not possess — life-satisfying refreshment. The Lord told her to go get her husband and thus deftly exposed her immorality. She countered by trying to get Him into a religious argument that would have provoked most Jews to rise up in anger and indignation and condemn her. The Lord instead exposed her shame, thirst, and efforts to flee from her sin and gave her the opportunity to worship the Messiah in spirit and truth. He took the data of the moment and used it to expose the heart of the woman, rather than merely condemn her behavior and exhort change. What are we to learn from His style of exposing a fool?

Exposing What Is Obvious

The fool is almost always angry or on the border of being angry. The anger may be directed toward self or others. In either case, it will be both obvious and unchangeable through reason, encouragement, and/or rebuke. All these efforts will either increase the rage or, worse, invite the fool to pour more venom on the one who tries to "help." What is required is a mirror that reflects the behavior and the apparent goal of intimidation or control. For instance, "Honey, right now your voice is loud and violent, and your words are rude. It seems clear you want us all to bow to your demand for power." Or, "John, your fury toward yourself is rather clear as you mutter words of despair and self-harm. If you want to talk, please ask, rather than setting me up to try to make this problem go away." The purpose of the exposure is to surface the rage as an issue, rather than flee from the anger as too intimidating.

Staying involved (with full intention of stepping out of the path of a charging bull) requires enormous courage. Obviously a calm, rational response to rage, such as the ones I mentioned above, is not devoid of ambivalence and passion. The person who stands up against intimidation may feel like her insides are crumbling or her own fury in the face of injustice is close to exploding. But something deeper than her own fear and rage compels her to enter the battle with strategic calm that is passionate with purpose. Just as a parent whose child's leg is gushing blood must shift into a crisis mode that takes her above the temptation to panic or faint if she is ever to get the child to the hospital, so a person who loves another whose soul is gushing sin must keep her head in battle if she is to be a catalyst for healing.

Expose with a mood that is matter-of-fact, strong, and benevolent. Such a mood is like passing a red cape before an enraged bull; it will incite and intensify the fury. When we "set up" the fool for further exposure, as the Lord did with the rich young ruler and the woman at the well, we set ourselves up for attack. We need to be prepared to move out of the way with a light step. This is the most difficult principle to describe because it requires such freedom of heart to operate with spontaneity, humor, and power.

One woman was often attacked by her husband for mismanagement of their finances. She was, at times, irresponsible with the checkbook, but her failure was no excuse for his violent temper and shaming assaults. The summation of many of his tirades was, unbelievably, a recitation of her inadequacies as a sexual partner. He often finished his assault with the statement, "I don't know why I married you. Your breasts are so small that even I am bigger than you." For years, she succumbed to his attacks and felt terrible shame.

Finally, after looking at her own hidden rage for herself and for him, she began to see his foolishness as a deep rejection of his maleness and a refusal to deal with his own emptiness and shame. She also saw her silence as a terrible failure of love. One night, in the midst of a terrible scene, the fool returned to his own vomit and went through the same litany. She looked him in the eye and said, "You know, sweetheart, you are right. I'm afraid your breasts are larger than mine. Honey, if you don't start a diet, we may end up getting you a bra for Christmas." She walked away, giggling internally and rejoicing in the Lord for empowering her wit and words, but full of sadness for her foolish husband.

Wise preparation will also include the "next step." She must be prepared for a whole new round of assaults. Will she (1) listen, (2) argue, (3) ignore his tirade, (4) go to another room, (5) leave the house, (6) go shopping, or (7) ask a friend to pray? Her choice must be consistent with the overall goal of offering the fool both tenderness (the merciful opportunity to repent and be reconciled) and strength (an unwavering commitment not to succumb to shame or intimidation).

Expose with an emphasis on the freedom of choice. The Lord left the rich young ruler with the offer to sell all that he owned and follow Him. He gave the woman at the well the opportunity to drink from water that would never leave her thirsty. Each of the ones He loved had to struggle with the awesome, awful battle of freedom. What do I want? What do I really want to do with this moment? My life? On one level, the fool hates with a passion anyone who attempts to take away his freedom, but despises even more anyone who puts him in a position to choose.

Exposure must leave the fool alone to wrestle with God. Its goal is to intensify the battle between the options of continuing in foolishness or facing his naked, shameful, hateful arrogance. This will likely not occur without the presentation of direct and indirect choice. Indirect choice occurs whenever the fool's intimidation does not work. It forces him to intensify his efforts or face the pettiness of his fury. Direct choice comes when the victim says, "Deal with your rage. I will no longer bear it or take responsibility for it," then leaves the fool on the stage of his arrogance with an audience of one—God. Exposure must be eventually followed, in other words, with consequences.

ENFORCING CONSEQUENCES

A second good gift for the fool is a taste of his own medicine, but one that is embellished by the paradoxical spice of both mercy and justice. As with the evil person, the consequence must have a measure of tenderness and strength that touches both the realities of dignity and depravity. The goal is to surprise and shame the fool but leave a wide-open door for restoration. What might that look like?

Consequences Should Confuse

Since the exposure of a fool's rage will likely intensify his commitment to shore up his fragile grandiosity, it is important to block his usual path back to control. One woman used to go through an orgy of self-hatred that compelled her husband to hover about her with solicitous concern. Years of therapy did little to break her foolishness. She seemed bound to shame and self-contempt. Her husband was exasperated and confused. After much failure, he stopped trying to help her, and her fury turned on him.

The energy of self-hatred and other-centered hatred swirled like tumultuous rapids. He anguished over what to do. Any conversation with her always focused on his failures, which he acknowledged were many. He was far from being the man of God he desired to be, but he was growing in strength and wisdom. During her most severe expressions of rage, he told her that he would only talk with her if there was some willingness to deal with both sides of the problem. She refused. After all, she had no responsibility for their problems; her anger was his fault.

The only remedy seemed to be detachment from her "disease," yet he intuitively felt that to shut down his heart was wrong as well. After much thought, he decided to pray whenever she went into a paroxysm of contempt. He got down on his knees in another room, and often tears streamed down his face like quiet rivers of passion. When she barged into the room where he was praying, her fury would intensify and she would berate him for his sanctimonious and self-righteous spirituality. He could not refute her attack. He agreed there was so much hypocrisy in his heart that it was near pointless for him to pray, but he continued to marvel over the grace that invited a heart as sinful as his to enter the glory of the presence of God. He bore her slap and offered his face to be hit again and again, yet he unswervingly refused to hover over her as he once did. Day in and day out she had to face a man strong enough to neither threaten nor revile, and tender enough to weep over sin.

Consequences that surprise the fool must violate what he anticipates. What is your normal response to his intimidation, shame, and hatred? Whatever you normally do, ask yourself if it is full of humor, wit, passion, sorrow, strength, and tenderness. If it lacks freedom and passion, then I would guess that whatever you do is as desirable as flat cola — it lacks fizz. Remember, this is a war. Preparation includes constructing scenarios where you practice the kinds of interactions you expect from the fool.

Do you suppose comedians just get on stage and tell jokes? Or do they hone their skills for years in small clubs and private gatherings before stepping into the limelight? It is never appropriate to excuse your failures to love boldly with the statement, "I just never think of what to say in the moment." If you can think of what you want to say later, then you can learn, over time, to gain the courage to say it in the moment.

Consequences Should Inflict Suffering

A fool will not repent unless he feels pain. The notion that a fool can be won by just "loving" him (defined as ignoring his harm, giving in to his desires, and being nice) is, in itself, foolish. Consequences must have a bite.

Consequences will, unfortunately, often involve elements of taking revenge now. No applied consequence will be so pure and perfect that it avoids the stains of fear and hatred. But if we wait for perfect motivation, love will be set aside until heaven. The key to differentiating between loving consequences and ungodly revenge is the degree to which restoration is desired. If one is somewhere on the continuum between demanding desperation, distant detachment, and disdainful disgust, then any boundary setting or application of consequences will be seeking revenge now. The person who desires reconciliation, on the other hand, may certainly struggle with ambivalence, but it will not propel him toward revenge. He may honestly hate his enemy's sin and the pain and difficulty of loving boldly, but the thrill of moving into another's life with divine purpose will be his deepest motivator.

Wisely applying consequences is an art and a science. Sometimes kindness, properly applied at the right moment and in the correct place, can be like salt in a wound. On the other hand, there are times when kindness must give way to indirect and direct force. Indirect consequences are often called natural consequences. The fool often expects his world to snap to attention when he wants a glass of water or does not want to answer a phone call. A natural consequence would be to not get up to answer the phone, but just let it ring — or let the checkbook go unbalanced until the fool bears the responsibility of a bounced check.

So many questions remain that need to be wrestled with. Should you get your own checkbook or credit cards in order to let the fool bear his consequences alone? Or should you go down in solidarity with the fool? Should you get out of the car and ask for directions, or stay and let him fume and flame in his blowfish rage? I simply cannot tell you. But keep in mind that the goal is to offer consequences that bear the slap without succumbing to either fear or hatred.

A direct consequence is often called a logical consequence. It is not merely letting the fool bear the natural effects of his harm; it is application of an external force that is fitting for the offense. For example, I cannot conceive of any situation where it is loving to let a fool physically beat you. I believe it is imperative for a violent fool to be held accountable before legal authorities for his crime. There should never be a warning or a "next time." Physical abuse must be prosecuted, and the sentence should include joining a therapy group for violent offenders.

Similarly, it is potentially life threatening in our day to overlook an unfaithful spouse. Adultery or any form of sexual immorality should be viewed as a serious breaking of the covenant of marriage. I would not argue that once immorality has been committed there is no hope for reconciliation, but the deceit and foolishness involved in order for immorality to occur are rarely recovered from without radical change. Few adulterers want to do much more than patch a leaky boat.

Often my work with an immoral spouse is hindered by the other mate who is either so enraged that I cannot get to the issues in the fool because of the noise in the environment, or so "forgiving" that the insipid foolishness momentarily quiets down in the glowing hope of getting things back to normal. I believe an adulterer should be under the careful and passionate eyes of a mature group of believers and involved with a therapist who is as keenly aware of the horrors of depravity as he is of the wonders of dignity. Rarely will this happen unless the wounded spouse is willing to seriously consider and plan for separation and divorce, if real change does not occur.

In the same way, an alcoholic, a sexual abuser, or a criminal should never be endured as simply a nuisance or a shameful secret that needs to be hidden. There are too many treatment centers and therapists who are capable of providing excellent care for a spouse or friend to feel helpless and alone. At some point, the logical consequence will be some form of intervention, in which the family, friends, or church will need to come together to compel the alcoholic to seek help, with logical consequences of such an unpleasant nature that breaking the addiction really is preferable to remaining in denial. There are many other situations which may require direct, forceful consequences, but they should all be preceded and followed by surprisingly merciful and indirect consequences. When the fool's pain is sufficiently high and something supernatural is working in his heart, then it is time to talk.

DISCUSSION AND WORKING
THROUGH REPENTANCE

A third good gift for the fool is a willingness to talk. But don't be naive. Repentance usually must begin with words, but talk is cheap. I don't know how to reconcile the tension. Repentance will manifest itself in words and deeds, and words usually precede action. God told His rebellious children:

> Take words with you
>   and return to the LORD.
> Say to him:
>   "Forgive all our sins
> and receive us graciously,
>   that we may offer the fruit of our lips.
> Assyria cannot save us;
>   we will not mount war-horses.
> We will never again say 'Our gods'
>   to what our own hands have made,
>   for in you the fatherless find compassion."
>
> "I will heal their waywardness
>   and love them freely,
>   for my anger has turned away from them."
>   (Hosea 14:2-4)

Words include an acknowledgment of our condition (sinful, downfallen, and desperate), our desire (gracious restoration), our intentions (for worship), and the absurdity of our pursuit of false protectors and gods in the light of the passionate Father heart of God. Discussions that attempt to convince the fool to be better or to do something different are almost always pointless and backfire into another skirmish of shame and intimidation. Conversation on a wide variety of topics is possible, but words that attempt to persuade, teach, exhort, or even encourage will be used against the one seeking restoration unless repentance has begun. The fool must show some signs of sadness, grief, or sorrow over sin before lengthy, penetrating, productive conversation can occur.

It is possible to live with a fool for decades before a meaningful, potentially life-changing discussion can occur. Does this mean the loving person should remain silent and ignore the fool until that day arrives? Of course not. Discussion of any issue or topic can and should occur, but a serious, heartfelt discussion of the fool's sin, damage, style of relating, and wounds ought not to precede or take the place of exposure and consequences.

In most cases, it will be the fool who initiates a discussion of his foolishness when he is paralyzed by the cumulative weight of the other's tenderness and strength. If this does not occur, the temptation to create conversations that are designed to get the fool "to see" is stronger than the most addictive drug known to humankind. The temptation must be resisted, fought, and fled from, however, or else the fool will trample over the pearls spread before his cloven feet. If and when a fool begins to feel some sadness over his sin, discussion should be poignant, penetrating, and visionary.

Acknowledging Dignity and Depravity
The power of words is immense. A word can soothe the soul or cut it to ribbons, and discussion with the fool ought to do both. When a fool acknowledges any level of responsibility or sorrow, it must not be merely accepted or quickly dismissed, but captured and underscored. Let me construct a possible dialogue that addresses both the dignity and the depravity in a fool's heart.

Assume that Kathy fits the description of a fool, and Ralph, her husband, has been the kind of man who has ignored her cruelty and given his energy to his work and children.

> KATHY: Honey, I am so sorry for how mean I've been
> to you while I've been working on this project. I hope

you're not too upset.

RALPH: Kathy, I am quite upset. Frankly, as much with me as with you. This has gone on for years, and I've failed you by ignoring it in the past. That is wrong. But I am encouraged, at least a little, by your willingness to admit that you have been mean. My question is, do you want to deal with this or are you looking for a quick absolution? If it is the latter, then I am far more upset than you can imagine.

KATHY (with slight disdain): Ralph! Do we have to get into one of these psychological discussions again?

RALPH (with a quiet strength and twinkle of a smile in spite of a sharp bolt of anguish): No, sweetheart, we don't. You are mean. In fact, you can be cruel and contemptuous. But I feel no compulsion to deal with your heart if it is that hard and cold. I trust and pray that the woman who asked me to forgive her will one day come to the surface far more. What would you like for dinner? I know you'll be busy with that project, but can I make anything in particular?

I believe Ralph's words have the potential to touch both the dignity that nudges Kathy to be the woman she is not and the depravity that hinders her from becoming the woman she, at some level, desires to be. Words of truth must not lack love, and words of tenderness must not be devoid of strength.

Opening the Door to the Wounds of the Past

Many fools have experienced profoundly disturbing, abusive pasts. The vast majority have likely been emotionally, physically, and/or sexually abused. The label "fool" is not a slur, a pejorative term that is meant to slip off the tongue with contempt. While it is wrong to deny their wickedness, it is equally wrong to ignore the reality of their past wounds.

If the fool is willing to talk, to open his heart to facing the issues of damage, then it is highly legitimate to open the discussion to the issue of what has led him to choose such a foolish path. The fool is not merely a victim whose painful past has forced him to inflict damage in the present, but he has likely been affected by the damage of past abuse.

Many times, the issue of the shaping events of the past will be best thought through with a trusted confidant — pastor, counselor, mentor — before it is discussed in depth with family or friends. One clue that reveals a fool's willingness to change is an openness to confess his sin to a trusted other and then to seek the kind of help that will enable him to grow in wisdom, discipline, and brokenness.

Envisioning Change

Discussion with the fool will also include prayer. Prayer is more than merely asking for help; it is the catalyst for change. Growth involves wrestling with God, laboring to put into words the realities both in us and outside us that we want Him to destroy and rebuild. The fool must be willing to struggle with God in prayer and with others who pray with him, asking God to destroy the strongholds of arrogance and unbelief that deter his growth in love.

Prayer is a context to ask for what we desire and listen for what He offers. It is the place to be stirred and silenced, broken and uplifted. Discussion and prayer must focus on what the fool's heart deeply desires. If his goals involve increasing pressure on those around him or demanding change in the circumstances that "make" him angry and selfish, then you know the fool is working his game. True repentance will lead to feelings of indignity and anger at the past damage, a desire to make restitution, and a renewed longing for purity and godliness (2 Corinthians 7:11).

Productive discussion will eventually open the door to spurring one another to love and good deeds. When this occurs, one knows the fool has fallen under the piercing arrow of repentance. Then, and only then, can a new intimacy come alive, impassioned by the hope of heaven.

CHAPTER TWELVE

LOVING A NORMAL SINNER:
Athletic Competition

❖

I am thankful that I am not required to dine daily with evil people or fools. It is clearly possible to go to war against them and do more than survive, but the daily grind of fighting against the assaults of shame, rage, and hatred is trying, even for the best-prepared and most-noble warrior. No one can escape dealing with evil people and fools in families, institutions, even Christian ministries, but it is a tragedy when one must do so often and across many different levels of relationships.

A friend of mine works for a religious organization that is run by very foolish folks. She works for arrogant men and women who vie for power and cut each other's throats as they frenetically work to preserve their turf and budget allocations. The veneer is pristine and placid, but the inside is full of dead men's bones. Unfortunately, she must deal with evil in her family as well. Her father severely abused her as a child and adolescent in every manner conceivable. He continues to deny any past abuse and is vindictive and verbally abusive. She was living with an extremely foolish roommate who punished her with coldness one minute and begged for more involvement the next. She was also in a dating relationship with a man who avoided commitment for two years, moving in and out of intimacy more times than she can count. For years, she lived the life of a self-hating fool who endured the abuse of others because it was the best that seemed available.

Years ago, she would have said that her destructive pattern of falling into abusive relationships was due to fear and insecurity, and to a degree, that was true. But over time, she found it also involved a stubborn commitment to find a few scraps of pleasure, no matter what the cost, in order to shut her heart to the pain involved in true change. She is repenting; change is freeing her to see and begin the process of dealing with her tragic relationships. One thing she has done is to pare down the number of fools and evil people she deals with in a normal day. She got a new roommate. She has largely cut off contact with her father and family. She gave her inconsistent Romeo the boot. And she is biding her time to find a better paying and less foolish environment to live out her calling.

After this significant change in her relationships, my friend said one day, "I've cut off involvement with many evil and foolish people after giving them the opportunity to deal with their damage, but as I relate to regular-type folks, I've found the battle is not over. In fact, it seems like it's just beginning." She is absolutely correct. A normal sinner may be easier to deal with than an evil person or a fool, but the battle is still real. There are enormous challenges in loving what the proverbs call a simpleton.

Normal sinners are people who are still capable of evil, and at times, indistinguishable from fools. Normal sinners include decent human beings who have rarely thought about the realities of living in a fallen world. They may be largely oblivious to the damage done to them and/or blind to the damage they do to others. Oblivious and blind people live precariously between foolishness and wisdom. They are not full-fledged fools, but over time, they may slide toward hardness and arrogance or become more deeply entrenched in denial, to be washed away when the storms of life descend.

Normal sinners also include those who struggle to comprehend what it means to live with wisdom in the face of the mysteries and confusion of life. They are not quite as blind as true simpletons, but because they are human beings, they do not consistently practice wisdom and are more likely than not to display the characteristics of a simpleton.

CHARACTERISTICS OF A NORMAL SINNER

The biggest struggles of a normal sinner are with envy, naivete, and poor judgment. The simpleton seems to lack the ability to see danger and make sound, wise decisions to avoid it. They seem to wander naively toward the precipice of terrible harm, but never quite choose the direction of foolishness or, on the other hand, prudence and wisdom. Simpletons are fence-sitters, but they have an openness to rebuke and wisdom that augurs well for them, if they are warned early enough to avoid the way that seems right but leads to destruction.

Envy

The simpleton is almost always inclined to judge the greenness of the next hill as more desirable than the color of the one he currently sits upon. What another person possesses is imagined as both desired and deserved. The desire is infused with naive hope that overtaking the next hill will settle all internal restlessness and dispel the internal ache.

I am amazed how often I still look forward to vacations or time off with an energy that borders on obsessive. Many times, anticipation draws me through difficult events with the thought, *Well, in a few weeks you'll be skiing, so keep breathing and make the best of this encounter.* There is nothing inherently wrong with looking forward to the enjoyments of life, but sometimes we simply do not look forward far enough to what will truly provide rest and joy.

Envy is fueled by the energy not only of short-sighted longing, but also of demandingness: "What I want, I deserve, because nothing is more important than the satisfaction of my desires." Envy seems to be one of the major causes of conflict and disorder in relationships (James 3:16, 4:1-3).

The evil person escapes the inner world of sorrow and longing by giving himself over to a cold, heartless violation of others. The fool is less effective in blocking out the internal war, therefore translating almost all pain, disappointment, and shame into anger. The simple usually do not succumb to cold violation or hot anger, but instead, pine after what they do not have and envy those who do. Sadly, envy comes so close to the hunger for something more—for a joy that is beyond our current struggle—but it stops short, settling on the here-and-now and the trivial rather than on the eternal.

The simple one feels more emptiness and desire, so consequently, is more human and involved. He has a greater capacity to feel, but unfortunately, the temptation is to weep with those who rejoice and rejoice when others weep. The simple sees the possessions, privileges, or peace of the other as a necessary solace for his inner struggle. The simple wants what he does not have and focuses on whatever looks like it might assuage his inner pain. Clearly, a key issue for the simple is the struggle between desire and demand.

Desire. All of us—believers, seekers, and unbelievers— live between the Cross and the coming Restoration. Our hearts feel a deep tug to erase the tension of tasting the Spirit today as an hors d'oeuvre and wanting to dine now at the banquet table of the Lord.

At a recent gathering, a few of us reflected on what heaven might be like in terms of our culinary obsessions. It was a succulent discussion. My vision of heaven is lying on the bottom of a huge vat of moist chocolate cake and eating my way out, without caloric intake, for several thousand years. That may not move you to anything but disgust, but each of us knows an inner hunger that is not satiated by any taste of legitimate or illicit earthly pleasure. We want more. And that is utterly consistent with how God made us. Our hunger for beauty, justice, and perfection is actually a reflection of our ultimate desire—God.

A major internal battle for us is that satisfaction is not available now, although a foretaste is available through worship. Worship is an experience of wide-eyed wonder and gratitude.

Worship can be orchestrated and legitimately enjoyed in praise gatherings or church services, but it is unlikely to bring forth the eternal fruit of the Spirit unless the heart has been plowed up through suffering. Brokenness in body and soul seizes us with the reality that where we are now is not our home. It robs us of the presumption that we are the master of anything and calls us to relinquish control and rest in the mysterious goodness of a God who does not condemn us for our pettiness and short-sighted envy.

At face value, nothing seems more absurd. God's economy of happiness is the mirror opposite of almost every experience in life. I learned early in life that weakness is an anathema. Tell a fat, slow, awkward kid that it is an honor to be chosen last for a pick-up game of baseball. Tell him the last will be first. Try to comfort him with the wisdom that weakness is a vehicle for the grace of God to shine, and your words will, at best, be ignored and, at worse, engender deep resentment. The same may be true of many adults, perhaps most, who battle with the same inner turmoil of shame and emptiness. The desire for something or someone who will take away shame and replace the emptiness with sensuous fullness feels like a throbbing nerve that will not stop hurting until we succumb to some pleasure that serves for a moment to both fill our bellies and satiate our deeper hunger.

The simpleton looks at the pleasures of life—be it a prostitute, a new car, a self-help book, or a packaged approach to curing shame and emptiness—and says, "Maybe! Just maybe, this might do it. At least, for the moment, I may find relief." The simpleton takes the tension of unfulfilled yearning and dissipates it through demand.

Demand. The demand of the empty soul is for satisfaction now, and, if that is not available, then relief. The eyes of the simple cast about their world looking for what will either fill the emptiness or dull the ache. The simple believe someone has found the key to happiness and the key can be possessed and used for their benefit, if only they can get their hands on it.

It might be argued that the self-help mega-industry is today's "vanity fair," offering pilgrims one answer or another to ills that will be healed only in heaven. This is a sticky issue, full of acrimony, accusation, and counter-accusation. For example, is it wrong to want the dark pallor of depression to be lifted in order to live a more happy, fulfilled life? Or on a mundane level, is it inappropriate to take tennis lessons in order to play better, win more, and have more fun? I wish the issue, let alone the answer, were simple. To this day, when I walk into a bookstore and see all the opportunities (including my own book *The Wounded Heart*) to recover from every ill known to personkind, I am tempted to retreat in despair.

Theoretically, we do not have to choose one course over the other — that is, working to recover from shame and past wounds or growing in holiness and wisdom. Practically, however, shame and past wounds are more deeply felt than the tug of holiness or the horror of sin. An unreflective consumption of the "recovery" entrees seems to lead to a riveting focus on one's current situation rather than promoting a passionate desire to know and enjoy God through all eternity.

People who are confused, empty, addicted, and full of shame certainly should not avoid a journey of reflection to gain a greater grasp of their inner world. But as they do so, they should be aware that any approach or person who takes away all deep uncertainty and mystery is a sidestep away from God, if not a replacement for a relationship with Him. Any approach that sees relief of human suffering as the basis of true worship, rather than the wonder of forgiveness as the key to deep change, has neglected the real problem, what we do with God. And any approach that cheapens sacrifice and service as basically neurotic and offers a sophisticated justification for self-serving pursuit of pleasure is a violation of the true route to joy. The task of growth is to pursue an unflinching honesty about self, world, and God, no matter what the results compel us to face or give up.

Other industries, both secular and Christian, also offer their wares in equal intensity — all with the allure of curing, or at least circumventing, inevitable human struggles with loneliness and shame. The simple look over the bevy of opportunities and salivate, or look at the one walking out of the vanity mall clutching a new toy and feel envy. Envy eventually leads to absurd convictions and actions. I know people who change wardrobes yearly based on some fool(s)'s determination about what is "right" to wear. Obviously advertising works. And what is the allure? "You too can be more beautiful and powerful if you own (fill in the blank)." The more we believe any material object can take away the struggles of the soul, the closer we live to the edge of foolishness.

It is also possible to be relationally or spiritually envious. I know many who presume with a vengeance that if they were married, a certain ache would go away. Many are not so naive as to believe marriage is a cure for emptiness, yet the conviction persists that it would take away enough shame ("I've not been chosen") and loneliness ("I won't have to buy a car by myself") to make life livable. Others continue to search the Bible and Christian literature for an answer — not for the issue of sin (for which the answer is forgiveness), but for emptiness. As they read, they tend to ignore or frankly be irritated at the thought that only heaven will be enough to fill them to the brim. The simple naively believe that more effort, faith, honesty, friends, or free time will bring happiness. Therefore, their envy is directed toward those who seem to have arrived and achieved an illusive joy.

Envy leads not only to foolish decisions, but it blocks the ability to weep with those who weep and rejoice with those who rejoice. In the same way that an evil person's coldness and a fool's anger keep them from empathetic involvement with others, a simpleton's envy dulls deep concern for others because it either compels him to rejoice that he is not suffering or look with possessive desire at someone who is happy. Over time and after major decisions to sin, envy will lead to foolish resentment ("Why can't I have that?") and perhaps to evil coldness ("I will take what you have because I don't want you to be happy"). It need not progress in this direction, however. If a simpleton's envy is exposed, he may enter his emptiness and admit that his heart is stricken with a disease that only forgiveness can heal and only heaven can perfectly restore. If so, then he is on the way toward wisdom.

Naiveté

A second major characteristic of the simple, normal sinner is a naive gullibility. "A simple man believes anything, but a prudent man gives thought to his steps" (Proverbs 14:15). The simpleton closes his eyes to internal and external signs that might alert him to danger, either by limiting his perspective or focusing so narrowly on one area of interest that little other information ever enters.

The "limited" naive have their head in the sand. It is their choice to live in denial, ignoring or misinterpreting the realities of life to keep from being disturbed. Naiveté is not a genetic endowment, although with a few friends the extent of their gullibility is so great that I am, at times, inclined to believe it is. One is not born naive; it is learned as a means of tuning out unpleasant data and thus avoiding interactions with others when inconsistency or veracity might be challenged.

For example, a gullible client was told by her husband that he would be working very late for a few weeks and not to wait up for him to get home. At times, she would awaken at 2 a.m. and he would not be home. Other times, he would get home late and smell of alcohol and perfume. Once she asked him what kept him so late and why he bore the odor of sin, and he concocted a story of business deals and the need for entertaining in comfortable eating establishments where waitresses occasionally got a little too close.

I recall the look in her eyes when she said, "But the Bible tells me that 'love believes all things.' What am I to do if I don't trust him?" Her eyes were plaintive and desperate. Somewhere in her soul she knew the truth, but she wanted me to join in her denial. There are times I wonder what it would be like to be able to see the world as simply a wonderful place, where people can be believed and promises are kept—where relationships are rarely, and then only mildly, strained by sin. Denial-based naiveté is an attempt, again, to build a better world than the one in which we live, without panting desperately for the one world that will be enough.

The "focused" naive are driven, compulsive performers who serve a task or ideal so completely that it buffers them from the disturbing realities of life. The activity may be thoroughly legitimate, like ministry, skiing, or reading, but its consuming focus offers a form of detachment through a merger of the heart with an external distraction. Nothing is wrong with getting away to a mindless task like chopping wood or a highly focused enterprise like reading Wittgenstein, but when it is chosen as a means of dodging reality, rather than propelling us back into the battle, it is an attempt to create a safe, reasonably controllable world.

There is a great price for naiveté. The price is a loss of energy to pursue wisdom, a crucial skill in living. Wisdom is a keen grasp of the human condition in light of eternal truths, which enables the wise subtly to maneuver out of moral danger and unnecessary conflict and lovingly to use words to intrigue, rebuke, and draw others into a relationship with God. The naive often end up paying for their denial by attracting trouble and feeling helplessness when others attempt to control their life.

For instance, recall the woman mentioned in the previous chapter who experienced a great deal of shame when her husband humiliated her over the size of her breasts. For years, she believed him. She actually believed the beauty of her body and soul could be calibrated by a tape measure. She was a simpleton—one who naively believed that her husband was her judge. It should be of little surprise that her "case" never passed the court's approval. She was always guilty.

It took a long time to help her see the context for her gullibility and the deep-seated commitment to believe her husband's lies. She was far more than misinformed by a perverse male definition of beauty. She felt relieved that she was not "pretty." As long as she was homely, she reasoned, no one would use her or ask much from her. It was a payoff. As long as she had little to offer, then the world—and God in particular—had little reason (or right) to ask. It should come as no surprise that she suffered enormous abuse in her childhood. She was capable of being shamed and controlled because, in part, she was more than willing to let others decide what was and is true. If her hem was too short, she felt shame when it was pointed out. If her hobbies did not fit the picture of what an "ideal" Christian woman did in her free time, she dutifully followed the prescriptions of more knowledgeable "doctors."

Although her naive openness let in a great deal of illegitimate shame, it also served as the basis for significant change. Unlike an evil person, a normal sinner is able to be exposed and feel shame. And unlike a fool, the simple person does not immediately use shame as the impetus to build a wall of arrogance. The capacity to feel shame, even illegitimate shame, can be used by God to expose the hurt and the subtle hubris of the heart. Change for her came when she saw what her naivete was doing to others and herself. Even greater change occurred when she saw that her gullibility was an effort to construct a new world, because at core, she did not think much about a God who would let things go as they do.

In our counseling, shame was used as a guide to the scars of her past abuse and as a means of exposing her powerful commitment to self-protection. As long as I did not succumb to telling her what to do and left her to flounder with making decisions on her own, she grew in beauty and honor. As we explored her past hurts and her relational style, she came to grieve over her loss and, even more, over her failure to love. She was now guilty, without feeling guilt. She actually experienced the freedom of bittersweet joy.

Sadly, her marriage went to pot. It was a bittersweet sorrow for me. Her marriage, viewed as "ideal" in her Christian circles, shipwrecked on the shoals of his foolishness and the solid land of her honesty. In one sense, she went from being an abused, but naively happy, automaton to a loving, biblically ambivalent and mature woman. Naiveté may make reality appear more rose-colored, but it eventually takes away the integrity of the heart and the joy of loving. It defrauds the person of the reason and energy to look forward to heaven.

Poor Judgment
A third character flaw of the normal sinner is the propensity to wander into danger. It almost seems like the simple person is a lightning rod for trouble. "A prudent man sees danger and

takes refuge, but the simple keep going and suffer for it" (Proverbs 22:3, 27:12). In most cases, the greatest danger is in relationships. The simple person often ends up in relationships with fools and evil people. When that occurs, it is common for the normal sinner to be seduced and used. Even if the seduction and abuse is not sexual, it will often involve great loss.

An acquaintance of mine had a history of dating irresponsible women. One woman he dated had a long history of sexual conquests, and he appeared to be next on her list for a hit-and-run. I warned him, and though it was painful, he eventually broke off the relationship. Three months later, he was involved again with a smooth, sincere-talking con woman, who was trying to deal with her own history of living like a black widow. At the time I talked to him, he was struggling unsuccessfully to extricate himself from her lovely web. The history of painful relationships broke his heart. It made him lose confidence and joy in relating to women.

Intuition. The simple person seems to lack the radar to warn himself of impending personal harm. Personal radar is based on the ability to intuit, feel, and assess the patterns of behavior that make up a potentially dangerous storm front. The simple person is either unwilling or unable to use his intuition, feelings, or deductive powers to avoid potential danger. Intuition is based on a deep hunch that is garnered from imperceptible impressions. It is obviously not an infallible guide, but the data must be listened to in relating to others.

Children are often unusually gifted in listening to something that they are unaware even exists. I worked with a family who was in the midst of a traumatic, potentially marriage-ending conflict. Neither of the parents had mentioned the possibility of divorce, nor had either of them expressed to any of the children the severity of the marriage problems. For all the kids knew, they were going to talk to a "doctor." I interacted with the youngest child, age five, for a half hour. At the end of our time, she matter-of-factly asked me, "Are my parents going to divorce? They don't like each other." The older two children, ages eight and thirteen, gave no indication of any marital problems or fears of divorce. How was this child aware of the impending divorce? I am not sure. My guess would be a child's intuition based on a willingness to listen to what is inside.

Intuition involves the subtle interplay of perception and effect, but when intuition crosses into full-formed emotions, it is even harder to understand why the simple person chooses to ignore the internal data. Another acquaintance refuses to see anything really sinful in his own life. Consequently, he can only perceive hurt and insecurity in the lives of others. He has suffered through a number of work-related disasters by hiring people who have used him and harmed his business. I asked him if he ever felt anger at an employee's irresponsible behavior. He said he felt only concern and support because he wanted to be the kind of person who "believes in others." His naiveté led to poor assessments of others because he refused to feel or label his emotions accurately. If he had felt anger, he may have acted with the same concern and support, but offered more respectful limits and consequences, and thus avoided the damage done to his good name. Intuition and the feelings that come from relating to others is the fodder for the mill of deduction. The simple person seems remarkably unwilling to draw conclusions from observable data.

Deduction. For many, their intuition and capacity to draw conclusions from data may be stunted due to the risk involved in seeing reality. Deduction is the highly simple (but talking about it is anything but simple) process of forming big conclusions from small pieces of information. We do it every single day. I just looked at the weather report in the paper and it said it was going to be ninety-five degrees. My deductive processes started to whirl ("Given that my small air conditioner does not do real well at that temperature, and I see only two clients today, and I have to be at work most of the day, and both clients are real laid-back Coloradans, I think I will wear shorts—nice ones, of course, given that I am a professional").

Amazingly, the little pieces of information led to a big conclusion within a millisecond. In fact, until I wrote out what I thought, I was largely unaware of the elements involved in my choice. Nevertheless, it was a simple deductive process. Again, the process—similar to intuition and emotion—may be faulty, given an inadequate grasp of the small pieces of information ("It might rain today") or in making a transfer to a conclusion ("One of my clients might be very offended by a therapist wearing shorts—and for British audiences, that is short pants"). Nevertheless, one cannot live without using deductive reasoning.

Deduction is dangerous because it is perilously close to making judgments. It is, of course, different, but the similarity often scares many Christians. It is frightening because it requires enormous courage to draw conclusions, but not cast them in concrete. A judgment is any assessment that is finalized and unchangeable. Most of us either avoid making deductive conclusions because they seem too hard and fast, or succumb to passing judgments right and left. In either case, it is a failure of courage, a refusal to face the data, sum it up the best we can and then make life-determining decisions without setting our choice in infallible, arrogant concrete. If I am going to make a decision about who to marry, I want to know I am making the "right" choice. Unfortunately, I can never know for sure. But I have ways of making assessments. I can see how she handles conflict, loneliness, shame, loss, feedback, my sin, disappointment. I can observe how she relates to a broad range of people and situations. I can interact with her heart and assess whether I want to muddle through life with her.

Trusting my intuition and making judgments takes courage because it is risky. Personally, I'd prefer the arrogance of the fool or the refusal to draw conclusions of the simple over the freedom to fail—and fail badly. Let no one assume a wise person is immune to terrible bouts of sin and dreadful decisions. The wise still stumble and fall into evil deeds, foolishness, and the traps of the simple. A major difference is that the wise person is open to rebuke (Proverbs 15:31) and uses instruction to advance his walk in wisdom (Proverbs 9:9, 18:15, 19:20, 21:11). A wise person, however, is known for more than a willingness to profit from rebuke; there is a deep love and respect for the one who wounded him, for the messenger of truth has opened a door to glory. The contrast is remarkable. Rebuke a fool and he will hate you; rebuke a wise person and he will value you for eternity. We will have little struggle forgiving a wise person because his heart is so deeply appreciative of direct honesty and courage.

Bad judgment does not just happen. It has a context. The simple are unwilling to accept that nothing in this fallen world really works to end the sting of shame or the hunger of loneliness. Consequently, they are drawn (envy) to look in all the wrong places, including bars and churches, for an elixir that will satisfy. They then embrace the lies of our world (naiveté) and refuse to process the evidence of deceit (bad judgment), which leads them to the arms of the seductress and the dangers of death.

A simple person never remains simple for a lifetime. He either moves toward deeper foolishness or becomes even more solidified as a sluggard. We are in movement, either toward wisdom or toward evil. The simple will eventually be seduced to foolishness and all sorts of addictive enslavements or drawn toward wisdom and an enslavement to righteousness. It is our privilege, if there is any work of God's Spirit in our lives, to call to the simple to pursue wisdom and flee from death. The odd thing is that in calling to the deep parts of another, our own shallowness is exposed and we are wooed by wisdom to be as deep and authentic as those we are trying to bring to life.

Wisdom is coquettish. Wisdom seduces and draws us to taste more deeply her aroma. It is like climbing a mountain for hours, struggling against the constant strain of pulling one's bulk up another stiff incline, only to turn and catch a view of grandeur that is breathtaking. The crisp, rarefied air, the wondrous perspective, and unparalleled beauty of wisdom infuse the soul with a newfound energy to press on in spite of the cost to gain an even more sterling glimpse of God. The more one tastes of her mystery, the more her embrace is the only enslavement worth succumbing to. How are we to love the simple and woo them to the mountaintop? How are we to grow in the process?

HOW TO LOVE A SIMPLE PERSON

Giving good gifts to a simple person, although not easy, is a breath of fresh air compared to loving an evil person or a fool. The primary good gift for an evil person is to limit their opportunity to damage. It is similar to putting an enemy city under siege. Siege warfare is tedious because the soldiers are doing little other than waiting for surrender. The greatest gift to a fool is to expose his sinful direction (Ephesians 5:11-14).

Loving a fool is like guerilla warfare—hiding, setting traps, exposing, and then waiting for the next best opportunity to come out of the forest to love again. It is less tedious than putting a city under siege, but it requires unusual commitment to the cause, a willingness to be constantly on the move, and a high degree of "good-intentioned" craftiness.

Loving a simple person, in comparison, involves the civilized and artful warfare of an athletic competition. It is bloodless warfare. Nevertheless, it is a battle with a high goal (wisdom) and a great cost if lost (foolishness). The gifts to offer a normal sinner are covering over sin and instruction through word and life—that is, modeling in speech and deed a path of brokenness and bold witness for the gospel.

The Gift of Covering Over Sin

Our basic stance toward sin should be an utter clarity and honesty about the offense, without any mood of a cover-up. We must honestly face our enemies and their sin, whether they are evil, fools, or simpletons. Our first response to them, however, ought not be to limit their evil or expose their foolish direction. Our first response must be to presume that we are dealing with a simple person, rather than an evil person or a fool. No one has perfect discernment, nor are the categories of evil, fool, and simpleton so clear that a person can be labeled without doubt or question. The labels, too, are to be held with a deep tentativeness, always hoping our diagnosis is in error, looking for contravening data that may indicate we are dealing with a more caring, open, and less destructive person. Consequently, while we are observing data and forming and testing deductions, our mood must be to cover over sin.

Covering over sin involves the choice consciously and purposely to turn our eyes away from the transgression, without ignoring or denying the damage. Peter tells us, "Above all, love each other deeply, because love covers over a multitude of sins" (1 Peter 4:8). Love believes all things and hopes for change without stopping to rest in cynical despair or abject deadening of desire. Love does not attempt to stir up trouble, nor does it hatefully attack in order to demand change. Proverbs states, "Hatred stirs up dissension, but love covers over all wrongs" (10:12); and "He who covers over an offense promotes love, but whoever repeats the matter separates close friends" (17:9).

Covering over sin involves the choice to believe the best in the other. It acknowledges the failure, but focuses on the other aspects of goodness that can legitimately be enjoyed. There is obviously a fine line between a Pollyanna positivism that only accentuates the good, and a biblical optimism that believes, until significant information has been collected, in the other's growing capacity to see and deal with whatever brings offense. Our critical generation seems to know little about affirmation's power to call forth a nobility in the heart. Covering over sin enables all that can be admired in another to surface and flourish.

Covering over is never based on denial or fear. Whenever either factor is involved, the cover over has turned to a cover-up. Covering over never involves pretense. The leaders of God's people were condemned for making sin look less sinful than it is (Jeremiah 6:14, Ezekiel 13:10-11). Pretense, in this case, is excusing sin ("He didn't mean to do it. Given his background, he really couldn't help it") or pretending the wound did not hurt ("If I got upset every time someone attacked me, I wouldn't get anything done at all"). Neither attitude reflects true forgiveness or love.

The process of covering over without covering up sin involves the choice to limit our response based on *data, opportunity,* and *calling.*

Data. When we cover over sin, we make a conscious choice to wait, prayerfully and patiently, for the right moment to deal with an observable pattern of sin, using specifics of harm to help clarify a path of relating that may be destructive. Many times we may see sin, but we don't know the context of how it fits the larger patterns of the person's heart. Often we lose power to impact a normal sinner for good when we focus on a single offense rather than waiting to see a pattern develop. The simple person might easily write off an individual failure as an anomaly, but a full-fledged, well-developed pattern is more difficult to deny. A wise person resists the temptation to pluck young fruit and, instead, waits for sin to ripen on the vine. He covers over sin until the data of a significant pattern of failure is ripe and irrefutable.

Once we've been in a relationship long enough to recognize a specific action as part of a destructive pattern, it is imperative to expose our heart to God as an offering for His service. Part of one's conversation with God ought to involve questions of *character* ("What about my life might call into question my sincerity, integrity, or commitment? Does my friend know I struggle for him?"), *content* ("What do I need to say, and what is best to leave for another time?"), *methodology* ("What approach will best gain a hearing? How will I invite the person to interact about the data?"), and *follow-up* ("Once I've spoken, am I willing to pray, talk, or deal with the struggles that come up? If I am poorly received, am I committed to a friendship, irrespective of what is said or done?").

Let me illustrate what this might look like. I have a friend who over nearly fifteen years has seen me at my abysmal worst and dignified best. Over the years, in a deep bond of love and respect, we have plowed into topics that I would discuss with no other person on the planet. Many subjects and secrets remain untold on both sides, but few others, even from a glance, know as he does what is stirring in my heart. His character is unquestioned after years of evolving friendship.

Rebuke has occurred many times, but far less than might be imagined. The content of his rebukes has, at times, been eloquent and lengthy, but far more often the rebukes are direct, strong, gentle reflections of my sin. Good friendships use shorthand, rather than the formal documentation of a careful, litigious rebuke. He smiles, almost guffaws, at my foolishness.

Once I was caught up in the seriousness of a concern, feeling the near-Herculean proportions of my struggle, and his response was to fold his arms and retort, "Harrummph." I wanted to beat him, but his eyes were not contemptuous and his laugh invited me to step down from my lofty concerns and rejoin the rest of the sinful race. Perspective was gained in a moment, but far more, I saw another side of my demanding heart. Even more important, I was reinvited to the feast of grace, although I still was stained by sin. Since then, when I turn to a mood of lofty superiority, he retorts, "Harrummph," and I am back to the real struggle of climbing down into the arms of mercy. The methodology of his rebuke fits what would best expose my arrogance without violating my dignity. Obviously, each person is different. What might be confirming to one person might seem like an outlandish attack to another.

Timing. Covering over sin involves waiting for the right opportunity for interaction about a pattern of sin. There are few times when the sin is so clear and so important that it bears public exposure (Galatians 2:11-21). Wisdom waits for the pregnant moment when words can penetrate and expose with tender grace and lithe strength. Generally, the opportune moment is in private and also soon after the offense. The offense should be recent enough that its glow is still silhouetting the mountain and can't be easily ignored. I am not implying other data that confirms a pattern is wrong to bring up, but in most cases, the immediate example ought to take the bulk of conversation.

Calling. Finally, we should cover over sin unless we are called by God to deal with it directly. The calling to confront will likely be laced with confusion. There are many levels of friendship, intimacy, and commitment. You may ask, "At what point am I called to risk a relationship by opening the door to a difficult conversation?" There are at least two categories to consider when grappling with the issue of calling—*propriety* and *context*.

I am told not to harshly rebuke an older person, but to treat him like a parent (1 Timothy 5:1). Age and position should be viewed with respect and treated with dignity even when rebuke is necessary. In general it is best to leave a rebuke up to someone who is an equal of the one who has offended.

There may be occasion, however, when a so-called subordinate will have information about a presumed superior that no one else may possess. For example, Natalie, our office's receptionist, came to me one day and asked, "Are you aware that you seem very touchy and angry today? I thought I would let you know because your humor seems more biting than usual, and several times I've felt stung by your words." She was gracious and strong. Her demeanor and kindness compelled me to take a look at a part of my life that I might have been able to avoid if I worked with uncaring or fearful people. I praise God our staff is courageous and kind. Natalie was respectful, but she valued my life more than merely performing the task she was hired to do.

Calling is almost always conditioned by context—that is, depth of relationship. Confrontation, of any sort, requires a strong bridge to truck the heavy material across the chasm of potential shame and misunderstanding. Few acquaintance relationships have the strength to bear such a load. I am involved with a score of relationships in one venue or another— a marriage, three children, working relationships with about fourteen people, a number of grace-filled friendships, and a slew of acquaintance relationships. In most cases, I am not called to address the most significant issues of the heart with folks who are in acquaintance or service relationships, but there are exceptions.

For example, at work I do not believe it is possible or desirable to be everyone's best friend, but I do believe it is crucial that competence and work production is just one category and not the only issue of importance in office relationships. If I am to function as a Christian in the workplace, I must keep in the forefront of my mind that the highest priority is not productivity or even profit (though both issues are acceptable objectives), but God-honoring relationships that recognize others as more important than the tasks they perform. My central task is to do my business in such a way that I provide a context where everyone on my staff, including the boss(es), is invited to grow in wisdom and beauty. At times, even in service and work relationships, bold love will be necessary for growth to occur.

There are no absolute, irrefutable answers to the issue of calling. Many times God will simply set the circumstances in an alignment that requires a response and creates a burden that cannot be ignored. The only warning worth heeding is, don't confront if you love to confront. I think God prefers reluctant draftees to overeager zealots in the area of confrontation.

A person who stirs up strife is a fool. The calling to confront should be resisted and ignored until the burden is unbearable and God's voice is clear. I truly believe calling is a supernatural set-up where God draws the line in the sand, clasps His hands around your neck, and pulls you into the ring.

Let me illustrate the relationship between data, opportunity, and calling. There are many times when I am sinned against that I choose to turn my eyes because I know the time is not ripe. For instance, I was telling a story at a gathering of friends and said that I had been involved in some enterprise for about three years. My wife quickly said that it was only two years. I felt hot with shame and anger. I remember thinking, *Why must she correct the story so that it is precisely accurate?* I wanted to say something about "my wife, the calendar," but I held my tongue, felt my hurt, and chose to go on with the story without a jab at her. After our friends departed, I desperately wanted to let her know that I felt hurt and angry, but she had enjoyed the evening. I did not want to detract from her enjoyment, and I believe in my wife; she is not a mean-spirited woman who normally takes her anger out on me in a subtle, public fashion.

A few days later, the same thing occurred again. I let it pass. The next day in a normal conversation, with no one else around, she corrected several details as we made plans for the evening. I finally asked her if she was aware of how often she was editing my stories. She was stunned. We pursued the data, and eventually acknowledged significant patterns of harm in our relationship. She felt like I dominated conversations and, at times, was thoroughly bored with my rambling. It was a painful, but highly significant, conversation. She apologized for the hidden anger, but stood her ground regarding my demeanor in certain gatherings. I, in turn, did not back away from the hurt, but I took responsibility for my insensitive domination. As so often occurs in any confrontation, there are issues for both parties to face. In this case, we were both at fault and profited from seeing our failure of each other in a context of love. Covering over sin buries the sin in grace and waits to see if and when it should ever be discussed. Covering over sin will eventually lead in one form or another to the gift of instruction.

The Gift of Instruction

When a normal sinner is exposed, the experience may initially feel foreign and frightening, and lead to a degree of hardening and self-serving anger, but it will likely invite him to see the danger that awaits if he continues on a destructive path. In other words, the simple are open to instruction, if it is sufficiently persuasive.

Scripture tells us to "give understanding to the simple" (Psalm 119:130), "make them wise" (Psalm 19:7), and increase their prudence in dealing with danger (Proverbs 1:4). The simple need exposure about the direction of their steps and instruction about the path of life.

Teaching is an art of enormous value. The best teachers rarely tell. They invite, tantalize, intrigue, confuse, and draw forth the natural hunger to know. A good teacher anticipates the deep questions of the human heart and uses them as hooks to increase the commitment to learn in spite of the cost. Few ever arrive as a master teacher, but it is a high aspiration that should drive our commitment to grow in the skill of effective communication. I have been privileged to know a few master teachers. I watched one teach Hebrew grammar and syntax in seminary. He taught what many might consider a difficult subject in which to generate enthusiasm, but his classes held an energy and passion for the text and life that still fill me with awe. I learned from him to love the Old Testament in a way that continues to shape the texture of my thought.

Another master teacher is my mentor. A man whose "probing, relentless personal honesty and his passionate hunger for God are the impetus that propelled by desire to move into the damaged soul with the hope for deep, eternal transformation."[1] His knowledge of Scripture and the soul rivets my attention and increases my hunger to see what he sees and taste what drives him to continually cling to the gospel.

At times, I've hated my teachers and occasionally still do. They are relentless, passionate, utterly odd human beings who are consumed by the coming Kingdom of God. I've been to Israel with one and around the world with the other, and I cannot, for the life of me, understand what compels and drives either of them. It is not fame, fortune, pleasure, or ease. Nevertheless, both are willing to battle daily with all the plagues of humanness and sin. They are not superhuman or paragons of otherworldly virtue. They are skeptics, deep doubters of their own press, and centered on little other than the marvel of what it means to be forgiven. Their words have shaped my mind. Their lives continue to mold my hope in a future day that they see in a way that compels me to clamor up their faith to get a glimpse of their God. I serve the same God, but not yet with their passion or humanness.

I grieve for any who have not had my privilege. I've watched them when they thought that they were least desirable. I drank deeply from their tears and marveled at their freedom to love, poorly, but better than most mere mortals. I am called, as you are also, to be a master teacher, or at least a beginning lecturer, in a similar fashion. Our lives and our words are to capture the simple, in the simplicity and passionate wonder of the One who is wisdom, truth, beauty, and life. One may be a brilliant communicator, with the tongue of angels, or a poorly educated, monosyllabic bumbler, but if the gospel means more than anything else in life, then one's words will sparkle with a shimmering translucence of heaven and a visceral, passionate humanness that comes from brokenness.

The powerful voice is one that falters but perseveres. I will never forget talking to a man stricken with cerebral palsy. He radiated with passion. Each word was like a piece of the body of Christ, served in tender dignity — parabolic and mythic — that was both confusing and simply illustrative of a great truth. I listened, barely understanding, to a faith that transcended my own, and I was deeply envious of his wisdom. I am a public speaker. I travel the world. I am said to be good at what I do, but before me was a man who will never hold a pulpit, who is limited to a few square miles of this planet, who told me of Christ in a way that I can only hope to suffer well enough to comprehend.

The ability to instruct the simple comes, paradoxically, when one sees how simple — indeed, foolish and evil — one is capable of being. It is at the point that the heart feels it has no right to utter a word of counsel, that oddly enough, it is most likely not to offer the dribble of advice, but the broken communion of life-giving bread. The bread may be nothing more than a look or a hug.

The day I learned of my father's impending death, I eventually found myself on the doorstep of one of our neighbors. Our hearts had been intertwined by kids, common interests, time, and the risen Christ. I sat and told my story. They wept. Their tears were, for me, the tears of eternity. Somehow they drew me to rest in the sorrow of One who hates death more than I and who offered His death so that life might not be swallowed in the horror of hell.

Their tears that night instructed a man who wavered between wisdom and evil. I hated life and the God behind it, but their tender tears and strong eyes, unashamed by deep passion, drew me and invited me to dinner, to eat with kings and queens, yeomen and laborers, saints and sinners, who before me have bowed the knee to the King of kings. I was instructed, and without word or obvious spiritual activity, I repented. I returned to the banquet table with humble emptiness and passionate hunger. Bold love is like that. My neighbors don't know the term, but I am their debtor for modeling something about the Kingdom of God. Instruction of the simple is heard if it is backed up with brokenness. Those who teach, but do not taste sorrow and the realities of humanness, indeed obscure rather than instruct.

The emphasis, so far, has been on the quality of instruction, not on what is said. The areas of instruction, of course, include the entire fabric of the Bible, but that can be broken down to a few significant categories. Let me highlight a few areas that must eventually be thought through with a simple person.

Relationships. John says that one cannot love God and hate his brother (1 John 4:20). Where is the simple person living out the gospel or denying it by the way he conducts his relationships? Conversation should especially include a discussion of failures of tenderness (emotions, touch, acts of kindness, thoughtfulness) and failures of strength (self-discipline, faithfulness, perseverance, handling conflict, decision-making, discipline of children, setting limits in relationships). Each area highlights issues of the heart that must be addressed if the simple person is to remove his blinders and pursue wisdom.

Purpose for life. Growing in wisdom requires us to ask the question, "What is our part in the Kingdom of God?" Why are we alive and how are we living out our unique calling, gifts, and burdens? How do we wish to be remembered at our funeral? Many times I have asked a person, "To whom (beyond the Spirit of God) do you owe your spiritual life? Who has been your mentor in the faith?" If the answer is no one, then it is possible that the person has not chosen to be involved in a rich, discipling experience. Usually, there are older believers who can be asked to study the Bible with a person seeking wisdom, to pray and talk about his struggles to grow.

The question can be asked from a different vantage point, "Who could put your name on that list?" If again the answer is no one, then it presumes one has not chosen to offer his heart deeply to any in the matters that will last an eternity. Anyone who has been a Christian longer than a few months will likely meet someone who is younger in the faith. As most teachers know, the best way to learn is to find someone who will put up with how little you know and then teach you. The simple person must be challenged to be both a learner and a teacher of life so the pursuit of wisdom will not be abandoned in his blind, naive grasping for life.

Wrestling with God. God desires intimacy, and relationship with God does not come without a struggle. He is aware of that and invites us to know Him, to wrestle with the deepest issues of our life with Him. A simple person must be encouraged to see the Christian life as a war, not only with the world, the devil, and the flesh, but with God Himself. Indeed, our deepest battles will often be with Him, stripped to our bare rage, fighting to gain a blessing that we neither comprehend nor, at times, desire. He is faithful not only to give us what He knows we desire at the deepest core of our heart, but to do so in a way that is tailor-fit for the breaking of our evil, arrogant, and simple ways.

That is the wonder of bold love. To the degree we choose to enter the war, the process of brokenness will begin. Intimate combat with others is His ground for engagement with us. To the extent we face evil, foolishness, and simple ways in others, we will see those realities in our own heart. The crushing weight of sin will open our hearts anew to the wonderful relief of forgiveness. And then the process will begin again—loving, being humbled, flying free, until the good day comes.

The magnificence of bold love is that in its brokenness, surprise, and simplicity, it is a human gift that could come only from heaven. Bold love provokes disruption that leads to solace, repentance that leads to rest; but far more, it invites both giver and receiver to stare into the eyes of mystery, the wonder of the meaning of the Cross.

NOTE
1. Dan B. Allender, *The Wounded Heart* (Colorado Springs, CO: NavPress, 1990), page 8.

BOLD LOVE:
A Sword in the Heart of Death

N ow that you have finished the book, I would love
to know what one central thought remains in your
mind. I hope you have found some of the material
helpful, but no doubt, some of the concepts remain
unclear and confusing. Even more troubling than the confusion is the nagging fear that bold love might do as much harm
as good. I share that concern. Whatever has the potential to do
good has an equal, if not greater, possibility of doing damage.
If that is true with the Word of God, which has been used to
justify war, prosecution, inquisitions, torture, and strife, then
how much more of a possibility with mere human words. I
am certainly not comparing this book to the Bible in terms
of a life-changing message, but to whatever degree a work is
helpful, it bears equal potential to lead astray. There may be
no way to minimize the potential for harm, but indulge my
desire to describe again the heart of bold love.

I am most concerned about our potential to disguise
meanness and revenge deceitfully under the cloak of bold love.
I was recently told about an acquaintance, Jan, who was "boldly
loving" her mother. When Jan began to face the harm she had

suffered in relationship with her family, she cut off contact with her mother, claiming her mother was too damaging to relate to on any basis. A friend questioned the wisdom of her extreme response, and Jan refused to talk with her, claiming her friend was in denial. She became a one-woman SWAT team against anyone who challenged her definition of love.

The dispute with her mother was over the issue of past abuse: Did Jan's deceased father abuse her or was Jan lying? Her mother refused to believe her, so Jan cut off all communication. Jan's mother is a weak, indulgent woman who refuses to deal with any ugly, messy problems. Her refusal to address life as it is, is wrong. But there are strands of information that indicate her mother has a real concern for Jan and a willingness to creep slowly toward facing truth. Should Jan refuse to talk with her mother until she acknowledges the past abuse? I cannot answer definitively, but I suspect bold love is being used (or misused) in this situation as a bludgeon to make her mother pay for the years of uninvolved, non-protective mothering.

The person who chooses to love boldly must remain open to more data and feedback in order to know how to deal wisely with the offender. The cost will be an enormous struggle with doubt and confusion that results from refusing to come to premature certainty through arrogant self-assertion. The person who boldly loves will remain tentative in his or her direction without losing the courage to move forward. In the use of extreme measures, there will be even greater thoughtfulness, time, and interaction with others before one moves. A defensive, closed, angry retort—"You just don't understand. This is repentance for me to cut off ties with my mother"—likely indicates a heart motivated by revenge rather than by mercy and grace.

I wish the process of loving were clearer and more simple. In many cases, it is. It is merely offering someone a cup of cold water in the name of Christ. Other times, love involves all the sophisticated planning and technology of a war. One central point must be underscored: *Unless we have made it a lifestyle to offer cups of cold water, we will not be able to engage properly in the warfare that bold love requires.*

During the course of writing this book, I have been engaged in one of the more poignant battles of my life. My father was dying of cancer. His dying provided me with one of those few times when I believe God enabled me to live out something of the message of this book. I wish I could write a thick book detailing the many ways that I have boldly loved. I can't. But because I am concerned that some might interpret my thinking to support cruel attack and rejection in the name of bold love, I've decided to tell the very personal story of my father's death.

He was a man who, in ways, failed me terribly; in other ways, he loved me magnificently. I could have confronted him with his failures and, calling it "bold love," had a chance to destroy his soul. Instead, I loved him boldly, and I loved him well. I am grateful beyond measure for the grace of God that enabled my feeble attempts at love to accomplish something of eternal value in my father's heart—and mine.

My father was, in my estimation, a man of unusual integrity and kindness. But like many men of his generation, he refused to let anyone know his feelings or convictions. He was a religious man, but prior to his illness, he thwarted all efforts to talk about his faith. I know without a doubt that he loved me, but he would never put words to what he felt about me. In occasional phone conversations, I would say, "Dad, I love you," but he would somehow wrestle free of my grasp and the call would end by him saying, "Yeah. Well, I'll talk to you soon." In almost four decades of knowing him, I never once that I recall had a conversation with him about the big issues of life—doubt, insecurity, confusion, meaning, hope, loneliness, love, death, God. He was always for me and present, but silent and distant like a sphinx. That is, until the confluence of his illness and my efforts at bold love.

After the diagnosis revealed he had a short time to live, I began calling him on the phone every day. Sometimes our conversations were brief checkups, and other times, lengthy meandering. After calling for a week, he said, "This calling every day has to stop. I am doing fine. You are spending too much money for nothing. I'll call you in a week." I laughed.

The words floated to my mouth more easily than I could have imagined: "Dad, you know you are going to die, if not soon, then certainly later. I simply refuse to allow money to keep us from talking. I will live with many regrets about our relationship after you are dead, but I'll not live with the regret that we did not talk because I saved a few dollars." I did not tell him about the other regrets, but I was willing. For weeks, I prayed for the opportunity to talk about our relationship and his inner world. A few doors opened, and I slowly moved inside his struggles and fears.

I kept calling and pestering him with questions. During most calls, he would argue that I ought not call so often. I told him he could hang up on me at any point he desired, but I was staying on the phone as long as I wanted. The calls went on for months. I talked endlessly about what his illness and the prospect of his death brought up in me. I talked about prayer and my doubts, convictions that bolstered me, and loneliness. When he changed the subject, I asked if he preferred a more neutral and pleasant topic, and if he didn't answer, I would be silent until he made a choice. In many ways, we were beginning to dig out a new level of depth in a relationship that was scorched dry and hard in the baking sun of uncomfortability, busyness, and distance.

In a visit prior to his death, I prayed and planned some clever ways of talking with him about the gospel. Since he would not talk about his faith, I planned to audio-tape an interview with him about his early life experience in order to ask about the development of his core convictions. The hook was the likely reality that his three-year-old grandson would never be able to ask him those questions directly. He agreed. Before we taped our talk, I sat with him on our front porch step and asked him what he had been thinking about. He answered, "Death. I've been thinking a lot about what will happen after I die. I think I'll be in heaven, but I'm not sure. Frankly, I am scared I've not done enough."

No door could have been more widely opened to the good news that he had not done enough, nor could ever do enough, to erase the failure to love. We talked about the futility of earning love, using our relationship as an example. During the period of my adolescence, I failed him terribly in many shameful and tragic ways. I broke his heart so many times that he should have refused to let me matter, but instead he continued to love me. The comparison was not hard to draw to his relationship with God. I asked him directly if he had put his trust in the finished work of Jesus Christ as the only remedy for sin, or if he believed that his efforts were sufficient to make a claim on God's love and forgiveness. He said, "It is clear. I cannot earn a spot in heaven." The next day, a close friend of my father, a trusted pastor, and I prayed for him and anointed him with oil. My father glowed with the joy of a man who could smell heaven was near. Few moments in my life are as poignant or wonderful as seeing him embrace faith in the living Christ.

In the days to follow, we talked about the things of life that were off limits. Many topics, sadly, still remained closed or answerable in a way that left me empty. Our relationship was never close to ideal. We had some painful and healing talks about our failure of one another. Even days before he died, I still fought with him to get him to see another physician. I believe God honored my unrelenting persistence with a closeness that was tangible and tasty to the soul. The eulogy I wrote for his funeral could not have been honestly read unless my father and I had struggled together in the labor of deepening love. I wrote:

> The poet Rilke said:
> But because being here is much and because
>   all this
> that's here, so fleeting, seems to require us
>   and strangely
> concern us. Us the most fleeting of all.
>   Just once,
> everything, only for once. Once and no more.
>   And we, too,
> once. And never again. But this
> having been once, though only once,
> having been once on earth — Can it ever be canceled?

My father was only once, but his life — his heart and passion to love — will mark every step of our "once" until we see him again face to face. He lived his life well — exceptionally well — and he drew many to his quiet, tender, giving heart. I have met no man in my life who was more consistently and deeply in love with his family. He believed in us. At times when the data of my life gave him no rational basis to keep believing, his tender and obstinately dogged heart chose to believe and offer forgiveness after forgiveness. He was my first and most consistent taste of God's grace.

Of all the things I profoundly respect about my father — his perseverance, his fierce loyalty, his tender heart — I will always be most dumbstruck by his willingness to sacrifice any pleasure or comfort for the sake of his family and friends. After his heart attack, he told me his biggest struggle was in not being able to drive Mom to an eye appointment. My eyes, as a thirty-eight-year-old man, see him, at times, as if I were a little boy. He was bigger than life and better than any dad could be. I do think he was exceptional, but I am not blind to his faults.

He was a man who struggled like most with his humanness and sin. He could be obstinate and stubborn beyond reason. Once his mind was locked into an opinion, it would be easier to dislodge a barnacle than his perspective. He was also intensely private. I will always wonder what was in his inner world. His personal doubts, dreams, and struggles were always off limits, or only hinted at, rather than open for the privilege of joining him in his journey. But without doubt, some of that was my responsibility as well. Many times, I did not ask the questions that I was most curious about.

In the last few months of his life, I asked him questions I had never asked before — questions about his past, his dating relationship with my mother, his dreams, his loneliness, his picture of what awaited him at death, about his relationship with God — and I found depths of passion and soul that will nourish my heart in the dark, questioning moments to come.

My father was aware of his faults and, far more, was aware that his hope for eternity rested not on his good and

*kind heart, or on the amount of sacrifice (though considerable)
he expended for his family, but solely on the forgiving grace
of God. My father embraced the forgiveness that comes from
knowing his sins were wiped away by the death and resurrection of Jesus Christ. His good heart was matched by a growing
awareness of his need for life in Christ.*

*My family and I are heirs of a legacy of love that is a
reward equal only to heaven. I will miss him terribly, but I
delight in the hope that we are heirs together of the grace
of God. And one day, I will again be face to face with his
unrelenting, stubborn, sacrificial love.*

*Though your body will soon be laid in the ground and swal-
lowed up by the earth — I cannot and will not say goodbye.
For you will be forever stamped into my "once."*

I love you, Dad.

In my efforts to love boldly, I was granted the opportunity
to know and enjoy my father at a profoundly new level. In one
sense, his death has been much harder to accept knowing that
we touched a mere cuticle below the surface. In other ways, I
smile at the thought of what that ol' boy is up to now.

A question remains: Why love? The price is so high, and
even when there are rewards, they seem so paltry compared to
the effort expended. Why do I continue to love boldly, or better
said, why do I bother facing how poorly I love? Words that I
wrote the day after my father's funeral sum up my answer.

*A warrior has died. Another passing gesture of grace is sur-
rounded by flowers and extolled in honor. My father is dead.
As I stared at his rock-like but tender face, waiting for the
final light of day to close over his frame, I felt an odd heaviness and lightness of heart. He is gone, never to return or
speak or smile or love in a way that was deficient but unlike
any human love I've experienced on this cold planet. The
heaviness feels like a lead weight that descends slowly through
my throat down into my heart. But what I am more amazed
by is a feeling of lightness.*

I spent so many hours dreading the moment I would see him in the casket. I concocted a plan for how I would handle the surge of horror on seeing him. But when I walked into the room that held my father's casket in the somber shades of funeral home gray, I felt unabashed excitement. I had not been with him for several months, and my first flash of emotion was anticipation of being with him again. I walked to his casket and put my hand on his face. I had wondered if I would be able to touch a dead body, even my father's, but the movement of my hand came as unexpectedly as my excitement.

I will never forget how cold his face felt. My last few moments with him alive I had put my hands over his leathery, pain-weary face and though he was dying, he was warm and present. The instant I touched his cold, dry face I felt a wave of joy that stunned me. What rang in my mind was the angel's words about our Lord: "He is not here." Somehow because Jesus conquered death, so had my father. He is not only not here, but his sojourn is over and he has ascended to the face of glory and mercy.

The victory bells are ringing for this warrior, and though I cannot hear or see the parade in his honor, nevertheless, I know the words spoken at his commendation: "Welcome, My good and faithful servant." The words will have thrilled his heart and he will beam his wonderful smile for eternity.

In an odd way, my father's cold face is a major reason for me to continue to fight on. I despise death. But even more I despise the one who tempted our forebears and sneaked death into the garden. I, too, will one day lie cold and inert to eyes that cannot see my "ringing in." But I will risk my present on the hope of what lies ahead. Paul said, "If only for this life we have hope in Christ, we are to be pitied more than all men" (1 Corinthians 15:19).

My father had a small inkling of the God he has now met. My glimpse is likely not much larger than his while on earth, but I will fight on, waiting for the day when my thin perspective will be made full.

Bold love is a taste of our eternal hope. Love well. Hope deeply.

AUTHORS

Dr. Dan B. Allender received his M.Div. from Westminster Theological Seminary and his Ph.D. in Counseling Psychology from Michigan State University. Dr. Allender has been an associate of Dr. Larry Crabb for almost fifteen years and taught with him in the Biblical Counseling Department of Grace Theological Seminary for seven years. He currently teaches and counsels with Dr. Crabb at Colorado Christian University near Denver and travels extensively to present his unique perspective on sexual-abuse recovery, counselor training and Bold Love workshops. He is the author of *The Wounded Heart* and co-authored *Encouragement: Key to Caring*. Dr. Allender and his wife, Rebecca, live in Littleton, Colorado, with their three children, Anna, Amanda and Andrew.

Dr. Tremper Longman III received his M.Div. from Westminster Theological Seminary and his Ph.D. in Ancient Near Eastern studies from Yale University. Dr. Longman is Professor of Old Testament at Westminster Theological Seminary. Dr. Longman has written many professional and pastoral articles and is the author of *How to Read the Psalms* and *Literary Approaches to Biblical Interpretation*. Dr. Longman and his wife, Alice, live near Philadelphia, Pennsylvania, with their three sons, Tremper IV, Timothy and Andrew.